Shaping Belief

LIVERPOOL ENGLISH TEXTS AND STUDIES, 52

Shaping Belief

Culture, Politics and Religion
in Nineteenth-Century Writing

Edited by
VICTORIA MORGAN *and* CLARE WILLIAMS

LIVERPOOL UNIVERSITY PRESS

First published 2008 by
Liverpool University Press
4 Cambridge Street
Liverpool L69 7ZU

Copyright © 2008 Liverpool University Press
'Allegiance: A Sermon' © 2002 by Rowan Williams

The right of Victoria Morgan and Clare Williams to be identified as editors
of this work has been asserted by them in accordance with
the Copyright, Design and Patents Act 1988.

All rights reserved. No part of this book may be reproduced, stored in a
retrieval system, or transmitted, in any form or by any means, electronic,
mechanical, photocopying, recording, or otherwise, without
the prior written permission of the publisher.

British Library Cataloguing-in-Publication data
A British Library CIP record is available

ISBN 978-1-84631-136-9 cased

Typeset by XL Publishing Services, Tiverton
Printed and bound in the European Union by Biddles Ltd, King's Lynn

This book is for our parents –
Norma and Greg Morgan, and Shirley and John Williams

Contents

List of Illustrations	ix
Acknowledgements	x
Allegiance: A Sermon *Rowan Williams, Archbishop of Canterbury*	xi
Introduction: Re-visioning Belief in Nineteenth-Century Writing *Victoria Morgan and Clare Williams*	xv

I. Religious Discourse: Transmission and Appropriation

1. Tell the Story: Re-imagining Victorian Conversion Narratives
   Andrew Tate — 3

2. 'Recognizing Fellow-Creatures': F.D. Maurice, Octavia Hill, Josephine Butler
   Hester Jones — 21

3. 'Filthy Lucre': Christianity, Commerce and the Female Bodily Economy in Seamstress Narratives of the 1840s
   Ella Dzelzainis — 39

4. Isaiah and Ezekiel – But What about Charley? An Essay on 'Wanting to Believe'
   Philip Davis — 57

II. Shaping Subjectivities: Belief, Aesthetics and Space

5. 'Repairing Everywhere without Design'? Industry, Revery and Relation in Emily Dickinson's Bee Imagery
   Victoria Morgan — 73

6. Poetry, Poetic Perception and Emerson's Spiritual Affirmations
   David M. Robinson — 95

7. Sacrificial Exchange and the Gothic Double in *Melmoth the Wanderer* and *The Picture of Dorian Gray*
   Alison Milbank   113

8. Church Architecture, Tractarian Poetry and the Forms of Faith
   Kirstie Blair   129

III. Mediating Culture: Inscribing Democracy, Class and Social Identity

9. Caricature and Social Change 1820–1840: The March of Intellect Revisited
   Brian Maidment   149

10. Feeling '*Ghost*like': Carlyle and his Exposure to the 'Condition-of-England-Question'
    Clare Williams   171

11. 'Getting Down into the Masses': Dickens, Journalism and the Personal Mode
    Juliet John   189

12. 'Scrupulously Empty Phrases' and the Silent Work of Matthew Arnold: Belief in the Action of Writing
    Kate Campbell   209

Index   223

List of Illustrations

9.1 Anonymous wood engraving and accompanying poem by 'W.E.', in *The Comic Magazine* (London: W. Marshall, n.d.), no. 19, pp. 194–5   153

9.2 Robert Seymour, 'Look Papa', from *Sketches by Seymour*, 5 vols (London: Robert Carlile, 1836), vol. 5, no. 36, 14 April 1836. Etching   156

9.3 C.J. Grant, a cut-down page from *Everybody's Album and Caricature Magazine* (London: Kendrick, 1834). Lithograph   157

9.4 A scrap from an unidentified album cut out from Grant, *Everybody's Album and Caricature Magazine*. Lithograph   158

9.5 Cut-down title page from C.J. Grant, *The Penny Magazine* 1 (London: Edward Lacey, n.d. [*c*. October 1832]). Lithograph   159

9.6 Anon. [C.J. Grant?], *Arithmetical Terms Being a Frontispiece to 'The Tutor's Assistant'* (London: no pub., n.d.). Lithograph   160

9.7 H.K., 'Reading and Understanding' (London: G.S. Tregear, n.d.). Lithograph   161

9.8 J.L. Marks, 'The march of Interlect or a Sweep & Family of the 19th Century' (London: J.L. Marks, n.d.). Engraving   162

Acknowledgements

We would like to say a special thank you to Juliet John, Hester Jones, Jill Rudd, Philip Davis and Dinah Birch for the help and encouragement they have given us during the course of this project. Also, thanks to Anthony Cond for his support and belief in this book. We would like to thank all of our contributors for their much appreciated commitment and patience, and for making this collection of essays possible. Finally, thanks to Peter Francis and all of the staff at St Deiniol's Residential Library, Hawarden, North Wales for their assistance and friendliness, and thanks also to the helpful staff at the Sydney Jones Library and the British Library.

Allegiance: A Sermon[1]

Rowan Williams, Archbishop of Canterbury

It is strange how we construct our icons of stability. Some of those figures we most clearly and deeply associate with stability and continuity were in their own lifetime regarded as deeply unreliable people. Winston Churchill is probably the most startling example in the twentieth century if you look at his early career. Something of the same kind might also be said of William Ewart Gladstone. If in the middle of the nineteenth century you asked 'Is this man reliable?' most 'reliable' politicians in the United Kingdom would have said, 'No'. This is a man who changes his mind, a man whose allegiances seem not wholly clear in political terms, even if they are in moral ones. We might well have asked, 'Where is the deepest loyalty in this man? Where is his allegiance?' Allegiance – it is a word you will be hearing in the prayers, quoting Gladstone's own phrase – 'an allegiance from the heart, rooted in the mind, governing the conduct.'

Where is the loyalty, where is the allegiance of William Ewart Gladstone? The implication of the whole of his life and witness is that loyalty is not best given by human beings to politics alone. Loyalty, allegiance, is best given to a particular vision of what is humanly proper, what it belongs to human beings to do and to be in God's world. We have become familiar enough in recent times with philosophical and cultural findings that suggest that all disagreements about humanity are in the long run political – they are all really disagreements about power. 'Who is to be master? That's the question,' as Humpty Dumpty asked Alice: a reductionism that sees all disagreement finally in terms of struggles about power is what a life such as Gladstone's challenges. In Gladstone's life, political risk is very much to the fore. His vision was nourished by something other than who is to be master.

Gladstone's deepest loyalty is indeed about something other than political struggle. It is nourished by Homer and Dante; it is nourished by

[1] St Deiniol's Library Centenary Sermon, 14 October 2002.

an *epic* vision. Doubtless some of those who heard the heroic speeches of Gladstone in later life might have thought the word 'epic' uncomfortably appropriate. Epic is about the long and the patient unfolding of truth through event. It takes time and there is no way for it not to take time. Interweaving, the ups and downs, plot and adventure: these are the essence of the human vision.

Gladstone's passion for the unity of Homer isn't just a cultural accident. It is about seeing the complexities in life resolved not by programme, not by the imposition of a successful strategy, but by the evolution and interweaving of complicated human lives – epic vision. His allegiance is shaped by that sense of a human narrative and unity that will only emerge in story and in relation. It is an allegiance rooted in the way that scripture itself works in the Christian vision. Because whatever may sometimes have been said across the history of the Church, the unity that belongs to believers is not finally a unity of system but a unity of story and relation. These are the people, not with whom we are in total agreement, but with whom God has given to us to discover the truth. These are the people with whose stories we are irrevocably involved. This is the epic of God's work in the world into which we have been called.

Gladstone's life and witness have a good deal to do with the hope of a unity that is something other than imposition of a system, a triumph of power. Gladstone's vision is a theological one grounded not only in Homer and Dante, but also in what he was reading, thinking and experiencing as someone living through the astonishing turbulence of Victorian Christianity. God save us from thinking about the lost golden age of Victorian religion! If you have spent more than five minutes studying the history of religion in the Victorian period you would know that our present difficulties are perhaps really a storm in a teacup.

Gladstone understood that politics is too important to leave to politicians. You might equally well say that politicians are too important to leave to politics. That is to say, the politician who matters, the politician who is able to crystallise moral vision, evoke imaginative energy in a society, is one who knows about more than politics. Such a politician needs a hinterland, an imaginative world that nourishes allegiances. We are perhaps most suspicious of politicians who seem to have least hinterland, least human world of their own. We may well look around and ask where is that hinterland, that inner landscape, in modern politicians. I'm not simply speaking about the United Kingdom but the whole of the developed world. Where is the inner world, the imaginative reference?

God has blessed us in giving us an answer as to where that might be found. St Deiniol's Library witnesses to an inner world, an extraordinary, variegated, exciting, exhausting inner world. We glimpse the world of a politician who knew about more than politics, who knew that to be a politician you had to care about more than politics. In the Library is the human epic if you will, the human ethic with an epic story of God's dealings with humanity and their climax and focus in Jesus Christ at its centre.

The history of this library has of course reminded us that this is not simply about political and public life but about the life of the Church. The vision, let's say, of an Alec Vidler (warden of St Deiniol's Library 1939–1948) and what he did for the life of this library is really all about teaching the Church to care about more than *Church* politics. The correspondence that Alec Vidler undertook when he was at the library, and the extraordinary network that he built up of shared wisdom, insight, awkward questions and brilliant answers has to do with the hinterland of Church life. The politics of the Church is a hidden, narrow and depressing business if it is not shaped by human vision, energy and imagination; by an *epic* vision, to use that word once again.

St Deiniol's Library is about epic, it is about the long story of human understanding shot through by the revelation of God: arrested, interrupted, summoned, woven together, split up again and then reconnected by the gift of God. It is strange to use such dramatic language, to postulate such a dramatic scene setting for the prosaic vision of books on shelves, but that is what this place is about: a place that provides an inner landscape for Christians.

The more Christians spend their energy looking suspiciously and with hostility at each other, the less their inner world may be richly developed. Church politics and secular politics have a good deal to learn from each other on how to do it – and how not to do it.

The spirit of William Ewart Gladstone still presides over St Deiniol's, committing this library to an epic vision of a humanity that is not all about the exchanges of power, but rather is about the discoveries of the epic interweaving of human imaginations, human failures, human visions, human faith. The question put to us by Gladstone and by this library is about our loyalty. What nourishes our allegiance? What is our hinterland as citizens and as Christians? What keeps our imagination vital and critical in this world?

We turn again today in thanksgiving and, I hope, in excitement to the epic of God's dealings with us – still incomplete because our lives are still being woven together. What that will produce in the future, God knows.

We know how God deals with us; we know the scriptures. God does not deliver a set of solutions, but first a net of relations. Into that net of relations God has drawn us, and in that you will find God and be found by God; there is our nourishment; there is what will 'nurture an allegiance coming from the heart, rooted in the mind, governing the conduct'.

Introduction: Re-visioning Belief in Nineteenth-Century Writing

Victoria Morgan and Clare Williams

The shaping of belief, or the forming of different ideas of unity, is something that can be described as typical of the nineteenth century, a period in which knowledge was obsessively categorized and the taxonomical urge was evident, seemingly, in all areas of life. William James argued in *The Varieties of Religious Experience* (1902) that the shaping force of ontological unity might be harnessed or reached through forms other than religion, observing: 'But to find religion is only one out of many ways of reaching unity; and the process of remedying inner incompleteness and reducing inner discord is a general psychological process, which may take place with any sort of mental material, and need not necessarily assume the religious form.'[1]

Yet the unifying principle of James's 'psychological process' still requires belief if it is to work; belief not only in what can be reconciled but also in the shape of unity that is to be reached. The particular climate of the nineteenth century, in which there was an increased diversity in religious groups as much as increasing secularization, was one that opened up a uniquely dynamic dialectical space in which such 'unity' might be challenged, fought for or reconfigured. Any study which seeks to understand the particularly dialectical aspect of belief during the nineteenth century should be necessarily open to the many different forms of belief that were being developed in the period. This in turn necessitates a recognition of the term 'belief' as social, cultural and political phenomena especially operative within the nineteenth-century period, rather than as bearing synonymity with a specifically religious conviction.

'Shaping Belief', our title for this collection, is a descriptor for the process of these phenomena and explores the pervasive call in the period for a re-visioning of religious belief. The diverse range of material in each of the book's chapters reflects, in different ways and to varying extents, how the energy that had once been contained within religion flowed out into society and its writings, to generate reconfigured articulations and experiences of belief. It also offers an exploration of how its channels were etched just as deeply in the application of theology to literary constructions of the self, as in the social, cultural and political activities of the period. The appropriation of religious discourse occurred in a new age of mass culture where political and cultural beliefs could be advanced with the resonant force of religion. Nineteenth-century anxieties about rapid industrialization, a de-personalized mechanization and fiercely contested ideas of democracy got caught up in the wave of reconfiguring traditional ideas of unity. The vigorous sway of belief that manifested itself within the psychological and physical landscapes of the period is evidenced by the bold assertion and expression of the new forms that writing was taking. Varieties of belief can be seen in writing of the nineteenth-century period as much in expressions of newly formed personal relations to ideas of the public as in the poet's individual search for an aesthetic of unity. Each anxiety about or articulation towards an idea of unity generated varying shapes of belief, and this collection presents some of the ways in which culture, politics and religion intersected to produce writing that bears evidence of such shaping.

Questions surrounding the nature, use and varying definitions of belief have always been and indeed will always continue to be of fundamental importance to nineteenth-century studies. The reasons for this rest not only within the specific context of the period itself and the vast range of cultural, political and religious beliefs that were developing in both Britain and America, but also because of the particular ways in which writers of the period responded to those beliefs and experienced the very act of writing and shaping those beliefs in an age of increasing secularization. Many important critical texts and anthologies have drawn upon the connections between belief and nineteenth-century writing, but have dealt with religious faith exclusively as a means of exploring those connections.[2]

However, the 'waning tide' or 'crisis' of faith many nineteenth-century writers encountered has subsequently become something of a clichéd paradigm within criticism on the period for the complex, interconnected and varied responses to versions of unity they produced. Within the current climate of nineteenth-century studies, a study of 'belief' in writing of the period requires a more interdisciplinary and fluid approach in order to take in a wider view of the dynamic energy that shaped it. Texts such as W. David Shaw's *The Lucid Veil: Poetic Truth in the Victorian Age* and J. Hillis Miller's *Victorian Subjects* achieved this in the allowance they made for a fluidity which terms such as 'truth' or 'belief' generate.[3] Shaw's book illustrated how the changing axioms of knowledge and perception within philosophy, science and religious culture of the nineteenth-century period flowed into, and was reflected within, attempts to represent 'truth' in poetry. The search for such 'truth', and the problems which writers of the nineteenth century encountered when trying to represent it in Shaw's study, is akin to Miller's notion of the unifying aspect of the search for belief. Miller argued that the idea of belief, evolving both diachronically between, and synchronically through, a dialectic of 'affirmation and denial', has perpetually recurred throughout the intellectual history of western civilization, and has provided humanity with a connecting point of unity within a universe of confusion. The desire to forge points of human interconnectivity or unity that the notion of belief articulates in different ways is not new. However, examining the points of connection between different forms of belief provides new ways of approaching the problematic cycle of 'affirmation and denial' in writing of the nineteenth century:

> Without denying that there have been vast gaps and new beginnings both in linguistic history and in cultural history, this affirmation and denial may by hypothesis be said to form the unity in disunity of any "period" in Western intellectual and literary history, even that of the Greeks. The distinctiveness of any historical period [...] lies in its special combination of certain recurring elements rather than in its introduction of anything unheard of before. The gaps and discontinuities making linguistic and cultural history a vast anacoluthon are within each synchronic expression, making it hetereogeneous, as well as in the diachronic movement from one expression to another.[4]

It is the 'special combination' of different forms of belief, and the ways in which they intersected in different areas of life during the nineteenth century, and were expressed in diverse ways, that makes writing of the period so particularly prolific. The precedent set by critics such as Shaw and Miller is instructive, drawing attention to the necessarily broad way in which the term belief can be employed to describe the movement of energy initially only associated with religiously inflected writing. Such a critical perspective allows us to describe the many different ways in which belief shaped and reformed itself through culture, politics and religion in different forms of writing, showing the new ways in which the concept of belief in nineteenth-century writing can be approached.

It could be argued that the precarious relation between belief and unbelief in writings of the nineteenth century not only anticipates the postmodernist age (already brought to bear later within the period itself in the philosophical writings of Friedrich Nietzsche) but also shows how from ideological plurality something else could be created. That something else took the form not only of new forms of belief, but forms of belief which, despite their differences and conflicts, appeared united in their desire for some kind of unity in the dawn of a strangely modern world. In the series of challenges to forms of orthodoxy or perceived versions of 'unity', modes of 'unbelief' were also demonstrative of the search for the unity that would in turn give shape to a cause. The tension between belief and unbelief has been described as being akin to a 'religious phenomenon'[5]: retaining some qualities of religious experience while being also, in some cases, emphatically secular. Belief in this sense is necessarily dualistic, alluding to two conflicting yet mutually generative or 'shaping' movements: the understanding of belief both as a concept (that is an idea with a unified form, which may be contemplated with scepticism or beheld with conviction) and as an experience (the processes the subject undergoes in his/her effort to believe, which s/he may encounter simultaneously in terms of conviction, scepticism, and interrogation.) Such a re-visioning of belief as a hermeneutical space between concept and experience allows for the fuller complexity of the themes examined within each chapter of this book to come more readily to the fore. Thus, the relation between writing about belief and the experience of it; how such intersections emerge and/or merge aesthetically; the practical implications which follow or flow from such belief; and how understanding nineteenth-century writings concerned with belief in different ways might inform our own, are all issues which the collection addresses in this experimental arena.

In the wake of postmodernism, there has been a notable reluctance to explicitly explore the question of belief, which has been seen as being an outmoded, chimerical and highly contentious concept. To many it immediately connotes a liberal humanist approach, interpretation being both circumscribed and distorted in terms of restrictive moral and religious frameworks. However, this collection reflects a current wave in contemporary literary studies with scholars now beginning to seriously reconsider the space/place of belief as a locus for the varying energies and tensions inherent in literature as well as in society more generally. Recently established connections between the nineteenth-century climate of belief and that of contemporary culture offer important insights into how we might reconsider the relevance of our own reading and understanding of the period. Philip Davis observes: 'In an age of so many competing, inchoate, or recovered frameworks of belief, so many standpoints and changes of view at the very origin of powerful feelings over a century later, the perspective of the Victorian years can shift, and shift again, within seconds of imaginative reading.'[6]

John Schad's pioneering work on Victorian poetry and literary theory posited an important connection between the self-reflexive, meta-textual space of poetry during the period and that shared by contemporary literary theory. Although not explicitly about belief, the 'third and almost ghostly figure or text' Schad encounters in the space between each poet and theorist he examines, from the 'looking-glass theology' of Christina Rossetti and Luce Irigaray, to the 'gospels' of Elizabeth Barrett Browning and Hélène Cixous, resembles in the book the shaping space which belief occupied and generated within the period.[7] The attention paid to belief and the discoursal space it generates has become a marker for a new self-reflexivity in theoretical debates across other disciplines.[8]

One recent study that has importantly come some way to opening up this debate within literary studies has been Terry Eagleton's *After Theory*, which addresses how those fundamental issues of metaphysics and religion, love and death, truth and objectivity, and morality, virtue and evil, have by and large been inadequately explored by theory. What Eagleton calls for is not the retrogressive idealism of a pre-theory age, but a courageous move towards embracing, critically, the big questions concerning human existence with a view to developing new ways of understanding them:

> Human history is now for the most part both post-collectivist and post-individualist; and if this feels like a vacuum, it may also present an opportunity. We need to imagine new forms of belonging, which in our kind of world are bound to be multiple rather than monolithic. Some of those forms will have something of the intimacy of tribal or community relations, while others will be more abstract, mediated and indirect.[9]

Eagleton's prescription supposes that in the wake of (and one might also add even because of) postmodernism, we are left in a space which is as much positive as it is potentially negative; a space in which we can re-create our understanding of the world just as much as we could potentially destroy it, as we are asked 'to accept that human life is a matter not of treading on thin air, but of *roughness*' (*After Theory*, p. 204). It is within the company of a contemporary perspective such as this that the present collection is offered, with the concept of belief not only opening up a creative space in its own right from which such questions can be addressed and explored, but also with the re-situating of the concept of belief specifically within the context of the nineteenth century; the period in which belief became less and less understood as an inviolable law and more and more experienced as an open critical space in which versions of 'unity' were magnified.

That unitary understandings of belief were being questioned in the nineteenth century caused both a destabilizing sensation of anxiety and creative energy of regeneration for many prominent social critics. John Stuart Mill, in his essay 'Utility of Religion', argued that the enlightened and conscientious intellectual was bound, both by his own individual interests and those of society, to ask the fundamental question of whether religious belief was necessary in modern civilization. Yet the fact that the essay was published posthumously in 1874, despite being written between 1850 and 1858, is a significant indication of Mill's own anxieties about his challenge to religious belief. Mill was fully aware that this was both an extremely difficult and potentially dangerous question to address, significantly observing that 'People must either have ceased to believe, or have ceased to rely on the belief of others, before they could take that inferior ground of defence without a consciousness of lowering what they were endeavouring to raise.'[10] In particular, Mill sympathized with the intellectual who became effectively paralysed in the fear that their alternative expression of truth might sacrifice the general good of mankind, where:

> It is a most painful position to a conscientious and cultivated mind, to be drawn in contrary directions by two of the noblest of all objects of pursuit, truth, and the general good. Such a conflict must inevitably produce a growing indifference to one or other of these objects, probably to both. Many who could render giant's service both to truth and to mankind if they believed that they could serve the one without loss to the other, are either totally paralysed, or led to confine their exertions to matters of minor detail, by the apprehension that any real freedom of speculation, or any considerable strengthening or enlargement of the thinking faculties of mankind at large, might, by making them unbelievers, be the surest way to render them vicious and miserable.[11]

Mill argued that religious belief could not necessarily be rejected simply on the grounds that it was untrue 'For, though the knowledge of every positive truth is a useful acquisition, this doctrine cannot without reservation be applied to a negative truth.'[12] Instead, he wrote about an idea of belief that seemed to harmonize his two pursuits of truth and general good, arguing that poetry and religion supplied mankind with a fundamental want: 'that of ideal conceptions grander and more beautiful than we see realized in the prose of human life'.[13] Consequently, he argued that 'the Religion of Humanity'[14] was able to fulfil this want by not only cultivating an active belief in participating in the progress and continual perfection of the general good (which for Mill meant both the good of the individual and of society), but also by calling on mankind to contemplate an ideal state of being that seemed mysterious in its infinitude of possibility.

However, the popular idea of the 'Religion of Humanity', of which Mill's was only one expression in the period, was not without its cultural, political and religious problems. For many, it was simply not enough. Of Mill's utilitarian reading of life, Thomas Carlyle revealingly observed 'I sigh with more sadness than you can imagine to think that this is the truest Truth now going; the softest "soft green of the soul" one has to repose on, this hard Macadamised highway!'[15] Indeed, Mill himself had already conceded in his 'Utility of Religion' that belief in religion would always hold out the advantage of life after death. Mill even allowed the religious belief of reunion with one's loved ones after death to remain tentatively present and almost co-exist with his 'Religion of Humanity':

> That loss, indeed, is neither denied nor extenuated. In many cases it is beyond the reach of comparison or estimate; and will always suffice to keep alive, in the more sensitive natures, the imaginative hopes of a futurity which, if there is nothing to prove, there is as little in our knowledge and experience to contradict.[16]

Thus while Victorian ideas revolving around the 'Religion of Humanity' certainly provided a belief through which Mill's contemporaries were able to write, it also inaugurated a range of conflicts in nineteenth-century writing that essentially revolved around endeavouring to negotiate a meaningful and satisfying relationship between self and world, between the individual intellectual writer and society, and between literature and social need. Questions generated by religion flowed out into other areas, such as those which were explicitly addressed on the place and function of the intellectual, art, and culture in society.

Such was the case for Matthew Arnold. In Arnold's poetry, notably in 'Dover Beach', a consolatory 'let us be true to one another!' was held up in front of the retreating and evaporating 'Sea of Faith'; in 'Culture and Anarchy', Arnold finds something more than a consolation in his articulation of a new belief in culture, which appears able to replace the Hebraism which Arnold perceived as being powerless in the modern age. Analogous to the drive towards perfection for which he takes Hellenism as a precedent, he proposes a belief in perfection, or 'right reason,' as it is manifested in culture:

> For we have seen how much of our disorders and perplexities is due to the disbelief, among the classes and combinations of men, Barbarian or Philistine, which have hitherto governed our society, in right reason, in a paramount best self [...]. But for us – who believe in right reason, in the duty and possibility of extricating and elevating our best self, in the progress of humanity towards perfection – for us the framework of society, that theatre on which this august drama has to unroll itself, is sacred.[17]

Arnold's belief in culture to some extent reinstates the distinctions between right and wrong which support not only the framework of society under consideration, but also the archaic, 'powerless' ones being discarded. Unlike Mill's re-visioning of belief, Arnold does not see himself as writing some kind of fallen prose, but rather believes that he is putting forward a definition of culture which he believes supersedes religion in its critical fostering of an expansive and infinitely diverse universality. While still connecting culture to religion in the sense that he views its directive aim as being 'To make reason and the will of God prevail',[18] for Arnold culture itself, rather than religion, is seen as the authoritative agent in

> determining generally in what human perfection consists [...] culture seeking the determination of this question through *all* the voices of human experience which have been heard upon it, of art, science, poetry, philosophy, history, as well as of religion, in order to give a greater fullness and certainty to its solution, – likewise reaches.[19]

In this sense, Arnold's expansive belief in culture enables him to courageously assert:

> But, finally, perfection, – as culture from a thorough disinterested study of human nature and human experience learns to conceive it, – is a harmonious expansion of *all* the powers which make the beauty and worth of human nature, and is not consistent with the over-development of any one power at the expense of the rest. Here culture goes beyond religion, as religion is generally conceived by us.[20]

Arnold believed in culture as a universally liberating force and argued for the exclusion of the term class as the necessary means of resisting what he observed as a degenerative, monopolizing and disingenuous mass culture. However, for his own part, Arnold overlooked the particularities of social class, and how such particularities affected the ways in which writers from different social backgrounds articulated both their individual and collective experiences of nineteenth-century society. For many working-class writers, for example, the dawning of a new mass culture appeared in the apocalyptic light of social regeneration, and moreover as a natural outgrowth of the workings of God's universe, rather than as a degenerative break from it. Such a perspective is dramatically illustrated by the autodidact Ebenezer Elliott in his poem 'The Press' (1840), where he radically continues the telling of God's creation of the universe with his belief in the press as a democratic medium of mass education and emancipation, declaring:

> O pallid Want! O labour stark!
> Behold, we bring the second ark!
> The Press! The Press! The Press![21]

The endeavour to express and make sense of an existing form of belief in what appeared as a new world and/or a new form of belief, while still living within the constraints of an old one, generated a ubiquitous struggle between belief as a concept and belief as an experience, a struggle which, in significantly different ways, affected all social groups and classes, and which provided the source of momentum for much nineteenth-century writing right across the literary canon. In the poems of Emily Dickinson, which bear the mark of the American Civil War era, maintaining the *ignis fatuus* ('foolish fire') of religious belief is increasingly difficult, and yet Dickinson still refuses to relinquish the concept of belief itself, observing:

> Those – dying then,
> Knew where they went –
> They went to God's Right Hand –
> That Hand is amputated now
> And God cannot be found –
>
> The Abdication of Belief
> Makes behaviour small –
> Better an ignis fatuus
> Than no illume at all –[22]

The concept of belief in itself, whether it was affiliated to political, cultural or religious convictions, always appears necessary as a space through which an individual can critically make sense of his/her experiences in the world, as well as becoming a vehicle for meaningful expression, giving form to these experiences. In the poems of Arthur Hugh Clough the abstract notion of 'Truth' is invoked as a stable embodiment of belief, which is not particularized to a religious faith or conviction. Instead it bears affinities with the expression of some kind of spiritual dimension which desires to believe in an unseen locus of meaning at which divisions of all manner are dissolved, with the recognition of a higher working unity. It appears that Clough is only able to write and thence move forward through life because of his crucial observation that:

> It fortifies my soul to know
> That, though I perish, Truth is so:
> That, howso'er I stray and range,
> Whate-er I do, Thou canst not change.
> I steadier step when I recall
> That, if I slip, Thou dost not fall.[23]

The desire to believe in a constant, stable 'Truth' presents itself ultimately as a belief in political and moral integrity beyond the implementation of religious orthodoxy:[24] Clough's 'Thou' is Christ-like, but peace is ultimately dependent upon the speaker's own will to 'recall' 'Truth' as an abstract something in itself.[25] For those who still believed in that religious orthodoxy however, the expression of belief was still just as critical and discursive, with the concept of belief often falling short of the experience of it, and yet still providing the means through which one could both find and develop a critical voice.[26] Such was the case in Joseph Ramsbottom's popular Lancashire dialect poem *Preawd Tum's Prayer*, which was significantly both written and turned to during the Cotton Famine (1860–1861), where the speaker deploys the rhetoric of prayer as both a private and collective space in which he can express his grievances and critically seek redress not only from God but by implication society as a whole:

> O th' things abeawt depend on Thee,
> O th' hedges, threes, an' th' prattier fleawrs,
> An' every buzzart, brid, an' bee,
> An' th' warmin' sun, an' th' coolin' sheawrs.
> Theaw knows aw've neaw done o aw con;
> An' while Theaw cares for o these things
> Theaw'll surely help a sthrivin' mon.[27]

Thus even with writers from radically differing social and political situations, the dynamic of belief gives voice to and relocates the individual struggle within a wider cultural context, both towards and also against predetermined versions of subjectivity and unity. Always challenging, the many diverse articulations of belief to be found in nineteenth-century writing offer a constant reminder that the dialectical relation with differing notions of unity is an enduring factor in articulations of human understanding and experience.

The collection is divided into three interconnected sections that allow for multiple approaches towards the dynamic dialogue stimulated by ideas of belief in nineteenth-century writing. The sermon given by the Archbishop Rowan Williams, at St Deiniol's Library, Hawarden, in 2002, serves as a cursory introduction to ideas of unity, with reference to William Ewart Gladstone's inner life and his preference for literature that nourishes unity and allegiance through 'epic vision', which his library at St Deiniol's reflects. The struggle with and for versions of unity and allegiance, for something to believe in, in writing under examination in each section of this collection, produces a dialogue around belief that is also in relation, in process. The first section of the collection brings together essays that explicitly deal with the question of how religious discourse was transmitted and appropriated to explore, challenge or assert religious, cultural or political beliefs. Andrew Tate explores different models of conversion and their shaping of radical personal change. Drawing on contemporary theories from the disciplines of religious studies, psychology and literature, he asks, 'What is conversion?' and 'How important was it in the Victorian age, beyond the enthusiastic chapels of non-conformist Christianity?' Beginning with the re-establishment of the Roman Catholic hierarchy in England and Wales in 1850, Tate explores stories of personal religious change and examines the patterns of structure that were developed in both public and private modes of describing conversion. Considering theological debates surrounding the subject of conversion and its representation in newspapers, tracts and religious periodicals, Tate significantly views religious conversion as a phenomenon that was an integral part of popular culture and also as one which could take on alternative modes such as rational conversion, cultural conversion and conversion as apostasy. Importantly, he considers the extent to which the reappraisal of theological aspects of conversion might challenge contemporary assumptions about identity, with conversion offering a space in which fragmentation and 'radical discontinuities' can be explored and accommodated.

Also on the theme of reconciling difference, Hester Jones's chapter considers the attempt to bring together faith and society in the late nineteenth century, by examining the work of Christian theologian F.D. Maurice and its influence on Christian social reformers Octavia Hill and Josephine Butler. Jones importantly argues that although these figures have been criticized for displaying a 'conservative' and 'custodial' relation to those they worked with (something which has been construed as a lack of commitment to reform), the theological ideas of kenosis and of 'reciprocal fellowship' in Maurice's writing show an 'embodied complexity' through which the work of Hill and Butler can be viewed, a model which is instructive to a contemporary climate committed to diversity and pluralism.

Whilst Jones offers a constructive understanding of the theological basis of reciprocity and mutuality, reading this as being powerfully employed in writings and activities of women of the period, Ella Dzelzainis examines how the appropriation of religious discourse in connection with the medicalization of women's bodies produced a reconfiguration of female identity which could be used as a site for protest against political economy. The production of a fundamentalist Christian critique of political economy in the seamstress stories written by

Charlotte Elizabeth Tonna and Francis Paget presents a religious opposition to the attempted redefinition of the concept of luxury in the political economic debate of the eighteenth and early nineteenth century. Dzelzainis illustrates how Tonna and Paget drew on the teachings of St Augustine and St Paul to argue that Christianity rather than commerce was the real agent of England's progress as a civilized nation, and uncovers the ways in which the seamstress stories suggest that, just as the female bodily economy needed to be monitored and regulated, so too did political economy. Furthermore, she argues that their acceptance of R.D. Grainger's medico-moral understanding of the female body provided both authors with the model through which they were able to criticize the laissez-faire ethos of nineteenth-century commerce.

Philip Davis's essay considers the importance of belief in relation to the act of writing. Looking in particular at George MacDonald's novel *Wilfred Cumbermede*, the essay explores the problems engendered by wanting to have something to believe in, focusing on how the everyday individual, when situated within the destabilizing context of an increasingly secularized age, encountered and struggled with religious belief in terms of a counter-productive paralysis. However, Davis moves on to argue that this articulation of 'wanting to believe' actually produced a different form of belief. In the light of this, Davis analyzes the importance of William James's philosophy of pragmatism for moving the nineteenth century out of and beyond its impasse of doubt with the reintroduction of the term 'faith'. Davis's essay asserts that in James it is argued that one needs to have faith in the possibility of bringing belief into being through individual efforts of provisional formulation: that one needs to have the will to believe in something, even to make that something realizable in the world.

The second section of the collection focuses on the importance of ideas of subjectivity in relation to different kinds of cultural, political and religious beliefs and the ways in which they could be mediated by aesthetics and rearticulated in a formal space. Victoria Morgan's essay considers Emily Dickinson's critique of religious orthodoxy, namely the legacy of New England Puritanism, by focusing on Dickinson's use of bee imagery and its cultural associations with Protestant models for both community and industry. In view of current critical debate, which seeks to emphasize Dickinson's engagement with and commentary on the social, political and religious climate of her day, this essay draws on the various contemporary and transatlantic, inherited influences on her poetics. Moreover, the essay considers the radical re-positioning of belief within the context of production, or notion of 'employment' as poet, in Dickinson's work, connecting spirituality with writing. Crucially, Morgan traces the three elements of industry, revery and relation which are forcefully connected with the bee in Dickinson's work, and considers the extent to which this delineates an alternative 'design' or 'space' for belief within the schema of her poetics.

The productive relation between subjectivity, religious discourse and poetry that perhaps defines the mid-nineteenth-century is also explored in David M. Robinson's essay. He argues that, for Ralph Waldo Emerson, the religious impulse and the poetic impulse were always intertwined, if not indistinguishable, as both were expressions of the reach of the intellect towards similarities, analogies, kinships and ever-expanding recognitions of holistic unity. The essay explores how Emerson interrogates his earlier theory of inspiration and imaginative creation based on receptive vision on more naturalistic and pragmatic grounds, which were influenced in part by the examples of scientific categorization and development that were transforming the modern understanding of the natural world. Robinson shows how Emerson progressed to form a new conception of the poetic imagination, which attempts to give an account of the possibilities and limits of a conception of poetic vision, and by implication, of religious affirmation, as the product of desire, will and discipline, rather than the purely passive reception of insight.

Whilst Robinson's essay explores the ways in which Emerson's poetics project an aesthetic towards unity and oneness, Alison Milbank explores how the aesthetic of the gothic double can be an ultimately redemptive trope for the formation of a managed subjectivity within the context of nineteenth-century anxieties about maintaining social order. Tracing the idea through gothic literature, from Charles Maturin's *Melmoth the Wanderer* in 1820, to his great-nephew Oscar Wilde in *The Picture of Dorian Gray*, Milbank argues for the theological justification of the fissured self through the idea of sacrificial exchange. Thus, rather than viewing the fissured self as a primarily secular phenomenon, Milbank crafts a powerful reading of biblical discourse, exploring ideas of sacrifice and mutuality to support a potentially radical critique of nineteenth-century social relations.

Continuing on the central role of aesthetics in the shaping of subjectivities, and also specifically during nineteenth-century gothic revivalism, Kirstie Blair explores the formative relation between church architecture and religious poetry. Focusing on church architecture of the 1830s and 1840s and Tractarian poetry, the essay considers the extent to which such aesthetic spaces operated as formal 'regulated' structures, and how the centrality of reserve as a theological principle, were to give expression to the outlet for religious feeling. Looking at works from very different theological perspectives, such as Isaac Williams' poem 'The Cathedral' and John Ruskin's *Seven Lamps of Architecture*, Blair examines how architecture and poetry became fundamentally connected within the period. Blair argues that the 'central space' for religious feeling which church architecture and poetry came to represent was also the locus for immense controversy and debate as these aesthetic spaces were increasingly being perceived as a 'major power in the shaping of belief'.

The final section of the book addresses the issue of culture, and its authority, within an age of increasing anxieties about cross-class fluidity and the assertion of competing versions of democracy and unity. Brian Maidment's essay explores how mass literacy was conceived in light of the complex series of shifts in attitudes towards science, education, literacy and class mobility in the period between 1830 and 1860, which generally go under the shorthand title of 'The March of Intellect'. By focusing on caricatures and graphic satire that sought to represent the March, Maidment argues that a 'new visual language' was produced to mediate and accommodate the emerging issues surrounding questions of social interaction and diversity during the nineteenth century. He examines the repertoire of tropes, motifs and stereotypes used by caricatures to figure beliefs about social change, and suggests how these represent the complex or even fractured nature of middle-class understanding of debates about literacy and social change.

The concern with fractured social identities is brought sharply into focus by Clare Williams in her examination of Thomas Carlyle, and his involvement in the 'Condition of England Question', which addressed not only the condition of the working classes but also its implications for the rest of society. Williams argues that Carlyle, in addressing this question, experiences a serious crisis of social identity, wherein his own cultural beliefs were conspicuously challenged and tested against the pressing backdrop of social unrest and competing ideas of democracy. Reconsidering the perspective of reading Carlyle's rhetoric of labour as a purely reactionary and conservative critique, Williams critically explores Carlyle's endeavour to authenticate his own projected literary identity as social critic and validate his own mystified outlook of contemporary social relations.

Juliet John also engages with questions concerned with the relation between democracy, class and social identity through her exploration of

Dickens' vision of mass culture. John's essay innovatively examines how, in Dickens' journalism, his use of a particularly personal mode of address was intricately connected to a form of mass culture which attempted to incorporate humanistic beliefs within an increasingly commercialized social context in the hope of reaching a cross-class audience. She explores how Dickens tried to reconcile and articulate, both in mass journalism and through his performative personality, the contradictions seemingly endemic in any seriously committed engagement with the cause of popular education in a new age of mass culture. Such a critically receptive approach calls for a reassessment of many of the cultural assumptions of the 'current postmodern, mature age of mass culture', if a greater understanding of both Dickens' own cultural beliefs and those of nineteenth-century society is to be reached.

The concern with education is also taken up by Kate Campbell's essay, which argues against prevailing approaches to Arnoldian culture which position it as virtually a belief in itself and as something marked by its detachment from society. Considering Matthew Arnold's dedication to praxis, whereby cultural production is a means to the transformation of society, Campbell takes the view that culture is valued as a medium of exchange both for the spreading of ideas and as an aesthetic field. Campbell argues that, in this sense, belief in culture meant belief in the possibility of socio-political transformation, where culture was believed to enable the due articulation of intellectual and aesthetic forms of liberalism, with transformative import.

Notes

1 William James, *The Varieties of Religious Experience: A Study in Human Nature* (1902) ed. by Martin E. Marty (New York: Penguin, 1985), p. 175.
2 For notable examples of texts dealing with notions of belief in nineteenth-century writing through a religious framework, see: Mark Knight and Emma Mason, *Nineteenth-Century Religion and Literature: An Introduction* (Oxford: Oxford University Press, 2006); Andrew Dix and Jonathan Taylor, *Figures of Heresy: Radical Theology in English and American Writing* (Eastbourne: Sussex Academic Press, 2005); David Jasper, ed., *The Critical Spirit and the Will to Believe: Essays in Nineteenth-Century Literature and Religion* (London: Macmillan, 1989); Hilary Fraser, *Beauty and Belief: Aesthetics and Religion in Victorian Literature* (Cambridge: Cambridge University Press, 1986); and G.B. Tennyson, *Victorian Devotional Poetry: The Tractarian Mode* (Cambridge, MA: Harvard University Press, 1981). See also the anthology by R.L. Brett, *Poems of Faith and Doubt: The Victorian Age* (London: Edward Arnold, 1965).
3 W. David Shaw, *The Lucid Veil: Poetic Truth in the Victorian Age* (London: The Athlone Press, 1987), and J. Hillis Miller, *Victorian Subjects* (London: Harvester Wheatsheaf, 1990).

4 J. Hillis Miller, 'The ethics of reading' (1981) in *Victorian Subjects*, p. 250.
5 See Philip Davis, *The Victorians* (New York: Oxford University Press, 2002), pp. 4–5.
6 Davis, *The Victorians*, p. 533.
7 John Schad, *Victorians in Theory: From Derrida to Browning* (Manchester: Manchester University Press, 1999), p. 3.
8 Slavoj Žižek's contentious uses of Christianity as a model to support dialectical materialist thinking is evidence of recent philosophical self-reflexivity on issues of belief. For example, see Slavoj Žižek, *On Belief* (London: Routledge, 2001).
9 Terry Eagleton, *After Theory* (London: Penguin, 2004), p. 21. All further references cited in the text refer to this edition.
10 John Stuart Mill, 'Utility of Religion' (1874), in *Collected Works of John Stuart Mill: Essays on Ethics, Religion, and Society*, ed. by J. M. Robson (Canada: University of Toronto Press, 1969), vol. 10, p. 403.
11 Mill, 'Utility of Religion', p. 404.
12 Mill, 'Utility of Religion', p. 405.
13 Mill, 'Utility of Religion', p. 419.
14 Mill, 'Utility of Religion', p. 422.
15 Thomas Carlyle, in a letter to John Stuart Mill dated April 1835, in *Thomas Carlyle: Letters to Mill, Sterling, and Browning*, ed. by Alexander Carlyle (London: T. Fisher Unwin, 1923), p. 113.
16 Mill, 'Utility of Religion', p. 427.
17 Matthew Arnold, 'Culture and Anarchy' (1869), in *Matthew Arnold on Education*, ed. by Gillian Sutherland (London: Penguin, 1973), pp. 164–269 (p. 263). All further references are taken from this edition.
18 Arnold, 'Culture and Anarchy', p. 167. Arnold quotes Bishop Wilson.
19 Arnold, 'Culture and Anarchy', p. 168.
20 Arnold, 'Culture and Anarchy', p. 169.
21 Ebenezer Elliott, 'The Press' (1940), in Brian Maidment's *Poorhouse Fugitives: Self-Taught Poets and Poetry in Victorian Britain* (Manchester: Carcanet Press, 1987), pp. 54–5.
22 R.W. Franklin, ed., *The Poems of Emily Dickinson: Reading Edition* (Cambridge, MA: The Belknap of Harvard University Press, 1998), p. 582, #1581. Although the date of this poem is estimated at 1882 in both T.H. Johnson's 1975 and R.W. Franklin's editions, it bears a remarkable resemblance, in its concern with the absence of God, with poems Dickinson wrote profusely during the 1861–1865 American Civil War era.
23 Arthur Hugh Clough, 'It Fortifies My Soul to Know' (1862), in *Clough: Selected Poems*, ed. by J. P. Phelan (New York: Longman, 1995), p. 269.
24 Clough's satirical comment on capitalist appropriation of the Ten Commandments, 'The Latest Decalogue' (1862), is an example of his concern with the precarious connection between religious orthodoxy and the sustenance of political and moral integrity in society. See Francis O'Gorman, ed., *Victorian Poetry: An Annotated Anthology* (Oxford: Blackwell, 2004), pp. 262–3.
25 For an interesting contrast to this, see Clough's more devotional poem 'Say Not the Struggle Nought Availeth', in O'Gorman, ed., *Victorian Poetry*, pp. 227–8. Significantly, the sustaining of a Christ-like redemptive agency of 'light' within this poem proved enough to make it into a popular hymn.
26 For arguments on the essentially discursive nature of Christianity and its links to postmodernism, see Luke Ferretter, *Towards a Christian Literary Theory* (Basingstoke: Palgrave, 2003).
27 Joseph Ramsbottom, 'Preawd Tum's Prayer' (1864), in Maidment, *Poorhouse Fugitives*, pp. 86–90 (p. 90).

I. Religious Discourse:
Transmission and Appropriation

1. Tell the Story:
Re-imagining Victorian Conversion Narratives

Andrew Tate

> [T]he Churches for a long time have practically forgotten that the conversion of the world is the great business assigned them [...]. They have ceased to regard the conversion of men as their peculiar, great, and only business in the world; for they are, evidently, living for other ends.
> Charles G. Finney, 'Why London Is Not Converted', 1850[1]

Dramatic calls to conversion are alien to most liberal, contemporary readers. However, during the mid-nineteenth century, conversion narratives – in sermons, fiction, music and art – were a commonplace element of popular culture. In a sermon to the 'members and visitors of the Christian Instruction Society' at the Tabernacle, Moorfields, Charles G. Finney (1792–1875), a distinguished American evangelist, challenged the assembly to dedicate themselves to the task of converting the world, beginning with London. Finney's zealous message – taking the 'great commission' of Matthew 28 as its text – was delivered in June 1850, and foreshadowed a decade in which religious belief in Britain would experience some radical challenges, including the re-establishment of the Roman Catholic hierarchy, and a new wave of popular revivalist activity. Charles Haddon Spurgeon (1834–1892), for example, rose to prominence as a preacher who emphasized the necessity of spiritual second birth. Spurgeon's emotive, conversion-focused sermons, heard by thousands every week from the pulpits of New Park Street and the Metropolitan Tabernacle, are part of what Callum Brown, in his controversial secularization thesis *The Death of Christian Britain* (2001), has named the 'salvation economy' of Victorian Britain. Borrowing the term from Albert Bradwell's *Autobiography of a Converted Infidel* (1844), in which a new believer repudiates his former resistance to God's grace, Brown defines the 'salvation economy' as 'the machinery of ideas and agencies by which the discursivity of evangelical piety dominated public culture'.[2] Conversion, in short, was not just a part of the grammar of Victorian theology but also an animating presence in the popular imagination.

4   *Shaping Belief*

This chapter examines the shifting concept of radical religious change and its representation in early and mid-Victorian Britain. What is conversion? How important was it in the Victorian age, beyond the enthusiastic chapels of non-conformist Christianity? The chapter will explore the ideas of eminent Victorian 'converts' of various kinds – Spurgeon, John Henry Newman (1801–1890) and John Ruskin (1819–1900) – and narratives by less well known figures. Where Callum Brown emphasizes the socio-historical processes that produced conversion, my argument will explore the intersections of theology, sociology, religious practice and literary representation.

'No Longer Myself': Theologies of Transformation

'[C]onversion,' reflects Jacques Derrida, 'ought to be the surprise of an event happening to "myself," who am therefore no longer myself'.[3] The unsettling thought of radical personal change may have been crucial to a long-repressed nineteenth-century religious discourse, but it is also one that continues to haunt the postmodern imagination. In his study of the covert tradition of 'Christian unreason' in literature, science and philosophy from Darwin to Derrida, John Schad suggests that for the latter (specifically in the peculiar essay, 'Circumfession') 'conversion is a name for the radical discontinuities that beset identity or being; it names, if you will, "The Importance of Being Someone Else", or rather the inevitability'.[4] Narrating dramatic personal change presents the interpreter with a series of problems about the meaning of the transformation. '[T]he experience of conversion', notes Heather Henderson, 'points toward a central problem of the autobiographer [...]. How can he assert the continuity of his personality over the course of time?'[5]

Does the 'surprise event' of conversion imply insincerity or is it evidence that the original, firmly held conviction was entirely erroneous? John Henry Newman, perhaps the most famous convert of the nineteenth century, isolates this question in his *Apologia Pro Vita Sua* (1864). He does not, however, associate the problem with his own conversion to Roman Catholicism but with a critique of the 'anti-dogmatic principle' of liberalism: 'persistence in a given belief is no sufficient test of its truth: but departure from it is at least a slur upon the man who has felt so certain about it'.[6] Significantly, almost a decade and half before joining the Roman Catholic communion, Newman had arrived at the conclusion that conversion is a gradual process, analogous to the growth of plants, rather than a sudden or dramatic transformation of identity:

> When men change their religious opinions really and truly, it is not merely their opinions that they change, but their hearts; and this evidently is not done in a moment [...]. This we see in the growth of plants, for instance; it is slow, gradual, continual; yet one day by chance they grow more than another, they make a shoot, or at least we are attracted to their growth on that day by some accidental circumstance, and it remains on our memory. So with our souls.[7]

The organic imagery of this sermon might be interpreted as an attempt to challenge the traditional hegemony of Evangelicals on the importance of personal transformation through repentance and public confession of Christ.[8] Newman's disdain for the sudden and unexpected conversion of formerly profligate individuals is an indirect, but nevertheless incisive, denunciation of the Evangelical mode of calling for conversion. This, Newman implies, engenders a subjective sense of forgiveness without the authority of the Church and constitutes a mockery of its sacraments. Newman's argument is based on an audacious re-reading of the conversion of St Paul, who, he argued, underwent a gradual conversion that was concluded, but not begun, on the road to Damascus. He observes that as Saul, persecutor of Christians, he was without equal for his zeal and religious obedience, and that he was a strict follower of the Law. Newman notes that these remained key aspects of Saul's character after his conversion to Christ and his change of name and were 'merely directed to other and higher objects, and purified; it was his creed that was changed, and his soul by regeneration'.[9] Newman's emphasis on the developmental nature of St Paul's dramatic transformation was informed by his suspicion of the Evangelical tradition which had been so vital in his own religious heritage. Yet it also indicates some of the problems we might have in describing the nature and legitimacy of different conversion experiences.

Asserting a stable definition of conversion is not easy, even, as Roland Robertson has noted, within the limits of the Christian tradition. However, its core characteristic, throughout Christian history at least, might most accurately be described as 'the idea of self-revision relative to God'.[10] A.D. Nock, in his highly influential 1933 study of religious transformation in ancient and early Christian civilizations, described conversion as a 'reorientation of the soul' and the 'deliberate turning from indifference or from an earlier form of piety to another, a turning which implies a consciousness that a great change is involved'.[11] As a social phenomenon, conversion implies a radical reassessment of identity and the relationship between the individual and the society of which it is a part. In the Gospel accounts of both Matthew and Mark the first assertion of Jesus's ministry was 'Be converted!'[12] A number of words are used in the New Testament to denote different forms of conversion. *Metanoeín* and *metánoia* indicate the divinely influenced 'change of heart' that leads to salvation. Michel observes that these words take precedence in the New Testament over *metamélomai*, meaning to feel regret or to repent.[13] The sentiment of remorse, as Michel notes, does not always lead to a full repentance or 'conversion', and this is illustrated with reference to the sense of guilt experienced by Judas after the betrayal of Christ which resulted in suicide rather than spiritual re-birth.[14] James Walter makes a further distinction between *metánoia* and *epistrophé*, arguing that the first word emphasizes the intellectual processes and intentions that inspire action, whilst the latter indicates 'the visible characteristics of an external act'. He also notes that these terms are almost synonymous and can both be appropriate translations of the Hebrew *shub*, used in the books of Isaiah and Jeremiah to call Israel to turn away from sin and return to God for salvation.[15]

Since the eighteenth century, 'conversion' has most often been associated with Evangelical Christianity. Bebbington argues that a particular emphasis on the necessity of the conversion experience is one of the 'priorities' of the Evangelical tradition from its origins in the 1730s to the end of the twentieth century.[16] In his groundbreaking study of conversion narratives ('a biography of a genre'), D. Bruce Hindmarsh claims that a reappraisal of spiritual autobiography might challenge common assumptions about modern identity. These Evangelical stories of personal change, he argues, 'bore witness to a religious understanding that was only ever a vector of the Enlightenment [...] that did not succumb to the pathological elision of community, contingency, or faith that is typical of the modernist autobiography'.[17]

The matrix of nineteenth-century religious debate produced many dynamic accounts of faith re-discovered, lost or transformed which were widely published as print culture became increasingly accessible. John Wolffe has argued that literature was the most obvious medium for Evangelicals, in particular, to make use of because it was 'a natural extension of their own consciousness of being a people of the book, drawing inspiration and authority from the study of the Scriptures'.[18] Testimony was a crucial element of Victorian religious life: new converts stood before congregations recounting their salvation stories; short pamphlets, often anonymously written, described reasons for joining, or leaving, particular churches. The 'reality-shaping power of language', as Brad Kallenberg has described it, has a specific theological precedent in the narratives of the life of Christ. He observes that Jesus is made distinct from the Old Testament prophets by his ability to heal through words.[19] How, then, do conversion narratives, by necessity retrospective, operate? Can modern-day, sociological models of religious experience help us to understand conversion without traducing its theological nature?

'Conversion Motifs': John Ruskin and the Sociology of Conversion

If Newman is the most famous convert of the nineteenth century, John Ruskin might well be its most distinguished '*un*-converted man', to use his own phrase. In 1858, the great critic of art and society underwent what he described as an 'unconversion' from the Evangelical tradition of his youth for which had been an articulate advocate. The first major public assessment of this *bouleversement* was detailed in Letter 76 of *Fors Clavigera*, published in April 1877, almost twenty years after the event. In this narrative Ruskin describes his departure from a Turin gallery where he had been studying the gorgeous (and Catholic) art of Paolo Veronese, a place of spiritual and physical affirmation where he had been filled with a sense of a painter's 'God-given power', to a Waldensian chapel that is characterized by a sermon given by 'a little squeaking idiot' who believed that 'all the people in the world out of sight of Monte Viso, would be damned': 'I came out of the chapel, in sum of twenty years of thought, a conclusively *un*-converted man.'[20]

Ruskin wrote a number of accounts of this intellectual and spiritual crisis: separate conversion narratives appear in his private correspondence of 1858 with his father, John James Ruskin, and friends including Robert and Elizabeth Barrett Browning, and Charles Eliot Norton; it is also represented in his 'Notes on the Turin Gallery'. The last of these individual readings of the crisis is included in the third part of his uncompleted biography, *Praeterita* (1885–1889), where Ruskin refers to his unconversion from Evangelical dogma as the 'Queen of Sheba crash', in reference to Paul Veronese's painting that precipitated this radical change.[21] Michael Wheeler, whose *Ruskin's God* (1999) is the most thorough and sophisticated account of its subject's theological journey, rightly warns that the 'crash' is too 'easily caricatured as another simple case of Victorian "loss of faith"'.[22]

Describing a movement away from a religious tradition as conversion might be deemed perverse. However, as Wheeler notes, Ruskin explicitly (and subversively) drew on the language of his Evangelical background to describe an experience apparently counter to its claims.[23] The writer's failure to transcend a Puritan idiom resonates with Callum Brown's emphasis on the defining 'salvation economy' of the era and illustrates the difficulty of using the term 'conversion' in Victorian Britain. Throughout the 1850s the problem of conversion divided the believing community of Great Britain. To state that a person was a 'convert' had a number of contrasting meanings in different social circles: in Oxford Tractarian circles, for example, it was likely to indicate secession from the Anglican communion and admission to the Roman Catholic Church. For Evangelicals, however, the epithet was rarely used to describe an individual's new institutional affiliation. Rather it was bestowed to indicate the movement of a soul from damnation to salvation through sincere repentance and confession of Christ. The lack of consensus on how an individual was to find salvation informed the other major religious debates of the decade regarding biblical authority and historicity, and conflicting images of regeneration became a key feature of the literature and art of the period, even in work that was not consciously 'religious'.

Much of the most crucial late-twentieth-century research on religious conversion was conducted by sociologists and social anthropologists. In particular, Victor Turner's work on ritual models of personal transformation has influenced research in a number of disciplines, including religious studies and English literature.[24] In the late 1970s important work was produced by James Beckford, Sallie McFague and Brian Taylor. McFague's work contrasts with that of Beckford and Taylor as her criticism explores theologies of conversion rather than the social conditions and consequences of its production.[25] More recently, interdisciplinary work has been undertaken by scholars including Lewis Rambo, Christopher Lamb and M. Darrol Bryant, Martyn Percy and Gauri Viswanathan.[26] In an article written in 1981, John Lofland and Norman Skonovd identified six key types of conversion. These 'Conversion Motifs' are Intellectual, Mystical, Experimental, Affectional, Revivalist and Coercive. The last of these is irrelevant to the present discussion as it relates to the primarily twentieth-century phenomenon of 'brain-washing', often associated with religious cults and oppressive political regimes.[27] However, the other five categories defined are pertinent to Victorian religious discourse and provide a useful framework for introducing a number of the fundamental elements of 1850s conversion narratives.

The 'Intellectual' motif indicates a conversion that is reached privately, through engagement with literature, for example, or perhaps through listening to a number of sermons, and with little reference to the believing community. Lofland and Skonovd suggest that this model of faith is relatively new and is a result of the increasingly personal nature of religion in the western world. This motif was, however, also a significant element of Victorian religious experience. One of the earliest references to conversion in Ruskin's writing describes a religious transformation that was arrived at primarily through intellectual engagement with Christian texts. In his diary for 31 October 1848, Ruskin reflected on a discussion he had held that afternoon with the father of his schoolfriend, Edmund Oldfield:

> I was sitting with Mr.Oldfield for an hour, and permitted to question him respecting the origin of his faith. It was a deliberate conviction, attained by careful reading and examination of all *serious* and dignified objections to Christianity, as well as of the evidence for it, begun about the age of twenty six, in shame at not being able to render a reason for the faith taught him from a child. Afterwards he had rested secure, quoting the words of an aged clergyman to some questions put to him respecting his faith: 'I was in doubt about the foundation of my house; I took a candle and went down into the cellar, and ascertained that all was perfectly safe. Since then I have lived in the pleasantest of the upper parts of the house: I don't live in the cellar.'[28]

The intellectual conviction of this reflective and rational approach to religious commitment contrasts with the anxiety of the age. There is a strong resonance between this intellectual decision as the basis of conversion and the aforementioned New Testament *metánoia*, indicating the divinely induced change of heart. As Mr Oldfield was the father of a schoolfriend we can assume that his conversion, at the age of twenty-six, occurred some decades earlier, in the context of a society that was significantly less troubled about its religious identity. The suggestion that to 'live in the cellar' of faith was unhealthy appears to be a rejection of the doubts of historicist scholars who were challenging the integrity of the biblical narrative as a contemporaneous and accurate account of key moments in human history. Neither the creation of the world nor the details of the life of Christ were taken for granted by these critics. The Evangelical hermeneutic which had formed the basis of Ruskin's worldview since childhood was the defining influence on his work during the late 1840s: *Modern Painters* II (1846), published two years before this conversation, and *The Seven Lamps of Architecture* (1849), appearing some months later, both feature apologia for the Evangelical tradition. Ruskin reached the summit of his intellectual commitment to Evangelicalism during this period, culminating with the publication of *Notes on the Construction of Sheepfolds* in 1851. His response to Mr Oldfield's conversion narrative illustrates this unequivocal intellectual sympathy:

> I then made some observation on the great distinction between this evangelical trust in Christ and all other, including any confidence in man: he then said, 'I believe there is but One great Difference, and that is, between him that serveth God and him that serveth him not; and that is implied by what St.Paul says: "Grace, mercy and peace be to all them that love our Lord Jesus in sincerity". If any man love *not* the Lord Jesus let him be anathema maranatha.'[29]

The use of the lower case 'evangelical' implies a broader sense of the term than a specific reference to the Puritan tradition of that name. Rather, he uses it to distinguish between genuine or Gospel-inspired Christian commitment from insincere conversions. Ruskin was certainly no latitudinarian at this time, and he believed that there could be no possible ambiguity regarding an individual's conversion to Christ: a soul was either inside the fold or was living in a state of corruption. This sense of assurance was undermined in the 1850s as Ruskin became less convinced of Protestant teaching on salvation and the authenticity of conversion. Disdain for the doctrine of justification by faith, that became so crucial to his work in the 1870s and 1880s, also guided him away from approbation for 'intellectual' conversion.

The 'Mystical' type of conversion is most obviously associated with the Damascus road encounter with the divine that led Saul to become St Paul, and in a sense is the 'classic', if not in reality the most common, mode of transformation. Theophany, a moment when God reveals himself, in some palpable way, to the individual or to the community, is a common feature of 'Mystical' conversion narratives. Intense emotional and sometimes even physical experiences are often integral to this motif. Ruskin's encounter with Veronese's 'Queen of Sheba' has elements of such a conversion.

'Experimental' conversion relates to active participation in a religion by an individual as a means of deciding whether to become a committed member. Although Lofland and Skonovd relate this type primarily with twentieth-century 'new age' groups that thrive on curiosity and which are often free from authoritarian structures, many Victorians experimented with different forms of worship, moving between church and chapel to listen to the latest highly esteemed preacher. In an anonymously published pamphlet, entitled *The Religious Tendencies of the Age* (1860), one writer advocated a full experiential encounter with specific religious practices as the only means of true understanding. Cool rationalism, he argued, was not the basis of a decision for or against a mode of worship:

> Do not imagine that you understand a religious system because you have mastered its history and can explain its doctrines [...]. You should try to divest

yourself for a time of your previous notions and to assume the feelings of others; you should read not merely their standard theological works, but also their ordinary devotional manuals; you should haunt the village chapel and the village procession, and endeavour in every way to enter into the feelings of the worshipper.[30]

The growing access enjoyed by wealthy Victorians to the Continent, and the tradition of the 'Grand Tour' in particular, exposed travellers to forms of worship and religious practice that were quite unlike their own modes of belief. Attending a Mass, for example, would have been very different in a culture that was predominantly Roman Catholic from one in the militantly Protestant environment of 1850s England. In July 1856 the *Evangelical Magazine* observed that the increasing opportunities for international travel would influence the religious identity of the nation. The writer suggested that this 'traffic' was potentially both enlightening and a threat to Protestant liberty:

> As the traffic among the nations becomes augmented, the difficulties of language will disappear, and literature will attain a tenfold power of enrichment as well as of a diffusion. The great law embodied in the proverb of Solomon applies in all its force to this case. 'There is that scattereth and yet increaseth.' The interchange of thought between races of the most various mental constitutions and habits is a process that cannot fail to be suggestive.[31]

'Affectional' conversion is precipitated by friendship or familial bonds with active members of a religious group. Lofland and Skonovd argue that emotional attachment can have the same influence as the intellectual sympathy, divine encounter, or 'experimental immersion' associated with the other motifs. For the Victorian Church, the 'affectional' motif was perhaps a means of holding members rather than actually gaining new ones. The social pressure to remain within the faith tradition in which an individual was brought up was, and is, often strong. The opprobrium conferred on those who seceded from the Church of England to Rome, for example, was highly potent and individuals were denounced in sermons and pamphlets for their act of apostasy. Charles Kingsley's censure of John Henry Newman in an article published in *Macmillan's Magazine* in January 1864 is arguably the most prominent example of such public defamation. However, the attempt to shame those who abandoned the Protestant faith was common. In a pamphlet entitled *The Folly of Going to Rome for a Religion* (1846), the Reverend A.G.H. Hollingsworth censured the conversion of 'Miss R.' to the Roman Catholic faith. He attacked this convert's lack of intellectual rigour and suggested that her earlier 'low church' affinities signified an insecure religious identity. His denuciation, however, indicates the desire of many Protestants for a stable site of authority:

> At first her own refinements, or her reason, or her feeling of some inward and ecstatic religious sensations were her sole guides to truth [...]. Every one that professed to love the Saviour of the world was her co-religionist. No difference could be perceived between methodist and presbyterian, churchman or baptist, so long as all these different dissenters and nominal churchmen could be fused together at a tea-party [...] she looked round for something more fixed, and of a firmer consistency, and found, as she thought, in these western regions nothing but Rome, which, in its intense exclusiveness, gave a well-defined though gloomy and uncharitably embattled citadel to her wandering soul.[32]

Other pamphlets in this popular genre included the Reverend W.E. Scudamore's *Letters to a Seceder from the Church of England to the Communion of Rome* (1851) and the Reverend Henry Alford's *An Earnest Dissuasive from Joining the Communion of the Church of Rome* (1846).[33] Public shaming was an important ritual for the Protestant community with its missionary rationale and an accompanying need to sustain its existing membership.

The 'Revivalist' motif is the final category to discuss. This involves the conversion of many people in the context of emotionally charged meetings. Revivalism is given little credence by modern critics and it is often argued that relatively few conversions occur within these meetings. Certain post-war studies suggest that the impact of this kind of missionary activity is significantly less dramatic than claimed by evangelistic organizations.[34]

Whether or not revivalism ever engendered significant numbers of conversions it was certainly a vital element of Victorian Church history. The foundation of the Evangelical Alliance in 1846 encouraged inter-denominational missionary activity, and many of these endeavours were distinctly revivalist in style. At the end of 1852, for example, the Reverend James Haldane issued an *Invitation for United Prayer for the Outpouring of the Holy Spirit* at a meeting to be held on New Year's Day 1853. This summons, published as a short pamphlet, attempted to galvanize the Protestant community with the observation that 'the Pope is making a daring onset on our [...] faith'.[35] Roman Catholics were clearly not included in Haldane's call to all 'who love the Lord Jesus in sincerity' to participate in a prayer meeting for the 'outpouring' of the Holy Spirit. This kind of assembly was designed to dissipate the variety of doctrine that existed even within the Evangelical community.[36] Although the principal objective of this particular rally was not the conversion of non-believers, the confident expectation that the Holy Spirit would become manifest and enact a transformation of those present locates it as part of the revivalist movement.

Spurgeon's meetings in the Music Hall of the Surrey Gardens and later in the Metropolitan Tabernacle were characterized by the presence of vast, emotionally stimulated crowds and by his dramatic sermons, delivered in impassioned rhetoric that emphasized the narrow road to salvation. Spurgeon was undoubtedly part of the tradition of 'revivalist' preachers, though he disliked the epithet: 'Whenever I see a man who is called a revivalist, I always set him down for a cipher. I would scorn the taking of such a title as that to myself.'[37]

Yet the objective of Spurgeon's ministry was unequivocal. He wanted to convert his listeners, and he very rarely preached without a challenge to accept faith in Christ as the sole means of salvation. He also believed that genuine revival was a fundamental promise of scripture, and, as a biblical literalist, he was confident that prophecy would be fulfilled in accordance with the word of God.[38] Significantly in 1858, the year of Ruskin's apparent 'unconversion' from the Puritan tradition, Spurgeon and other Evangelicals told their congregations of a dramatic revival of religion in America. Reports were made that thousands of people had turned to the Christian faith, and this was interpreted by certain groups as an unmistakable act of the Holy Spirit.

On 28 March 1858, preaching at the Royal Surrey Gardens, Spurgeon described the conditions necessary for a similar revival to the one that had apparently swept across the United States, exemplified by 'towns in New England where you could not, even if you searched, find one solitary unconverted person'.[39] Interestingly, Spurgeon represented the intensification of religion as an opportunity to compete with Rome, emphasizing the distinctly Protestant character of revival. Hostility towards the Roman Catholic Church was still strong some eight years after the re-establishment of the hierarchy: 'if we for once could outvie old Rome, who kept her monks in her sanctuaries, always at prayer, both by night and by day, – if we together could keep up one golden chain of prayer [...] then might we expect an abundant outpouring of the Divine Spirit from the Lord our God'.[40] One famous historian of nineteenth-century revivalist movements, J. Edwin Orr, has argued that the American revival was followed by a 'similar movement' in the United Kingdom in 1859.[41] However, Bebbington has since challenged Orr's conclusions. He argues that Orr failed to distinguish 'between spontaneous popular revival, deeply rooted in the community, and meetings carefully designed to promote the work of the gospel.' Orr's work, he suggests, relies too heavily on R.C. Morgan's magazine, *The Revival*, which 'created the impression that a single phenomenon, revival, was already aflame

14   *Shaping Belief*

throughout Britain'. The reality, claims Bebbington, was that 'its range was severely limited'.⁴² The history of conversion is a space of debate and contest, open to re-interpretation and new perspectives.

Apostasy and Public Profession

Lewis Rambo, acknowledging Lofland and Skonovd's vital work, has developed a further typology of conversion. One notable category featured in Rambo's work that is not included in the 'Conversion Motifs' essay is 'Apostasy'. This indicates the repudiation of a previous set of beliefs in favour of a new worldview. Rambo argues that this is a significant form of conversion because the 'dynamics of leaving a group or of loss of faith constitute an important form of change, both individually and collectively'.⁴³ In *Praeterita* Ruskin famously described the Turin crisis as his 'final apostasy from Puritan doctrine'.⁴⁴ This is something of an exaggeration. However, it is a useful example of the ways in which the term was used to describe a mode of conversion.

In the 1850s apostasy was often associated with those who had not lost faith but, being disillusioned with fundamental aspects of Protestantism, had chosen to enter the Roman Catholic communion. Just as thousands of pamphlets and sermons were issued to condemn these conversions, so too were many accounts given in defence of personal religious change. In 1858 one convert published *Churches, Sects and Religious Parties; or, Some Motives for my Conversion to the Catholic Church*, withholding his name and identifying himself simply as a 'Master of Arts, formerly a Clergyman of the Established Church'. Significantly, the pamphlet begins with a rejection of the charge that converts to Rome were weak men unduly influenced by Pusey and the Tractarian movement. The writer also notes that secession to Rome was not recognized by most Protestants as 'conversion', indicating spiritual rebirth and salvation, but described instead as *'perversion'*, a parody of the interaction between man and God.⁴⁵

His reasons for entering the Roman Catholic Church indicate that for many the Protestant tradition could no longer offer spiritual assurance. Catholicism offered a permanent understanding of truth, not influenced by the *zeitgeist* or by denominational division:

> I wanted a *theology*, and I found it only in the Catholic Church. I needed a *faith*, which should be something better than a mere system of opinions, and I found it there. I had all along sought for a *religion* which should be something more than mere sentiment, and here alone again I found it [...] universal truth was enshrined in a Church which more than realized all the dreams of

Kosmopolisan – of world-regard – embracing in her large and generous heart the whole of humanity – all the families, tribes, and tongues of the human race, without distinction of race, or lineage, or tongue, or nationality, or the thousand other differences which divide mankind.[46]

The public narration of conversion is extremely important, both to the individual who has undergone the change and to the community which he or she has entered. As Rambo argues, 'stories as they are retold orally and composed as autobiographies become the paradigms by which people interpret their own lives'.[47] This anonymous account, though written rather than spoken, provides a coherent reinterpretation of a life, locating it in a specific doctrinal frame of reference, and integrating the individual's identity in a *'Kosmopolitan'* religious community. The Roman Catholic Church harmonized the confused voices of the post-Babel world, and many converts desired transcendence from the conflicting tongues of an increasingly pluralist society. The conversion narrative is also an important act of reinforcement: the religious transformation becomes more 'real' when restated, both for the narrator and for the reader/listener. Brian Taylor maintains that in describing the momentous change, individuals in 'a quite literal sense [...] talk themselves into the experience of conversion in the past through engagement in the experience of accounting for conversion in the present.'[48] This, in Rambo's terms, 'biographical re-shaping' creates a powerful sense of regeneration, an opportunity to abandon the limits of the past and to enter a new, more authentic state of selfhood.[49]

A crucial part of the narrative process is a repudiation of the rejected hermeneutic or mode of belief. For the writer of *Churches, Sects and Religious Parties*, this is discernible in his careful contrast between the theology of growth with which he associates the Catholic Church and the aridity of 'dead Protestantism'. Repudiation is so vital as it emphasizes the separation between the identity of the past and present as converts wish to establish the integrity of their new religious selfhood and to maintain the sincerity of their transformation. Yet, as another anonymous convert to Rome observed, also 'a late Clergyman of the Anglican Communion', the intellectual transition was rarely swift or conclusive: 'How hard it is to get rid of the Protestant mind in which we have been educated!'[50]

This method of 'casting-off' the old form as a means of vindicating the new was not peculiar to those who relinquished Protestantism. The sense of becoming a new creation, fundamental to Evangelical conversion, was often perpetuated in public testimony as the convert described the sinfulness of his pre-regenerate self, as if describing a completely separate individual.⁵¹ This rhetoric of newness is also a feature of narratives constructed by those who inverted the apparently popular trend of movement to Rome. In 1851 a pamphlet entitled *Papal Aggression in England and Defection from Popery in France* was published, featuring the first-person account of a French priest's recent rejection of Rome. The writer argued that he remained a Catholic, as did all true believers but that the corrupt decisions and practices of his former Church would precipitate the judgement of God unless the believing community interceded for a renewal of private and corporate holiness.⁵² The pamphlet was published within a year of the so-called act of 'Papal Aggression' and there is a clear agenda for bringing the story of a Roman Catholic priest, who now rejected the Papacy, to the turbulent milieu of Protestant England. It was a narrative of conversion appropriated to warn people away from the call of Rome, using one individual's private religious experience as anti-Catholic propaganda.⁵³

Conclusion: Saving Conversion

'Conversion is paradoxical', observes Lewis R. Rambo: 'It destroys and it saves [...]. It is created totally by the action of God, and it is created totally by the action of humans.'⁵⁴ Victorian iterations of conversion are no less slippery than those of the pluralist, postmodern era. Yet if we are to understand nineteenth-century Britain, we need to re-appraise the irreducibly theological nature of its popular culture, however much it might offend our contemporary sensibilities. From a purely secular perspective, conversion narratives illuminate the 'practice of everyday life', to borrow Michel de Certeau's famous phrase, operating in a world that is no longer our own. In theological terms, by contrast, the form of spiritual autobiography known as the conversion narrative is vital in connecting disparate religious communities to a grand narrative of God's redemptive action in history. Whether we privilege the secular or the sacred versions of these accounts, our encounter with figures such as Newman, Spurgeon and Ruskin – as well as the host of anonymous converts – is enriched by the 'surprise [...] event' of conversion.⁵⁵

Notes

1   Charles G. Finney, 'Why London Is Not Converted', sermon delivered at the Tabernacle, Moorfields, 5 June 1850, http://www.gospeltruth.net/1849-51Penny_Pulpit/500605pp_whylondon_ntcnvt.htm, last accessed 23 November 2007.

2   Callum G. Brown, *The Death of Christian Britain: Understanding Secularisation, 1800–2000* (London: Routledge, 2001), pp. 35–6. Chapter 3 ('The Salvation Economy') offers a very useful exploration of this phenomenon in relation to the 'privatisation of faith'.
3   Jacques Derrida, 'Circumfession', in Geoffrey Bennington and Jacques Derrida, *Jacques Derrida* [1991], trans. by Geoffrey Bennington (Chicago, IL: University of Chicago Press, 1993), p. 124.
4   John Schad, *Queer Fish: Christian Unreason from Darwin to Derrida* (Eastbourne: Sussex Academic Press, 2004), p. 95. Schad invokes Derrida and the spectre of rebirth in an exploration of Oscar Wilde's lasting flirtation with – and death-bed conversion to – Roman Catholicism.
5   Heather Henderson, *The Victorian Self: Autobiography and Biblical Narrative* (Ithaca, NY: Cornell University Press, 1989), p. 14.
6   John Henry Cardinal Newman, *Apologia Pro Vita Sua: Being a History of his Religious Opinions*, ed. by Martin J. Svaglic (Oxford: Clarendon Press, 1967), p. 54.
7   John Henry Newman, 'Sudden Conversions', preached January 1832, *Parochial and Plain Sermons*, new edn, 8 vols (London: Rivingtons, 1882), vol. 8, pp. 225–6.
8   For a discussion of Evangelical influences in Newman's early life see Ian Ker, *John Henry Newman: A Biography* (Oxford: Oxford University Press, 1988), pp. 3–5.
9   Newman, *Parochial and Plain Sermons*, vol. 8, p. 227.
10 Roland Robertson, *Meaning and Change: Explorations in the Cultural Sociology of Modern Societies* (Oxford: Blackwell, 1978), p. 197.
11 A.D. Nock, *Conversion: The Old and the New in Religion from Alexander the Great to Augustine of Hippo* (Oxford: Oxford University Press, 1933), p. 7.
12 Matthew 4.17, Mark 1.15. See entry on 'Conversion' by James J. Walter in *The New Dictionary of Theology*, ed. by Joseph A. Komonchak (Dublin: Gill, Macmillan, 1987), p. 233.
13 O. Michel, entry on '*Metamélomai*' in *Theological Dictionary of the New Testament*, ed. by Gerhard Kittel and Gerhard Friedrich, trans. by Geoffrey W. Bromiley (Grand Rapids, MI: Eerdmans, 1985), pp. 589–90.
14 See Matthew 27.3. Kittel and Friedrich, ed., *Theological Dictionary of the New Testament*, p. 590.
15 Komonchak *et al.*, eds, *New Dictionary of Theology*, p. 233.
16 D.W. Bebbington, *Evangelicalism in Modern Britain: A History from the 1730s to the 1980s* (London: Unwin Hyman, 1989), pp. 2–3.
17 D. Bruce Hindmarsh, *The Evangelical Conversion Narrative: Spiritual Autobiography in Early Modern England* (Oxford: Oxford University Press, 2005), pp. v–vii. For other relevant studies see Avrom Fleishman, *Figures of Autobiography: The Language of Self-Writing in Victorian and Modern England* (Berkeley, CA: University of California Press, 1983); John Sturrock, *The Language of Autobiography: Studies in the First-Person Singular* (Cambidge: Cambridge University Press, 1993). See also George P. Landow, ed., *Approaches to Victorian Autobiography* (Athens, OH: Ohio University Press, 1979).
18 John Wolffe, *God and Greater Britain: Religion and National Life in Britain and Ireland 1843–1945* (London: Routledge, 1994), p. 176.
19 Brad J. Kallenberg, 'Conversion Converted: A Postmodern Formulation of the Doctrine of Conversion', *Evangelical Quarterly* 67:4 (1995): 335–64 (350).
20 John Ruskin, *The Works of Ruskin*, ed. by E.T. Cook and Alexander Wedderburn, 39 vols (London: George Allen, 1903–1912), vol. 29, p. 89.
21 Ruskin, *Works of Ruskin*, vol. 35, p. 497.

22 Michael Wheeler, *Ruskin's God* (Cambridge: Cambridge University Press, 1999), p. 126. Chapter 6 ('Solomon's "Christian Royalty": A Rite of Passage in Turin', pp. 125–52) explores the 'unconversion' in unparalleled detail.
23 Wheeler, *Ruskin's God*, p. 149.
24 Victor W. Turner, *The Ritual Process: Structure and Anti-Structure* (Chicago, IL: Aldine, 1962).
25 James A. Beckford, 'Accounting for Conversion', *The British Journal of Sociology* 29 (1978): 249–62; Sallie McFague, 'Conversion: Life on the Edge of the Raft', *Interpretation* 32 (1978): 255–68; Brian Taylor, 'Recollection and Membership: Converts' Talk and the Ratiocination of Commonality', *Sociology* 12 (1978): 316–17.
26 Lewis R. Rambo, *Understanding Religious Conversion* (New Haven, CT: Yale University Press, 1993). See also Rambo's contribution to *The Encyclopedia of Religion*, ed. by Mircea Eliade and others, 16 vols (New York: Macmillan, 1987), vol. 4, pp. 74–9. *Religious Conversion: Contemporary Practices and Controversies*, ed. by Christopher Lamb and M. Darrol Bryant (London: Cassell, 1999); *Previous Convictions: Conversion in the Present Day*, ed. by Martyn Percy (London: SPCK, 2000); Gauri Viswanathan, *Outside the Fold: Conversion, Modernity and Belief* (Princeton, NJ: Princeton University Press, 1998).
27 John Lofland and Norman Skonovd, 'Conversion Motifs', *Journal for the Scientific Study of Religion* 20 (1981): 373–85 (375).
28 *The Diaries of John Ruskin*, ed. by Joan Evans and John Howard Whitehouse, 3 vols (Oxford: Clarendon Press, 1958), vol. II, p. 370.
29 *The Diaries of John Ruskin*, p. 370.
30 Anonymous, *The Religious Tendencies of the Age* (London: Saunders, Otley, 1860), pp. 24–5.
31 Anonymous [J.G.], 'Hints to the Christian Tourist', *Evangelical Magazine* 34 (1856): 390–3 (390–1).
32 A.G.H. Hollingsworth, *The Folly of Going to Rome for a Religion in Two Letters to a Friend* (London: Hatchard, 1846), pp. 3–4.
33 W.E. Scudamore, *Letters to a Seceder from the Church of England to the Communion of Rome* (London: Rivington, 1851); Henry Alford's *An Earnest Dissuasive from Joining the Communion of the Church of Rome (Addressed to the younger members of the Church of England, and especially to students in the universities)* (London: Burns, 1846).
34 Lofland and Skonovd, 'Conversion Motifs', p. 380.
35 James Haldane Stewart, *Invitation for United Prayer for the Outpouring of the Holy Spirit* (London: Hodgson, 1852), p. 2.
36 One minister, the Reverend Dr Chalmers, argued that the aspirations of the Evangelical Alliance were missionary rather than ecumenical. *On the Evangelical Alliance; its Design, its Difficulties, its Proceedings and its Prospects (with Practical Suggestions)* (Edinburgh: Oliver, Boyd, 1846), p. 5.
37 Charles Haddon Spurgeon, *The New Park Street Pulpit and the Metropolitan Tabernacle Pulpit, containing Sermons preached and Revised by the Rev. C.H. Spurgeon*, 42 vols (London: Alabaster, Passmore, 1856–1896), vol. 4, pp. 161–2.
38 See 'A Revival Sermon', preached by Spurgeon on 26 January 1860, at Exeter Hall.
39 Spurgeon, *The New Park Street Pulpit*, vol. 4, p. 161.
40 Spurgeon, *The New Park Street Pulpit*, vol. 4, p. 164.
41 J. Edwin Orr, *The Second Evangelical Awakening in Britain* (London: Marshall, 1949), p. 5.
42 Bebbington, *Evangelicalism in Modern Britain*, p. 116.

43 Eliade, ed., *Encyclopedia of Religion*, p. 74.
44 Ruskin, *Works of John Ruskin*, vol. 35, p. 492.
45 For a discussion of the semantic slippage of the words 'pervert' and 'perversion' in relation to conversion see Schad, *Queer Fish*, p. 94. Schad also acknowledges a debt to Jonathan Dollimore's *Sexual Dissidence: Augustine to Wilde, Freud to Foucault* (Oxford: Clarendon Press, 1991) and Kenneth Burke, *The Rhetoric of Religion: Studies in Logology* (Berkeley, CA: University of California Press, 1970).
46 Anonymous, *Churches, Sects and Religious Parties; or, Some Motives for My Conversion to the Catholic Church* (London: Dolman, 1858), pp. 4–5.
47 Rambo, *Understanding Religious Conversion*, p. 158.
48 Taylor, 'Recollection and Membership', p. 319.
49 Eliade, ed., *Encyclopedia of Religion*, p. 77.
50 Anonymous, *Some Account of the Reasons of My Conversion to the Catholic Church* (London: Levey, Robson, Franklyn, 1847), p. 39.
51 I explore these issues in more detail in 'Evangelical Certainty: Charles Spurgeon and the Sermon as Crisis Literature', in *Reinventing Christianity: Nineteenth-Century Contexts*, ed. by Linda Woodhead (Aldershot: Ashgate, 2001), pp. 27–36.
52 Anonymous (M.R.), *Papal Aggression in England and Defection from Popery in France* (London: Hanbury, 1851), p. 5.
53 For a detailed survey of Protestant and Roman Catholic relations in the period, see Michael Wheeler, *The Old Enemies: Catholic and Protestant in Nineteenth-Century English Culture* (Cambridge: Cambridge University Press, 2006).
54 Rambo, *Understanding Religious Conversion*, p. 76. Also quoted in Sara Savage, 'A Psychology of Conversion – From All Angles', in Percy, ed., *Previous Convictions*, pp. 1–18 (p. 14).
55 Derrida, 'Circumfession', p. 124.

2. 'Recognizing Fellow-Creatures': F.D. Maurice, Octavia Hill, Josephine Butler

Hester Jones

From the perspective of a post-colonial, post-Christian, and even perhaps post-secular, twenty-first-century culture, there is much in nineteenth-century thought that seems uncongenial, lacking the confident commitment to diversity and pluralism which we now take virtually for granted. Post-modernity, indeed, has been constructed out of its resistance to a narrative of linear and rational progress, a narrative few now feel happy to accept. Many of its pivotal thinkers and writers, therefore, also seem limited by the constraints of their self-understanding, whether it is in the construction of gender, the commitment to nationhood and empire, or the upholding of social hierarchies. We do not look to this period for the voicing of paradox or challenging complexity, whether in doctrinal or artistic areas.

However, it is possible to find, in the work of a number of Christian theologians and reformers, attempts to bring together faith and society in such a way that paradox and self-contradiction are virtually unavoidable; indeed, in ways which seem at points positively to defend such inconsistencies, and whose theology and social practice set out to exemplify the dangers of coherence. In this essay, I shall look at some of the ways in which one theologian and one social reformer illustrate this intention, and suggest that, though both have been criticized and disparaged for their want of systematic political engagement and ambivalent relation to socialism, each nonetheless offers our own period an example of embodied complexity, a commitment to challenging what each saw to be the potential for destructive stagnancy in the cultural systems of their time. Each understands Anglican theology and practice as polemically non-dogmatic, as responsive to the particular, the circumstantial and the immediate, in ways that seek to bring together word and world in harmony. Neither is usually considered as a writer, and neither would have regarded themselves primarily in this way; yet for both, the former in particular, the word was central in their understanding of incarnation and kenosis.

I shall also begin to consider how the work of the former, F.D. Maurice, in his influence on the latter, Octavia Hill, and on subsequent social reformers, among them Josephine Butler, offers a surprisingly helpful response to a frequent problem that is raised by feminist theologians and social theorists in their consideration of such nineteenth-century figures. This concerns the role of the theological idea of kenosis, or the understanding of divine self-emptying, in the incarnation of Christ, when it is applied to the question of social reform and engagement. Kenosis, while potentially challenging traditional masculine roles in its image of the servant Christ, can sometimes endorse more repressive role models in social or gender areas. As a model for women, also, as feminists such as Sarah Coakley or Daphne Hampson have pointed out, it runs the risk of recommending a self-sacrifice, a submission to others, when those patterns of behaving are themselves sometimes in need of challenge.[1] In many respects, both Maurice and Hill seem to endorse conservative views about social relating, and the former in particular was at pains to distance himself from the desire of some Christian Socialists to bring about social change and political reform. That was not his intention, and his best-known work *The Kingdom of Christ* makes this abundantly clear.[2] However, his emphasis on the mutually responsive work of the Spirit, which is often located in divine and human friendship, focused above all in his account of the 'Trinity in Unity', offers a vocabulary of reciprocity, mutuality and even equality in relating between people of different classes, genders, sects and kinds, that is of value not only to his own readership but also today.

F.D. Maurice's work experienced considerable hostility, criticism and neglect in his own day. Matthew Arnold declared, with withering wit, 'He passed his life beating the bush with deep emotion and never starting the hare' and Gladstone, more temperately acknowledged, 'I found him difficult to catch and still more difficult to hold.'[3] Jules Lechevalier similarly observed, 'Mr Maurice's system is a very good one for bringing men in, but it is all door',[4] not least because to some he appeared predominantly as an insubstantial 'dreamer' while to others he became associated with the so-called Christian Socialists and their agenda to break through the insular walls of an increasingly individualistic and inward-looking church, in order to redirect Christian commitment to society and the needs of the poor. Maurice's work broke the mould of its own time, at the cost of fairly widespread indifference, misunderstanding, and, in his expulsion from King's College London over his understanding of eternal life, even professional ignominy. Yet, his constant reworking of Neo-

Platonist thought, introduced to him by his tutor Julius Hare, brought him to the work of the poet Coleridge, like himself a Unitarian for a period, though, unlike himself, raised an Anglican. Coleridge was of course in turn extensively influenced by seventeenth-century divines and, in particular, the latitudinarian Platonists such as Jeremy Taylor, the accumulating and iterative rhythms of whose work can be traced in those of both Coleridge and Maurice. Taylor, like Coleridge and Maurice, was responding to a culture in which war and the fear of war had led to considerable fragmentation and instability; but such latitudinarianism was not simply opportunistic, but a response to the intrinsically assimilative and organic nature of Anglican Christianity. In other words, Maurice in fact embodies an aspect of Anglican tradition which has persisted robustly, not least on account of its willingness to inculturate and engage with the traditions in which it is to be found. This may account for one reason why his work has endured, despite fluctuations of taste and understanding, while that of others has declined.

Central to an understanding of Maurice's work, in particular, his most enduring, *The Kingdom of Christ*, is its reiteration that, as Stephen Prickett has incisively put it, 'the vigour of this unique universal spiritual society [the church] depends on the dialectic of tensions within it. [...] Maurice's chosen title illustrates this tension.'[5] However, as Jeremy Morris observes, the 'threefold classification of the divine order of society', that is, family, nation and Church, 'remained central to Maurice's account of institutions throughout his life'.[6] As Morris points out, this scheme involves an 'implicit hierarchical orientation towards its highest level, the Church, or universal society', with the family occupying a prominent role on earth. This hierarchy can be seen in many forms in Maurice's work, among them, in his comfortable acceptance of the use of militarism to defend the nation of England on the grounds of his inhabitants' belief in its superiority, or in his opposition to union action or to universal suffrage. Such an hierarchical understanding of a fixed social order, so central and yet existing in such tension with the equal emphasis on dynamic fluidity and movement in divine revelation, is crystallized in Maurice's focus on the Fatherhood of Christ, about which much has been written. However, as I have already suggested, there is a sustained effort in his work, perhaps attracting less critical attention but recurring frequently, to work towards a language which reconciles these two contrary movements, the sustaining of social hierarchy and the discovery of the divine amidst fluidity, mutual discovery and meeting. This movement is often located in the use of the metaphor of friendship, to embody a movement between people and between God and man which not only complicates the 'assumption that there is an inherent gradation in forms of human society and religion', but offers a model of relating which is not exclusively dependent on hierarchy or on subordination, though often using such order as a point of departure.

I shall give a few examples of how Maurice brings this idea into play, before going on to suggest that a similar dynamic may be observed in the work of his disciple Octavia Hill and, though I shall allude only briefly to this, also the work of the reformer and campaigner Josephine Butler. First, in the relatively late work *The Friendship of Books*, Maurice sets out the ways in which a book may befriend the reader:

> A person is presenting himself to us, one who may have the right to judge us, but who is willing to be judged by his peers. That, you see, is because the *We* has become an *I*. All his apparent dignity is dissolved; we can recognize him as a fellow-creature.

Here, Maurice's definition of such literary friendship is consummately incarnational and kenotic. It is defined, initially and characteristically, against a misapprehension: 'I do not mean that we are in any special danger of looking upon them as our enemies.' Such friendship is to do, rather, with reciprocated conversation, the word which answers and raises from the dead:

> If books are only dead things, if they do not speak to one, or answer one when one speaks to them, if they have nothing to do with the common things that we are busy with – with the sky over our head, and the ground under our feet – I think that they had better stay on the shelves; I think any horse or dog, or tree or flower, is a better companion for human beings than they are.[7]

Such a claim, from a writer generally thought to be tentative to the point of invisibility, is confident, even uncompromising, despite the qualifying 'I think'; the accumulating array of examples, increasing in unlikeliness as it progresses, testifies to the overwhelming importance of 'common things that we are busy with'. Books, according to Maurice, must speak to their reader, and they must convey the living Word, the word that is life. But not only this: they must 'answer' the call of the reader, not with a self-concealing 'we' but with a vulnerable and particular 'I'.

For Maurice, the claim to an 'objective' stance indicated by such a use of 'we', denuded of the vulnerable particularity of a single self, turns the living word into 'dead things in stiff bindings'. Many years earlier, even before the *Kingdom of Christ* was published, Maurice had in 1828 brought out the *Sketches of Contemporary Authors* in which he distinguishes the poet-prophet, who 'enlarges the prospects of mankind' with his imaginative genius, his original and yet common voice, from other lesser writers whose products diminish, confine and condescend to their readers. Pre-eminent among the former, unsurprisingly perhaps, Maurice includes Wordsworth, undergoing himself some critical reassessment, who, in a period of revolution where 'the hearts of men were enlarged by the reception of a vast hope', 'of this inbreathed Spirit [...] has endeavoured to see, in his own breast and in the less artificial classes of mankind, the being of his species as it is, and as it might be.' He has, in short, 'done more than any English writer of modern times to correct this narrowness and meagreness of feeling'; 'the exuberant sympathies of the poet gush out on every grain of sand'.[8] Here as elsewhere in his writing, Maurice makes use of images of expansion and liberation to describe the effect of such poetic sympathy; genius, for him, is revealed in the releasing of the ties and boundaries of the self. The poet-prophet looks to Christ, the 'Liberator, Absolver', as the *Kingdom* has it.

In using the form of literary 'sketch', Maurice brings into service a methodology more often encountered in comic, satirical or journalistic contexts: a form of perhaps polemical or broad-brush writing, indeed, which he takes pains, in the *Friendship of Books*, to criticize for its potentially diminishing effect on human relating and being. In taking on this more popular form of criticism, and subjecting it to his method of organic and responsively gradual reading, Maurice challenges the polarity present in his culture between cultural registers and between intellectual disciplines, seeing poetry as an important context for theological and religious reflection and discovery.

Given this, it is perhaps surprising that an account of the poet Coleridge is absent from the *Sketches*. However, perhaps because of the potential offered by the poet for close identification, Maurice was in fact ambivalent about his influence and significance throughout his life. According to Strachey, for example, he believed that 'Coleridge was not a thorough Platonist; his disregard for facts and preference for diagrams was not Platonic but Aristotelian. Socrates was a very plain, matter-of-fact person.'[9] Maurice did, though, append to the second, 1842 edition of *The Kingdom* a dedicatory tribute, addressed to Derwent Coleridge, the poet's second son, in which he acknowledges, though again with some ambivalence, 'the books of Mr Coleridge are mainly interesting to me as the biography of one who passed through the struggles of the age to which we are succeeding, and who was able, after great effort and much sorrow, to discover a resting-place.'[10] Such an effort of painful and strenuous discovery, itself becoming the end of such searching as much as the means to it, comes close also to the movement characterizing Maurice's own life, with its own distrust of the satisfaction that comes with reaching any conclusion that may distort or misrepresent the nature of the enquiry. Maurice goes on to mention Coleridge's journal *The Friend* and infers that 'he had been convinced that society is a reality, and that it would not become more real by being unmade and reconstructed'; Maurice concludes that though incomplete, 'its merit is that it is an inquiry, that it shows us what we have to seek for, and that it puts us in the way of seeking.' Such incompleteness, a withholding from conclusive judgement, is a cardinal virtue to Maurice, and one peculiar to Coleridge: rather than offering a final word on its subject, it directs its reader 'to honour others of the most different kind, belonging to our own and to former times', without wanting to 'get a moral' from them. At one with truth, it claims no need to separate itself from its reader, but aims to unite with him or her in the universal search for further discovery of revealed being.

Readers of Maurice often quote his remark reproduced in the *Life*, 'the desire for unity has haunted me all my life through', in order to highlight the importance of the idea of unity to Maurice's theology. Important it is, but it is worth considering the remark in the context in which Maurice placed it in what his son calls one of his 'autobiographical attempts'. The remark continues, 'I have never been able to substitute any desire for that, or to accept any of the different schemes for satisfying it which men have devised.' Frederick Maurice concludes, 'in other words, the great wish in the boy's heart was to reconcile those earnest faiths which the household presented', referring to the schism in the Maurice household between his father's Unitarianism and the Evangelical and other versions of Anglican commitment embraced by his sisters.[11] Maurice's wistful longing for unity – whatever such a word might mean for himself or others – is inseparable from his awareness that conflicting and even irreconcilable points of view will always exist; such difference is not, in his view, to be either ignored or confronted, but can only be accommodated by a slow process of conversation, listening and responding. Indeed, so strong is this belief, that for Maurice any self-identification with unity as an end in itself, or, more, belief that it has been achieved, is understood as evidence of self-delusion, a will to power and therefore proof of fragmentation and isolation. Much of his work, consequently, engages with the attempt to acknowledge such difference but maintain the desire for a language that accommodates it, at the cost, or even, I suggest, with the desire to sustain, a degree of inclarity and incompletion.

Such a valuing of a disharmony that points to a higher, spiritual wholeness, does not always win approval, as I have already suggested. According to a letter by Hill's sister, with what seems like a surly humour, Ruskin complained to Octavia (at this stage an avid disciple of both men and apparently keen, though perhaps foolishly, to reconcile the one to the other), that he found Maurice's writing 'like a man who did not see clearly, and was always stretching out, moving on in the right direction, but in a fog'.[12] Ruskin here seems almost to parody the desire in Maurice not to risk the arrogance of a claim or an assertion: the kenotic emptying of content in Maurice's mode of expression perhaps struck Ruskin as either precariously close to an affectation, or as simply unhelpful. Ruskin goes on to encourage Hill to turn her attentions away from both art and books and towards work with 'people': and the vying of the two men, the theologian and the doubting critic, are perhaps here used as material to substantiate this emerging trend in Hill's self-understanding.

Indeed, Maurice certainly seems to melodramatize his own 'desire' for unity in the phrase 'throughout my life', and acknowledges its poignant frailty in his repetition of the word, 'desire', which remains as unassailably private as the 'schemes' for its satisfaction are inadequate and impersonal. But without both poles of the dialectic the truth, which remains in the movement between them, can not be discovered. Maurice goes on to say in the passage already mentioned, with a complicating refinement, that 'Trinity in Unity' is 'in the centre of all my beliefs; the rest of my spirit, when I contemplate myself or mankind.' Here, stillness and movement, singleness and multiplicity, exist in a paradoxical relation with one another: spiritual 'rest' is at the 'centre', yet the centre cannot be approached other than by means of many 'beliefs' and a process of unfolding 'contemplation', an activity leading the speaker to move within himself and between himself 'and mankind'. This echoes the comment about Coleridge's struggles which led to a 'resting-place', quoted previously: Coleridge's 'resting-place' returns Maurice to his own struggles for self-understanding, which in turn are given meaning through their engagement with Coleridge's own tortuous yet meaningful 'biography'. Maurice uncovers, in other words, an understanding of dynamic difference and relationship at the heart of the self and of mankind, and of such difference, united in the ground of being, also being the ground of fellowship between the isolated self and the universe.

Furthermore, in a long letter to his mother, Maurice sets out the nature of his faith, and uses two traditional symbols of religious enlightenment, the mirror and the ladder; but both depend for their effect on a double movement. First, he says, 'I have seemed to see myself in a double mirror, one human, one divine [...] when I could feel a reflection back [...] all became true and real again and I have felt a happiness at times which is almost new to me.' He goes on,

> It seems to me that all relations acquire a significance and become felt as actually living and real when contemplated in Him [...]. At first, each relation seems to be a step on a beautiful ladder set upon earth and reaching to Him, prefiguring that heavenly relation; and afterwards, if that top step be apprehended, a descending ladder set in heaven and reaching to earth. But I am afraid I am growing incomprehensible, though, I thank God, I have a meaning.[13]

'Meaning' here looks both to the fulfilment of language and of personal identity in Christ, a fulfilment which is anticipated in the moment of meeting between author and reader; the speaker's words are inadequate embodiments of his dimly grasped perception; but they are also shadows of the truth which derives from God.

Maurice suggests here that his language fails as he imagines the culmination of spiritual seeking; but at the same time, as that pitch of perfection is approached, the descending ladder of kenotic grace reaches down to repair the fog, as Ruskin called it, and meaning, which derives from the divine, is enacted and discovered. It is almost as if Maurice's meaning is assured, not challenged, in its elusiveness, for if it were more accessible no ladder of grace would be needed, and its truth, which depends on its coming from Christ, would be diminished. Revelation of truth is always for Maurice essentially organic and evolutionary; as Stephen Prickett puts it, not 'breaking in from the outside, but rather as the discovery of the indwelling of the supernatural growing up and out of the particular, the concrete, and the ordinary.'[14] Writing of his experience of being taught by Julius Hare at Cambridge, Maurice attributes to him the discovery that 'there is a way out of party opinions which is not a compromise between them, but which is implied in both, and of which each is bearing witness.'[15] 'Party opinions', as expressive of the sectarianism and the passion for systemization that Maurice saw as characterizing his age, are merely the externalized form of the selfish ego; they are unavoidable in his view, but are in need of the descending ladder or the responsive voice of grace which constantly works to expand, enlarge and adulterate the drive of the self.

Maurice pursues the theme of 'Trinity in Unity' more fully, of course, in the *Theological Essays* that led to his dismissal from King's College London; and the essay of this name concludes with another paradoxical and terse account of the attitude which may lead to unity. Of the

Unitarians, he concludes, with a wonderfully convoluted triple negative enclosing his meaning in layers of hermeneutic uncertainty:

> while *we* use the doctrine of the Trinity in that way, I am certain we shall not believe it, whatever we may pretend. While *they* think they know what that awful name 'Father' means, because they can pronounce it, or what that wonderful word 'Unity' means, because they can fight for it, they will not only not enlarge the circle of their convictions, but they will lose those that they have.[16]

The italicized pronouns enact the battle between sects that Maurice deplores, doctrine used 'as weapons against other men'. And the process is not a static one; faith not enlarged, he implies, leads to faith lost. His proposed alternative is, as so often, to indicate by the means of contrasting analogy the restricting consequences of such sectarian narrow-mindedness: 'they shall be such as sick people want who sigh for the morning; as poor men who toil in mines; as captives want who are chained together in loathsome prisons; and I have no fear of them coming to acknowledge the whole name which we confess.' The essay concludes with lines by Milton, including some that beautifully imagine when

> long Eternity shall greet our bliss
> With an individual kiss.[17]

Closely related to Coleridge's elaboration of the nature of unity is, as the title of the journal, *The Friend,* perhaps suggests, the idea and the experience of friendship, about which the earlier poet wrote much, and whose use of the term both looks back to its rehabilitation by the latitudinarian Jeremy Taylor, and is also at points appropriated and transformed by Maurice.[18] The word of course encompasses a range of meanings and experiences, but, as Gurion Taussig has suggested, Coleridge responds to an application of the term to literary hermeneutics elaborated by the German theologian Schleiermacher, for whom 'a friend enjoys a privileged, divinatory understanding of another's mental processes'. Therefore, 'whether as listener or reader, Schleiermacher's actively sympathetic "friend" participates in the inner life of the speaker/author-friend, overcoming the usual barriers to an understanding of another's subjectivity.'[19] As Taussig and others have noticed, however, such a marrying of friendship and sympathy (an idea developed by David Hume in particular) risks leading such a friend into a subordinate relation with more dominant figures, one which blurs the boundaries between one person and another; a poem such as 'Frost at Midnight', indeed, seems to end by concluding that such sympathetic friendship may never be fully realized.

However, friendship offers Coleridge, and Maurice, an image of a social relation which organically spans both the sphere of intimate male friendship (often eroticized in Coleridge's case and, it has been suggested, perhaps in Maurice's too) and also the wider realm of both political and spiritual endeavour. However, while for Coleridge friendship offered a substitute for familial security, as Thomas McFarland has remarked,[20] a symbol of unity above all, for Maurice it includes the difference, the otherness, without which unity cannot be substantially encountered.

The work of the two social reformers, Octavia Hill and Josephine Butler, the former a warm admirer of Maurice, though both different from him in many respects, can also be seen as illustrating an attempt to 'shape belief' in such a way that neither the shape nor the belief loses its integrity or predominates over the other; like Maurice, both women came in for a considerable degree of censure, and both, I suggest, work to find ways of accommodating and moving beyond endemic social subordination and hierarchy. All three attempted reform without seeking to be or perceiving themselves, as, radical, let alone revolutionary. All, in fact, denied that such was their intention, and all have subsequently been criticized by twentieth-century social programmers and socialists for their want of a more challenging or sustained political and social engagement. To a greater or lesser extent, each also pursued through their work a critique of what was to become a dominant force in the Church, the Tractarian movement, a movement whose hugely successful renewal of spiritual energy was gained at the cost of ecclesiastical insularity, for all its subsequent involvement in social justice, a rootedness in the past and an intractable emphasis on the structures and assumptions deriving from the university.

But no less insular, or 'selfish', to use the word Maurice often brings into service, is the vision of evangelical salvation as depending upon private faith and conviction. Maurice, Hill and Butler all explicitly claim to offer an account of Christian ministry that 'lives' through the bringing of the 'kingdom of Christ' into the world as it is now. In different ways, they radically oppose theologies which defer expectation of the kingdom to an imagined future, whether within or beyond the temporal realm. Theirs is, in the familiar phrase, a realized eschatology, but they also persistently look to the parousia, the coming, as a shape for their commitment to worldly endeavour. Each resists also the systemization of such reform: Maurice and Hill, because they perceive the creation of such systems as inevitably distorting of the work of the living Word in the world at hand. Much of Maurice's work, in one way and another, struggles to articulate the reasons for such resistance: in a different context, Hill continues this struggle, incurring considerable criticism for what seemed to a subsequent generation of 'socialists' to be her condescending moralism and unhelpful individualism. David Owen echoed the distaste for such potentially patronizing moralism expressed by socialists such as Beatrice Webb and Henrietta Barnett in his judgement that her approach 'today is almost incomprehensible'.[21] However, in this section I shall suggest that Hill's approach, as expressed in her personal letters and in her more public writings, few as they are, illustrates a more complicated thinking around the problems raised by social reform. At its centre is a commitment to the redeeming effects of Christian love – such, of course, is probably uncontentious – but more than this, to the difference that is made by personal relationship, expressed in the attentive look of one person at another. Hill's writing shows surprising sensitivity and alertness to the ways in which such attention may be offered, both in physical and verbal ways, and also in the ways in which housing bears the marks of human vision.

Octavia Hill is usually remembered in connection with her co-founding of the National Trust, but most of her life's work was in fact dedicated to the 'steady and gradual improvement of the people and the houses' within what had been impoverished areas of London.[22] Such conversions were funded by wealthy acquaintances and patrons, initially by her one-time friend John Ruskin, left wealthy after his father's death; the tenants were required to pay rent punctually, and she, their landlady, obliged to maintain the upkeep of the property. Although this contract was sometimes prosecuted with what seems like punitive thoroughness, Hill set out to infuse it with a spirit of Christian communion and fellowship; her original vision was of a house in which 'I may know everyone, and do something towards making their lives healthier and happier',[23] and throughout her life she held on with conviction to a belief in the ability of personal fellowship to transcend differences of class and circumstance. 'You cannot learn how to help a man, nor even get him to tell you what ails him, till you care for him', she writes in one of her 'letters to fellow-workers';[24] in her thinking, 'help' and 'indifference' are almost on a par with one another in relating to the poor, if personally attentive relation is lacking. Such an emphasis encourages us to challenge the view of her work as thoughtlessly condescending or patronizing.

Yet at the same time, Hill also became an advocate for the improving effect of space in inner-city life, campaigning to reclaim space from development and to enlarge and make beautiful what spaces already existed.

Good social relations did not merely require that housing should be better equipped, but that it should enable family identity to flourish, for

> it seems as if a certain amount of quiet and even of isolation make family life and neighbourly kindness more possible. People become brutal in large numbers who are gentle when they are in smaller groups and know one another [... furthermore it is hard] to give a block home that stamp of individuality [...] and the power of developing the individual life. [...] The dweller in towns must accept the law of considering his neighbour rather by sacrifice of his individual joy, than by development of individual varied capacity.[25]

Of importance here is the perception that space permits and does not obstruct the creation of individuality, where 'the lower classes', as she puts it, 'can get the individual feeling and notice which often trains in humanity'. 'Individuality' here is, of course, a term which is often used, and which may seem to pre-empt a more collective or genuinely just social vision, based on a commitment to equality and human flourishing. Hill, indeed, like Maurice and Butler, cannot imagine such flourishing occurring in a vacuum; by 'individual life' she means something closer, I think, to Maurice's idea of organic and original growth, something natural and dependent on the formation of mutual relationship. Such fellowship, as she calls it, occurs amidst the acknowledgement of particular social and class differences; without such an understanding, the moment of meeting between diverse minds is without a context and a space in which it may be realized.

Hill wrote rather little, but the *Life of Octavia Hill, as Told in Her Letters*, edited by C. Edmund Maurice, illustrates the persistence of her commitment to infusing social action with personal encounter and even friendship. Indeed, it is prefaced with the epigraph:

> Not what we give, but what we share;
> For the gift without the giver is bare.

Her reputation has presented her as a 'giver' to the point of no return, but her letters seem inclined to redress this imbalance, acknowledging the extent to which she has been informed by those to whom she has given, and articulating an identity shaped in the course of this interaction.

A letter 'to a friend', dated 4 July 1858, observes:

> I would rather take up wholly a few individuals or pictures or books, and love and know and study them deeply, than have any more superficial (though wider) sympathies; and my trial is, that I have to tear myself away from this intense grasp and absorbing interest, to love and know and help in fresh and fresh directions. I have often felt like a perpetually uprooted plant. Only somehow in looking back, I find continuity and deep inner relation between the various works and times of my life, and always find the past a possession because in memory I have it still.[26]

Here Hill suggests, with the unusually weighted phrase 'intense grasp and absorbing interest', that a focus on the single occupation, for all its appearance of naturalness and humility, risks selfish interest, while undertaking work in 'fresh and fresh directions', while seeming to risk repetitive superficiality, in fact leads the self, through the working of restorative memory, into a deeper understanding of the dynamic and ever-moving unity at the heart of things. An unnatural fragmentation becomes the opportunity for reflection on an invisible, but deeply felt, 'inner relation', discovered and expressed through epistolary friendship. A month later, Hill writes in similar vein, but with a still more impassioned conviction:

> If we were all less self-occupied, what a depth of beauty and order we should see in [...] the momentary lighting up of an eye, or the slight quiver of a lip, which we lose perhaps in a fit of self-contemplation; [...] then I would wish most lovingly to grasp the whole purpose of each life [..] to watch, not unaiding, the struggle with [evil...]; to look at all, not as one standing aloof or above, but as fellow-worker, fellow sufferer; to trace the same tendency to evil and good in myself.[27]

Here, the careful negation ('if we were all...') cloaks any pretence to moral superiority, while the possibility of a regard for another person that is 'not unaiding' and yet makes no claim to condescension, instead becoming merely a 'fellow-worker, fellow sufferer', is imagined, while also accepted to be an impossibility, for as long as self-involvement remains an unavoidable aspect of the human condition. Hill's language wrestles with her own inner conflict, as the word 'grasp' once again conveys both the philosophical detachment and understanding suggested in 'watch', but also acknowledges the drive towards selfish possession owned in 'self-contemplation'. Such writing, I suggest, is honest in its sense of the real difficulty of relating to other people with a heart free from the desire to grasp; yet the desire also to move towards a relation of fellowship, one that creates a space in which such commonality may be imagined, is equally real.

In 1855, Octavia writes to Emily, her sister, and attempts to describe a sermon by Maurice on 'What peace was it which he gave', a topic at the centre of Maurice's thinking. Hill recounts Maurice exhausting possible answers to the question, and concluding:

> The sense of a friend, a deliverer, the revelation of a Father, would give them really a peace which the world did not give, and could not take away. I forget how it came in, but Mr Maurice mentioned Christ's look to Peter which made him weep, and contrasted it with Judas's remorse.

She then apologizes that the sermon 'is now confused in my mind with

Kingsley's, and with several things I have been reading'. The substance of the sermon, in other words, has been lost in the fog, as Ruskin put it, of his style of pursuing it.[28] But it is nonetheless significant that Octavia's memory concludes with the detail about Christ's look to Peter, in contrast with the non-personal, 'self-contemplating' remorse of Judas. Nothing in this account fully indicates the nature or the signs of divine 'peace'; the 'look' of Christ to Peter comes close, but we are not told what this look conveys only, its effect, that of Peter's tears, and the 'sense of a friend, a deliverer'. Maurice often, indeed, juxtaposes two such terms, and the intention is not a sentimental one, nor one blind to the cramping effect of power imbalance on the equality and mutuality of true friendship. His claim, rather, is that within the peace and unity of Christ, such a tension is held and resolved: that the joy of egalitarian friendship is made possible only with and through a difference in power – between Christ and Peter – which is deliberately released. In this sense, then, Christ is both fellow-friend and divine 'deliverer', and the two antagonistic terms depend on one another for their effect.

Such instances from Hill's personal correspondence suggest, I think, a desire to approach a relationship with others, whether family, friend or 'the poor', that found moments of fellowship in an acknowledgement of power and 'self-contemplation'. Such examples may also be found, though taking sometimes a different form, in her various essays and letters that addressed a more public readership. In such letters, it is hard, amidst her accounts of all the properties that Hill 'reformed', 'improved' and, above all, 'converted', not to draw parallels with the march of empire and its accompanying work of evangelism running concurrently overseas, and to find it as equally disturbing for its assumptions of cultural superiority. Her powerful and vivid accounts of entering the slums to claim rent described predominantly in the 'Letters to Fellow Workers', indeed read much as a personal crusade against darkness, dirt and chaos, as she sees it, both physical and moral. The Christian Socialists were in fact by no means straightforwardly enlightened in such areas, and Kingsley is of course notorious for his racism.

However, Hill writes at various points against those who seek 'over the whole world for some new good work and cannot see the holiness of that which is near them'; and the 'near' also includes the self. At points, such a modest particularity of aim seems to confirm Hill as conservative in her understanding of gender; she opposed women's suffrage, and like Maurice, often expressed somewhat surprising conservatism. But her understanding of what constitutes the 'near at hand', or the 'home' sphere, so often recommended as the proper location for female work, is also surprising in its elusiveness. The letter already quoted to Miss Howitt continues, despite acknowledging that 'it is very delicious to find people owning their home work as first and most blessed', 'all people who are obeying the best part of the nature that has been given them, do, more or less, belong to it [...and] know themselves to be bound into a society by that gift, by being children of Christ and heirs of God'. This follows a letter written a few months earlier in which she declares with passion that 'we want all generous and good work recognized as Christ's [...] the tendency is for doubters to think the best work is done by unbelievers; to think our faith cramps our labours and narrows our hearts. [...] we care for good as good.'[29]

Such care, even amidst a language of crusade, is also demonstrated through narratives that work towards moments of meeting, focusing on a look exchanged or a demonstration of fellowship with the tenant from whom Hill is also eliciting rent. For example, in the essay originally published as 'Homes of the London Poor' in 1875 in *Macmillan's Magazine*, Hill describes herself attempting to reach one tenant down 'kitchen stairs, broken and rounded by the hardened mud upon them, the foul smells which the heavy foggy air would not allow to rise met me as I descended, and the plaster rattled with a hollow sound as I groped along'. It is a true urban inferno, assaulting the senses and deadening individual response. 'Truly a wild, lawless, desolate little kingdom to come to rule over.' Eventually, Hill discovers her quarry:

> She was sitting on the floor at tea with another woman, the tea being served on an inverted hamper. I sat down on an opposite hamper, and told her I was sorry that I had never made her acquaintance before. To which she replied, with rather a grand air and a merry twinkle in her eye, that she had been 'unavoidably absent'; in other words, some weeks in prison.

On another visit, Hill is taunted by an angry tenant, to which Hill responds with silence; 'Perfect silence would make her voice drop lower and lower, until at last she would stop, wondering that no violent answers were hurled back at her, and a pause would ensue.' Within such a pause, Hill then engages with her, and a resolution is made.

Hill recognizes that without such acknowledgement, peace between the classes, or between any whose interests are opposed, can never be achieved. The account of her 'descent' into this desolate kingdom, a kind of urban hell, presents herself in the role of Christ, humbly occupying a 'hamper'; but she is in turn rewarded with a discovery of humanity, often enacted through humour – 'with rather a grand air and a merry twinkle in her eye'. The terrifying beast within the 'wild, lawless kingdom' turns out to be capable of irony and self-aware mockery, picking up Hill's genteel speech and trumping it.

A letter written in 1867 seems initially to indicate a condescension of approach which has already been mentioned, declaring that when 'gifts are given and received by the same person they are ennobling. It is the greediness of the recipient that is the awful result at present; and the helpless indolence of expectant selfishness'. However, it continues: 'let us give better things; sympathy, friendship. Intercourse; let us be friends, and then we can give with comparative impunity. For the hearts of people always feel the spiritual gift to be greater if it be genuine at all.' Hill perceives, that is, that such 'selfishness' comes about from underpaid work, which in turn generates 'thanklessness'; and then 'we blame him for his alternate servility and ingratitude;' with adequate work, however, 'one day we shall be able to give to our friends among them as we give to one another [...] and be sure that he who gladly receives today will tomorrow give more gladly'.[30] Here, as so often, mutual exchange, not selfless charity, is the character of the kingdom towards which Hill looks, and signs of which she discerns even among the rubble created by the neglect of the rich. Such a vision also leads her to realize 'how much we owe to those who have consented to be served by us', and to reflect ruefully that 'when all confess mutual dependence, and glory in mutual service', many also speak in admiration of those who 'starve in silence', 'as if that silent starvation were not the most awful protest against all who might have been near friends'.[31]

Hill is as conscious as Maurice of the ease with which such a vision may be deployed, and the challenge of realizing it; the moment of reaching such a fellowship, potentially always present within the world and within society, requires a kenotic emptying, both of giver and receiver. Hill does not speak of grace, but such is her implication; that in the self-giving of the wealthy, and in the readiness to receive in such a spirit of the poor, the kingdom is renewed. Such friendly fellowship and mutual exchange, however, are dependent on the reaching out of those with power and wealth, and such expansion, as Maurice often calls it, is only a step away from a colonial appropriation of the other.

Hill's reform project is informed by a desire for reciprocal fellowship whose rhetoric she inherited from Maurice, in turn absorbing its assumptions from Coleridge and earlier theologians. Hill is not, I think, alone in this more complex use of a language that has often been understood, in particular by more recent feminist social historians and theologians, to be 'custodial' rather than 'egalitarian'.[32] Josephine Butler's writing about her experiences with prostitutes in the oakum sheds of Liverpool, for example, employs the rhetoric of friendship in a similarly qualified and kenotic manner, clearly aware of the limits to such a meeting between two people of radically different social classes, yet also claiming that such a moment was, within the economy of salvation, a possibility. There is a similar moment to Hill's account in *Homes of the London Poor* in Butler's *Autobiographical Memoir* where she describes herself descending into 'an immense gloomy vault' to visit the 'women and girls' picking oakum there. She 'sat on the floor among them'; and 'they laughed at me, and told me my fingers were of no use'; but 'while we laughed we became friends'.[33] Butler, like Hill and Maurice, makes the kenotic release of power a prelude to the mutuality of friendship, and acknowledges its temporary nature; but nonetheless holds to the possibility of such momentary meeting and exchange between individuals as essential to social change and reform.

I have suggested that these three writers and reformers, though perceived often as embodying a conservative and 'custodial' relation to those with whom they worked, nonetheless exemplify both a realism and a relational sophistication in their incarnational theologies and accounts of difference. Their use of the rhetoric of friendship, in particular, counters those readings that have perceived their attitude as exclusively condescending or individualistic. Further, such a use also challenges the tendency to regard their work as more conventionally endorsing the units of 'family and nation', suggesting that their boundaries of relation are both more fluid and expansive than such a vocabulary might imply.

Notes

1 See Daphne Hampson, ed., *Swallowing a Fishbone?* (London: SPCK, 1996).
2 Alec R. Vidler, ed., F.D. Maurice, *The Kingdom of Christ*, 2 vols, second edn [London: 1842] (London: SCM, 1958), vol. 2, p. 337.
3 Quoted by Charles E. Raven in *Christian Socialism: 1848–1854* (London: Frank Cass, 1968), p. 79.
4 Quoted by Edward Norman, *The Victorian Christian Socialists* (Cambridge: Cambridge University Press, 1987), p. 15.
5 Stephen Prickett, *Romanticism and Religion* (Cambridge: Cambridge University Press, 1976), p. 143.
6 Jeremy Morris, *F.D. Maurice and the Crisis of Christian Authority* (Oxford: Oxford University Press 2005), p. 154.
7 F.D. Maurice, *The Friendship of Books* (London: Macmillan, 1874), pp. 2–4.
8 A.J. Hartley, ed., *Sketches of Contemporary Authors, 1828* (London: Archon Books, 1970), pp. 35,41
9 Frederick Maurice, ed., *Life of Frederick Denison Maurice*, 2 vols (London:

Macmillan, 1885), vol. 1, p. 251.
10 'Appendix', *The Kingdom of Christ*, vol. 2, p. 350.
11 Maurice, ed., *Life of Frederick Denison Maurice*, p. 41.
12 Edmund C. Maurice, *Life of Octavia Hill, as Told in Her Letters* (London: Macmillan, 1913), p. 119.
13 Maurice, ed., *Life of Frederick Denison Maurice*, p. 131.
14 Prickett, *Romanticism and Religion*, p. 127.
15 Maurice, ed., *Life of Frederick Denison Maurice*, p. 56.
16 Edward Carpenter, ed., *Frederick Denison Maurice: Theological Essays* [1853] (London: James Clarke, 1957), p. 299.
17 Carpenter, ed., *Frederick Denison Maurice: Theological Essays*, p. 301.
18 See Taylor's essay *Discourse of the Measures and Offices of Friendship* (London, 1654).
19 Gurion Taussig, *Coleridge and the Idea of Friendship, 1789–1804* (Newark, DE: University of Delaware Press, 2002), p. 22 See also E.S. Shaffer in 'The Hermeneutic Community: Coleridge and Schleiermacher', in *The Coleridge Connection: Essays for Thomas McFarland*, ed. Richard Gravil and Molly Lefebure (Basingstoke: Macmillan, 1990), pp. 200–29.
20 Thomas McFarland, *Romanticism and the Forms of Ruin* (Princeton, NJ: Princeton University Press, 1981), p. 122.
21 David Owen, *English Philanthropy 1660–1960* (Cambridge, MA: Harvard University Press, 1967), p. 387.
22 Quoted in Robert Whelan, ed., *Octavia Hill and the Housing Debate: Essays and Letters* (IEA Health and Welfare Unit: London, 1998), p. 6.
23 Whelan, ed., *Octavia Hill and the Housing Debate*, p. 5.
24 Whelan, ed., *Octavia Hill and the Housing Debate*, p. 82.
25 Whelan, ed., *Octavia Hill and the Housing Debate*, 'Blocks of model dwellings: Influence on character', pp. 109–10.
26 Maurice, *Life of Octavia Hill*, p. 111.
27 Maurice, *Life of Octavia Hill*, p. 112.
28 Maurice, *Life of Octavia Hill*, p. 44.
29 Maurice, *Life of Octavia Hill*, pp. 184–5.
30 Maurice, *Life of Octavia Hill*, pp. 227–8.
31 Maurice, *Life of Octavia Hill*, p. 207.
32 See for example Jenny Uglow, 'Josephine Butler: From Sympathy to Theory', in Dale Spender, ed., *Feminist Theorists* (London: The Women's Press, 1983), p. 160.
33 George W. and Lucy A. Johnson, eds, *An Autobiographical Memoir* (London: Arrowsmith, 1909), p. 44. See Hester Jones, 'Josephine Butler: "The Still Voice of Silence": Prostitutes and Prophets', in Alison Milbank, ed., *Beating the Traffic: Josephine Butler and Anglican Social Action on Prostitution Today* (Easton: George Mann Publishing, 2007), pp. 69–89, for a fuller exploration of this use of the rhetoric in Butler's work.

3. 'Filthy Lucre':
Christianity, Commerce and the Female Bodily Economy in Seamstress Narratives of the 1840s[*]

Ella Dzelzainis

> Wealth flows into the country, but how does it circulate there? Not equally and healthfully through the whole system; it sprouts into wens and tumours, and collects in aneurisms which starve and palsy the extremities.
>
> Robert Southey, *Letters from England*, 1807[1]

In this vivid critique of nineteenth-century commerce, the Poet Laureate and High Tory, Robert Southey, reaches for the language of disease.[2] Wealth – or money – becomes blood circulating in the veins of the body politic. But unregulated commerce has produced a sick patient, where clots of luxurious excess in one part of English society create life-sapping, withering impoverishment in another. As 'one of the first, though by no means the last, to counterpose *moral* economy against *political* economy', Southey repeatedly and volubly condemned the latter through metaphors of illness until well into the fourth decade of the nineteenth century.[3] A leading critic of political economy, he provided analytical and rhetorical inspiration for those radical Tories who shared his dismay at the breakdown of paternalistic relations between rich and poor in the face of the manufacturing system and agreed with his moral diagnosis of England's ill health.[4]

However, as the full extent of occupational disease among young people and children of the labouring classes was revealed in a number of parliamentary reports in the 1830s and 1840s, Southey's lurid image took an increasingly literal turn. Metaphor yielded to pathology as medical witnesses gave testimony in investigations such as those by the Select Committee on the bill to regulate child factory labour in 1832 and the Children's Employment Commission in 1842, in the course of which

---

[*] I am grateful to Martin Dzelzainis, David Feldman, Hilary Fraser and Sally Ledger, all of whom have offered careful and incisive readings of this essay at various stages.

they heaped sensation upon revelation with their accounts of work-related deformity, disease and death. Widely publicized, the results of these investigations were deployed by opponents of the manufacturing system in their campaign against political economy. Fictional propaganda played a significant part in this campaign, with the parliamentary reports informing a number of tracts, novels and tales that sought to draw public attention to the degradation of the working classes in the face of unbridled commerce. Two of these stories – 'Milliners and Dress-Makers' by the pre-millenarian Evangelical, Charlotte Elizabeth Tonna, and *The Pageant* by the Tractarian, Francis Paget – were immediate responses to R.D. Grainger's disturbing account of the moral and physical condition of apprentice seamstresses in his 1842 Report on Millinery and Dress-Making, placed in the public domain by the Children's Employment Commission in 1843.[5] Despite significant doctrinal differences between Evangelicals and Tractarians, Tonna and Paget were united in their High Tory assertion of the claims of a Christian moral economy over political economy.[6] But the content of Grainger's Report, and the appended evidence on which it drew, added a further strand to their shared analysis. As an anatomist and physiologist, Grainger's interpretation of the seamstresses' plight was informed by his medical understanding of the impact of hours of stitching on their moral and physical constitution – or, as it was known, on the 'female economy'.[7] Accordingly, this essay examines the way in which early Victorian gynaecological accounts of the relationship between women's minds and bodies in Grainger's Report were filtered through a set of fundamentalist Christian beliefs in stories by Paget and Tonna. In doing so, the biologically essentialist account of the overworked seamstress in their fiction combined to draw all women – apprentices, employers and their wealthy clients – into a debate over vanity, luxury and avarice that identified the corrupt excesses of femininity with those of commerce. Sally Shuttleworth has noted how, in the nineteenth century, events in the social body were re-enacted in the female bodily economy, the ailments of the former being reproduced metonymically in the latter.[8] But persistently repeated throughout the debate over female labour in the early Victorian period was the axiom that the treatment of women was a reliable index to the civilized status of any nation: an axiom that invites an inductive and deductive reading in which contemporary analysis of the seamstress's condition doubles back as broader social critique.[9] I shall argue, then, that in 'Milliners and Dress-Makers' and *The Pageant* the figurative relationship between the social body and the female body is ultimately that of synecdoche, with its potential for a more complex and fluid movement between the general and the particular, the particular and the general. In consequence, Tonna and Paget's medico-religious prescription for female health is offered as an analogical cure for the diseased body politic, shedding its gendered connotations in this reversed, universal application.

R.D. Grainger's work as Sub-Commissioner began when the Children's Employment Commission was established in 1840. The Commission initially defined a child as anyone who had not completed their thirteenth year of age, but in February of 1841 this remit was extended to age eighteen. This brought dressmakers' apprentices, most of them articled between the ages of fourteen and sixteen, firmly within the scope of the inquiry. Grainger and his fellow Sub-Commissioners were instructed to investigate not just the hours, pay and conditions in the workplace, but also to assess the physical, spiritual and moral health of their subjects. The *Second Report* had been intended as an investigation of the 'poorer classes', but Grainger's Report focused on a class of young working women who had paid up to £60 for the privilege of a two- or three-year apprenticeship.[10] Based mostly in London fashion-houses, where they lived in as boarders to be trained in the making of luxury clothing for women of the higher classes, they were the daughters either of working-class families with social aspirations or of middle-class families fallen on hard times. But as the oral testimony given to Grainger confirmed, the girls' attempts to gain or retain social respectability came at the cost of working at least eighteen hours a day, sometimes on Sundays.[11]

In the supporting evidence to his Report, Grainger includes the testimony of ten medical men. Among the many ailments attributed to the seamstresses' excessive hours of sedentary labour in confined and stuffy rooms were consumption, inflammations of the eye, blindness, dyspepsia and deformities of the spine and shoulder. But, whether ophthalmologist, surgeon or doctor, each and every medical witness made reference to diseases and symptoms that they understood to be the result of damage done specifically to what they termed the 'female constitution', the 'female functions' or the 'uterine system'.[12] Dr G. Hamilton Roe's statement is representative:

> Among those who are dress-makers, the most common complaint is great constitutional weakness, indicated by that degree of pallor which only arises, in other cases, from the abstraction of a large quantity of blood, producing anaemia [...]. The uterine actions are almost constantly deranged; amenorrhoea and leucorrhoea are the most ordinary results. As these young persons commence this laborious occupation at the age of 14 or 16, when the great

change occurs in the female constitution, the most serious interruption to the functions of the uterus is likely to be produced; and daily experience shows that this is the result. Has no doubt that the action of the uterus is frequently permanently deranged.[13]

While he identifies the absence of menstruation (amenorrhoea) and abnormal discharge (leucorrhoea) by name, Hamilton Roe's reference to 'that degree of pallor which only arises, in other cases, from the abstraction of a large quantity of blood' indicates the diagnosis of another gynaecological condition: chlorosis.[14] What we would probably now term anaemia, chlorosis was understood in the nineteenth century to manifest itself not just through wanness but also through fatigue, loss of appetite, emaciation and fainting fits – conditions that were identified repeatedly throughout the medical testimony. It was a disease associated with puberty and particularly prevalent among girls like the sedentary seamstresses who lived in over-crowded, urban environments.[15] Furthermore there were several references in the evidence to hysteria – also understood to be a gynaecological ailment at the time.[16] Whether they described the young seamstress's bodily economy as 'completely disorganized', 'deranged' or in a state of 'disturbance', all these medical witnesses diagnosed a state of gynaecological turmoil that was directly attributable to the conditions of her labour.[17]

But the yoking of the mind and body in Victorian conceptions of the female economy meant that such a diagnosis went beyond the purely physical. In recounting the seamstress's menstrual disorders in such repetitive detail, the report had in fact revealed the fragile state of her sexual status and moral health to its readers. Nineteenth-century medical opinion widely held that in 'early childhood the speciality of the sexes is not yet developed, and the child is only boy or girl by anticipation'.[18] Rather, the pre-pubertal boy and girl appeared to share a 'common gender'.[19] This view was founded on the belief that it was not the genitalia alone that denoted sex. The individual achieved masculine or feminine status only at puberty, once he or she had acquired the appropriate secondary sexual characteristics and desires.[20] Thus, for the Victorian girl, the onset of regular menstruation signified more than just the accomplishment of puberty: it finally established both her sex *and* her gender. And since overwork deranged the seamstress's uterus, not just her health but also her womanhood and femininity were at stake.

In medical conceptions of the female economy, the uterus was central. As one doctor expressed it, 'all [women's] organs partake, more or less, in the condition of the uterus'.[21] There was, for example, a 'well-known sympathy' between the womb and the bladder, in addition to the 'intimate consent' which existed between the uterus and the stomach.[22] Dr Samuel Ashwell, a physician at Guy's Hospital, readily traced a link between chlorosis, amenorrhoea and phthisical diseases of the lung, such as consumption.[23] Moreover, just as the uterus could influence the other organs, so could the other organs – including the mind – influence the uterus. Any 'mental or moral agitation' could lead to uterine derangement and, similarly, the failure to establish normal menstruation could lead to a downward spiral of chlorosis, hysteria, inflammation, madness and melancholy.[24]

The link between hysteria and the seamstress had already been established in Thomas Laycock's *Treatise on the Nervous Disorders of Woman* in 1840: 'Hysteria is often seen amongst sempstresses, laceworkers, and others of the female population of large towns, confined for many hours daily at sedentary employments [...] who, from associating in numbers, excite each other's passions.'[25] According to Laycock, this excitation could have consequences even more dangerous than hysteria. He maintained that when young females of the same age were grouped together and influenced by the 'same novel feelings towards the opposite sex' there was a serious risk of sexual arousal and their 'being led to indulge in practices injurious to both body and mind'.[26] Dr Michael Ryan expresses a similar anxiety over girls' masturbation, but reverses the causal link. Hysteria itself could be the result of:

> an excessive sensibility, or irritability of the uterus, the abuse of venereal pleasure, strong and frequent emotions, voluptuous conversations, the perusal of licentious works, frequenting balls, theatres, dances, every thing that excites the general sensibility, and especially that of the genital organs, disorders of menstruation, masturbation, privation of sexual commerce after it had been long enjoyed, and chronic inflammation of the uterus or ovary. These diseases influence not only the brain and the uterus, but all other parts of the body.[27]

Thus women's moral health could be deduced from their physical condition – and vice versa. The entire female economy was at the mercy of the uterus, which accounted for the 'natural affectability' or 'susceptibility of woman, and her less mental and muscular power' when compared to the male.[28] Notoriously prone to seduction, young seamstresses, who worked so hard during the 'most important epoch of life' for women, were particularly unstable and in need of constant physical and moral monitoring if they were to stand any chance at all of withstanding the sexual temptations generated by their minds and bodies.[29]

Hence the various diseases with which the seamstresses in Grainger's report had been diagnosed were, with few exceptions, all understood to be the cause *of* and caused *by* uterine derangement. Not only were the diseases themselves mutually reinforcing, the girls were all of similarly young age and worked communally in close confinement. To underscore the implied moral dangers, Grainger quotes an extract from James Johnson's *Economy of Health* which asserts that 'the congregation of juvenile females, under such circumstances, conduces to anything rather than vigour of constitution or morality of sentiment'.[30] It is no wonder, then, that in his formal report Grainger felt able to make the apparently surprising claim that he need not 'speak of the causes which produce the immorality which is so proverbial among young dressmakers, except so far as they fall within the legitimate scope of this inquiry', as the appended medical evidence had announced the causes loudly on his behalf.[31] Furthermore, those doctors who in their evidence criticized the girls' lack of supervision on Sundays (staying in bed rather than attending church and wandering the streets due to meals not being provided by their employer) were not merely offering pious Sabbatarian platitudes.[32] These factors were fundamental to their understanding and diagnoses of the seamstress's frail physical, mental and moral health. To Grainger (himself an evangelical and a Sabbatarian) and his fellow doctors, religious instruction was essential in the fight to control the girls' biologically essential instability; their 'natural affectability'. It is important to stress that these beliefs about the female economy and the establishment of regular menstruation were not privy only to the medical profession, but were in the public domain. This was so much understood to be the case that one of Grainger's witnesses confidently asserted that it was 'unnecessary to dwell on the evils which result from the interruption of so important a function'.[33] Consequently, Grainger's Report blames not just the long hours worked, but also the apprentices' mostly female employers for their failure to provide moral and spiritual care *in loco parentis*.

In recent criticism it has become conventional to view the seamstress as an 'unthreatening' representative worker (because female, un-unionized and performing that most womanly of activities, stitching) through which the problems of industrial expansion could be discussed.[34] Ian Haywood, for example, considers that by the 1840s the needleworker had become a 'romanticized icon of social distress'.[35] Yet in sharp contradistinction to this figuration, the medical testimony to Grainger had revealed her to be a disturbing example of potentially uncontrolled – indeed 'deranged' – femininity. Moreover, the Report had revealed a fundamental ideological contradiction. The Children's Employment Commission had instructed its Sub-Commissioners to ascertain whether the girls under investigation were schooled in the 'domestic habits usually acquired by women in their station' or whether their work had 'rendered them less fit than those whose early years have not been spent in labour, for performing the duties of wives and mothers'.[36] They were required to check whether the girls had been 'instructed in needle and other household work'.[37] Yet contrary to the Commission's assumption that the ability to sew was one of the reliable measures of fitness for marriage and motherhood, Grainger had instead identified an estimated 15,000 girls in London alone for whom this archetypal signifier of the feminine was arresting their development into women and leaving them open to vice. Unsurprisingly, the public reaction to this portrayal of the seamstress was one of moral panic.[38] As I shall now show, in their alarmist fictional responses, Tonna and Paget's understanding of the seamstress's particular predicament led them to emphasize female instability in general. Their remedy was to place all women in a web of mutual surveillance and self-regulation founded on a Christian moral economy, in the belief that this would also put a brake on the commercial excesses of the marketplace.

As Boyd Hilton has noted, the 'affinity between evangelicals and Tractarians has long been something of an historical commonplace'.[39] Although relations between the two groups became more antagonistic in the 1840s, the tales produced by the Evangelical Tonna and the 'Evangelical-turned-Tractarian' Paget reveal key shared religious convictions: belief in the truth of scriptural revelation and original sin; advocacy of social paternalism as a shield against apocalypse; and a loathing of political economy.[40] Both of them rely heavily on the information in the Grainger report, footnoting extracts and quoting it at length.[41] But for anyone wishing to propagandize on behalf of the apprentice in fictional form, the problem was how to convey the full extent of the physical and moral threat to the economy of the young seamstress, but without indecorous reference to either the gynaecological or the libidinous.

Tonna's 'Milliners and Dress-Makers' makes discreet allusion to uterine derangement through her description of 'that universal air of languor, that absence of healthy glow, that reed-like attenuation of figure' that marks the apprentice seamstress ('Milliners and Dress-Makers', p. 402).[42] The girls are tired, pale and lacking in secondary sexual characteristics, and Tonna's middle-class female readership would have had no difficulty in recognizing these symptoms of gynaecological disorder. Besides the girls' many fainting fits, more overt reference is found in the final chapter, where Tonna cites Grainger's reference to 'great constitutional weakness, indicated by a degree of pallor, or bloodless condition of the body' ('Milliners and Dress-Makers', p. 416). No doubt the moral implications of this bloodlessness would have been plain enough to the Victorian reader. But Tonna goes further by embedding the mind–body axis of the female economy structurally in the story. She does so by introducing a *pair* of heroines, Ann and Frances King: one sister suffers physically, the other morally.

As daughters of a yeoman farmer in reduced circumstances, Ann and Frances are compelled to seek work in London's West End. Ann's three-year apprenticeship as an improver (that is, she already had some experience in needlework) costs £30, while Frances has been articled for five years for a premium 'something larger' ('Milliners and Dress-Makers', p. 402). The first part of the story follows the fortunes of Ann who, on her first day, encounters the entire gamut of unhealthy conditions in the workplace as identified by Grainger. The girls stitch from 6am to 2am; the poor ventilation is made worse at night by gaslight; tea is 'sickly slop, and slices of coarse bread with a scraping of rancid butter' ('Milliners and Dress-Makers', p. 403). One girl is of 'deformed appearance' ('Milliners and Dress-Makers', p. 403) and another faints for the second time around midnight, by which time Ann is so tired that she is advised to stand in order to continue working.

Ann's physical decline is rapid. Within a year she is 'wan and sunken' ('Milliners and Dress-Makers', p. 405) and suffering from a long list of complaints: pain in her shoulder blades; palpitations; a mist over her eyes; a choking in the throat; sickness and loss of appetite; pains in her limbs; headaches; and fainting fits. The doctor has seen her six months previously, when he diagnosed fresh air, exercise and food at regular hours – a prescription for disorders of the uterus that Ann is unable to follow because of the terms of her apprenticeship.[43] Ann's eventual fate is to be taken back by her father, Mr King, to the countryside and an early death from consumption. But Ann's belief in the power of the mind over the female body is indicated by her moral diagnosis of her own physical symptoms. When working late in the evenings, an elderly assistant reads aloud to the girls. The first time, Ann expected a reading from the Bible, but instead hears 'a tale, the very meaning of which she can hardly make out, but where murder, and violence, and situations of fearful peril, and bursts of unbridled passion, at the expense of filial and conjugal duty, make up the exciting compound' ('Milliners and Dress-Makers', p. 404). As the girls listen, Tonna asserts, a 'moral poison sinks deep into their minds' ('Milliners and Dress-Makers', p. 404). Similarly, in her discussion with the doctor, Ann herself offers a diagnosis of her condition that is partly spiritual ('Milliners and Dress-Makers', p. 406):

> For some time I went to church on Sundays, and that did me good, body and mind; but after a while, I was forced to lie in bed all the Sunday morning [...] left off going to church, because my spirits were bad, and I was over-persuaded by those about me that nothing was so good for me as merriment and amusement, which was out of our reach all the rest of the week. I regret it now, bitterly: I was better taught at home; but, oh! sir, the power of example is very great over the young, especially when nobody that they can look up to cares for them except as working-machines.

Brought up to be a dutiful Christian girl, Ann recognizes her own mental and physical need for constant religious observance and moral vigilance.

The more overtly sexual implications of Grainger's report are refracted through the figure of Frances. In contrast to Ann, Frances retains a 'comparative healthfulness' ('Milliners and Dress-Makers', p. 409) in her appearance. But, sent out unchaperoned on errands to match silks and ribbons, she is exposed to the temptations of the London streets. Her employer's failure to provide dinner on Sunday leaves her prey to seduction by men 'quite of a different rank, and more dangerous to a girl so much off guard' ('Milliners and Dress-Makers', p. 413). On learning of this, an indignant Mr King hands over money to Frances's employer, Mrs B., to pay for her meals on the Sabbath, but it is too little, too late. Victimized because of her father's complaints, Frances's fate has been clearly signalled by Tonna who chronicles her moral decline. She resorts first to one lover and, when rejected, acquires another. After this, she takes to drink; has her indentures cancelled; becomes a prostitute; and finally, found guilty of soliciting, dies in prison. Tonna tells the reader how her 'short career of vice' has marked her body: prematurely aged, her immorality 'has bloated her cheek and wrinkled her brow' ('Milliners and Dress-Makers', p. 413). Fully aware of the moral implications of the gynaecological evidence in Grainger, Tonna reconfigures the mind–body circularity of the female economy by using two characters to represent its component parts. At the same time, she confirms the connection between the physical and the moral: Ann's self-diagnosis in her conversation with her doctor acknowledges the role of the spiritual in her bodily ill-health, while Frances's descent into the 'abyss of wretchedness and guilt' ('Milliners and Dress-Makers', p. 414) is inscribed on her face.

Specifically addressing a mixed audience of 'the younger members of the higher classes of society' in *The Pageant*, Francis Paget is inevitably more restrained than Tonna in his references to gynaecological afflictions (*The Pageant*, p. vii). But there are several references to hysteria among the seamstresses in the story, and the girls' unestablished womanhood is implied through his description of them as having 'had no youth, but pass[ing] at once from childhood to sickness and decrepitude' (*The Pageant*, p. 90). And while the story focuses its attention on just one morally virtuous apprentice, Lucy Brooke (who, like Ann King, dies of consumption in the countryside), he introduces the disordered seamstress's vulnerability to bodily and moral disease by footnoting an excerpt from the High Church journal, the *Christian Remembrancer*, which warns of the human cost of luxurious finery and describes the 'cold, shivering walks, taken by half-starved, half-clothed, wan, sickly girls, creeping like evil spirits, vile, wretched, sinful, diseased, to their daily, nightly toil, polluted alike in body and soul' (*The Pageant*, p. 70). For Paget, moral responsibility for the pollution of the seamstress's economy lay with other women – the female employer and her lady clients – who failed to recognize their Christian duty toward her. This was an analysis with which Tonna agreed. In both their stories, Tonna and Paget build on the understanding of the female economy detailed by Grainger to make a link between women's proclivity for vanity, as exemplified by the demand for dresses at the height of the London fashion season, and the avaricious luxury that resulted from unrestrained commercialism and the worship of Mammon.

Through this moral analysis, both authors declare their opposition to the attempted redefinition of the concept of luxury by political economists in the eighteenth and early nineteenth century.[44] As two of political economy's leading thinkers, Adam Smith and T.R. Malthus, argued strongly that the spread of luxury was of positive benefit to the nation's prosperity and happiness.[45] Yet in making these arguments, Smith, Malthus and others were seeking to overturn a powerful tradition in Christian thought that posited luxury (or indulgence) as the cause of the Fall of Man. Arguing that original sin was the result of Eve's tempting Adam into sin, this tradition firmly established the rhetorical association of women, luxury and lasciviousness.[46] According to St Augustine, luxury was the result of prosperity and led inexorably to avarice – and it was Augustine who was cited by subsequent Christian theologians and political theorists 'as the source of their belief that the appearance of luxury signalled the onset of the death fever of civilization'.[47] Such was the resonance of this moral critique that not even Smith's devoted pupil, the influential Scottish philosopher and historian John Millar, was entirely convinced that a commercial nation's wealth could increase without immoral effects. In his *Origin of the Distinction of Ranks* (1771) he stated that 'it would seem [...] that there are certain limits beyond which it is impossible to push the real improvements arising from wealth and opulence'.[48] Citing the debauchery of Rome, he argued that too much luxury led to dissipation, and that this reversion to sensual indulgence diminished the rank and dignity of women. He did, however, suggest that in other opulent civilizations, such as France and Italy, religion had helped prevent this slide into immorality.[49]

It is against this backdrop, where luxury is associated with women and where their conduct, if unchecked by Christian moral principle, augurs a wealthy civilization's regression, that Tonna and Paget's remedy has to be understood. After his reference to the apprentices' 'proverbial' immorality, Grainger goes on to comment: 'It cannot be stated that, as a body, the principals in this business are careful to promote moral and religious conduct among those whom they employ.'[50] He refers to the girls being obliged to work late on Saturdays and stay in bed on Sunday morning rather than go to church. He adds that the houses where no meals except breakfast are served on Sundays deserve 'the severest reprobation'.[51] As already suggested, the medical evidence had spelled out the consequences of the employers' failure to act *in loco parentis* to their young apprentices, and Tonna and Paget readily condemn them in their turn.

Both writers create employers whose cruelties and moral delinquencies contribute directly to the trials undergone by their charges. Confirming St Augustine's cycle of prosperity leading to luxury thence to avarice, Tonna condemns the rampant greed in this 'commercial country' ('Milliners and Dress-Makers', p. 410). In 'Milliners and Dress-Makers', Madame A. tries to get rid of her apprentice, Ann, once her ill-health affects her efficiency. Mrs B.'s greed and spite contribute to Frances's downfall. Having described Frances's descent into prostitution, Tonna asks the reader ('Milliners and Dress-Makers', p. 413):

> Do you ask what wrought this painful change? It was wrought by THE LOVE OF MONEY. Not on her part, poor girl! she only desired to be taught a respectable business, that she might become the helper of her parents, and secure a moderate competence to herself. But the root of all evil was planted where her lot was cast; and for filthy lucre's sake the claims of justice were overlooked.

Tonna is joined in her attack on the pursuit of 'filthy lucre' – a phrase used by St Paul in his epistle to Timothy – by Paget who, as a Tractarian, believed political economy to be irreconcilable with Christianity.[52] Paget's mouthpiece in *The Pageant*, Sir Walter Blunt, condemns 'the competition and underselling' that constitute 'our avaricious commercial system' (*The Pageant*, p. 190). In *The Pageant*, this system is represented by the O'Raffertys, a pair of smugglers (also known in this period as 'the free traders') who own a dressmaking business. Mrs Rafferty refuses to take on more hands at the height of the season and we learn that, in consequence, one seamstress has gone blind and the health of the heroine is 'quite broken' (*The Pageant*, p. 112).[53]

In both stories, the female employer's commercial avarice leads directly to warnings of England's demise as a nation. Sir Walter Blunt's response to his niece's query about the belief that commercial prosperity was the sign of a nation's health and pre-eminence is to ask her if she can 'name one mighty city or nation whose terrible end and political annihilation are among the landmarks of history, whose down fall and ruin are not to be traced to these things' (*The Pageant*, p. 66). Having invoked the biblical fates of Tyre, Babylon and Amalek, Blunt insists that England's apparent power, glory and prosperity should in reality be interpreted as 'curses and judicial inflictions [...] the tokens that wrath irresistible is coming upon us to the uttermost' (*The Pageant*, p. 65). It is merely a sign of God's mercy that his 'bolt has not yet been launched forth against' the nation, in order that 'He may afford us the opportunity of being cleansed, and purified, and changed through suffering' (*The Pageant*, p. 67). Political and social convulsion is the cure for the sick English body politic. As Blunt, echoing Southey, tells Gertrude: 'there are forms and stages of disease in which the only chance of saving life is to be found in some remedy which for a while prostrates the whole system' (*The Pageant*, p. 65). The remedy is, of course, the assertion of Tractarian values and the primacy of the Church over the State. The substitution of the system of Christian moral economy for that of political economy was the only way to avert God's wrath.

Similarly for Tonna, known to her reading public as a fervent premillenarian who believed that divine vengeance was imminent and would precede the Second Coming, the failure of the higher ranks to fulfil their paternalistic Christian obligations toward the lower meant that England was in peril. In 'The Lace-Runners', the fourth story of *The Wrongs of Woman*, she describes England as resting on 'an awakening volcano'.[54] But in 'Milliners and Dress-Makers' national destruction is imagined in terms of a second deluge as the sins of the upper and middle classes are visited upon the working class. Only the Christian moral economy can serve as a 'breakwater' against the 'ocean' of greedy selfishness among the female employers and 'curb its force and prevent its bursting in, to bring ruin, destitution and death to the hearths of English cottages' ('Milliners and Dress-Makers', p. 417).

Evidently not just the apprentices but also their female employers were in need of regulation by others – but the question was how that regulation could best be effected. Along with other Tractarians, Paget rejected the idea of state legislation, which he saw as a usurpation of the authority of the Church.[55] In contrast, Tonna (who was a passionate campaigner for the Ten Hours Factory Bill) was willing to countenance it.[56] Nonetheless, for both the swiftest remedy lay in the hands of the dressmakers' female clientele. The wealthy woman was to follow the Christian (and specifically Pauline) precept to subdue her vanity and show solicitude in the placing of orders. Paget, for example, asserts that all 'right-minded persons' should decide 'whether they allow sufficient time to their dress-makers for the execution of their orders (as the *impatience* of customers presses more heavily on the work-women than the extent of the work)' (*The Pageant*, p. 189). His upper-class female readers were also to ask themselves 'whether they need as *many* dresses, as modern habits seem to require' (*The Pageant*, p. 189). The consequences of failing to be 'right-minded' are depicted in his story through the conduct of the aristocratic Augusta Blondeville. Warned by her more compassionate younger sister that seamstresses were being worked to death, she comments, 'The milliners are old enough to take care of themselves, and as for my dress, I must have it, and I will' (*The Pageant*, p. 53). The story ends with Augusta at the graveside of Lucy Brooke, whose death Paget attributes directly to Augusta's unreasonable demands: 'Thus met once more the VICTIM and the DESTROYER' (*The Pageant*, p. 186). Similarly, Tonna reminds her readers of how St Paul 'warned his female converts from paganism, "women professing godliness," against too great a love for "putting on of apparel," or adorning themselves in "costly array"' ('Milliners and Dress-Makers', p. 417).[57] She observes that among the 1,500 employers referred to in Grainger's report 'there are not a few who deeply deplore the cruel system of wrong and oppression [...] and who, if encouraged and upheld by the ladies of England, would pledge themselves to a line of conduct which at present they can only pursue under heavy disadvantages' ('Milliners and Dress-Makers', p. 415). As customers wealthy women should act forthwith, giving their patronage only to those houses which guaranteed a ten- or twelve-hour maximum day for their apprentices. If moral pressure was insufficient to make the avaricious employer recognize her duties towards her charges, then the commercial pressure of a boycott would force her to.[58]

Simultaneously blaming some women, therefore, while recognizing the power of others once mobilized in support of a cause, Paget and

Tonna promote a devout model of feminine conduct through a process of commentary and comparison that condemns women who fail to achieve it. To force home this message, each author holds up an example of selfish womanhood, figured as blood-stained and corrupted by vanity and luxury, from which the female reader is required to differentiate herself. Tonna deploys the biblical figure of Salome, whose vain exploitation of her sexuality leads to the shedding of innocent blood ('Milliners and Dress-Makers', p. 417):

> There is one female named, who went forth to the dance, as one of courtly splendour, and elicited even royal applause, while captivating a throng of nobles by her external appearance; yet who, in that very act, brought upon her soul the guilt of innocent blood. May God in His rich mercy deliver the daughters of England from such a snare!

Turning once more to the *Christian Remembrancer*, Paget spells out the human cost of a woman's luxurious finery and compares her guilt and complicity in murder with that other demonized female, Lady Macbeth: 'velvet and silk, purple and fine linen, all smell of blood, – "The perfumes of Arabia will not sweeten them"' (*The Pageant*, p. 69). Thus the medical knowledge that informs both of these stories resurfaces once more through these explicit allusions to the spilling of blood, whether that of St John the Baptist or King Duncan. Not just the seamstresses but all women were biologically unstable – and prone, therefore, to the vanity, luxury and lasciviousness of those deviant figures, Salome and Lady Macbeth, without the self-regulation that comes from Christian precept.

But for all the gynaecological and gendered specificity of the stories, both Tonna and Paget are also concerned to broaden their attack on luxury and avarice. For each of them the disquieting seamstress victim stands in for all the poor. In the final paragraph of her story, Tonna widens the application of her critique of greed through commentary on exploitative class relations, asking her readers 'How dare we profess [Christ's] holy Name, and assume to be partakers in the joy of his salvation, while lending ourselves to this worst of wrong and robbery, the wrong and robbery of the poor?' ('Milliners and Dress-Makers', p. 417). In his preface, Paget explains that the seamstress is a representative of all the 'humbler ranks' (*The Pageant*, p. vii) and later numbers himself among the rich, arguing that we must 'make up our minds to part from those accursed luxuries, or that still more accused covetousness which is plunging us to perdition!' (*The Pageant*, pp. 192–3). Paraphrasing Psalm 9, Paget reminds his mixed-sex, upper-class audience of the divine punishment that will be meted out to all those who have neglected the lower classes: 'The Lord will be a defence for the oppressed: even a refuge in due time of trouble. – For *when He maketh inquisition for blood He remembereth them*: and forgetteth not the complaint of the poor. – The wicked shall be turned into hell' (*The Pageant*, p. 115).

Ultimately, then, both writers shift attention away from the gendered particularity of the female bodily economy to the broader categories of rich and poor. For these High Tories, what the Christian moral economy meant above all was the stability of social and political paternalism, expressed through a hierarchical set of class relations founded on reciprocal duties and obligations.

These paternalistic conclusions can nevertheless be traced all the way back to the biologically essentialist view of femininity predicated on medical understandings of the female economy, as documented in Grainger's report, and which, in Tonna and Paget's fiction, furnished a solution to the predicament of the apprentice seamstresses. Just as the female body and mind needed to maintain a healthy equilibrium, so the answer to the problem was the achievement of a more balanced relationship between apprentice and dressmaker, dressmaker and client. The fashion-house workshop was to become a more morally protective environment – in other words, it was to function more like the home as the female employer fulfilled her duty to act as a mother *in loco parentis* toward those in her care. In her turn, the wealthy customer was to strive to emulate an ideal model of womanhood: actively Christian, modest in dress and character, and dutiful in her social relations. Her religious conviction and observance would be the means through which she would achieve self-regulation. This would lead to the regulation of others as recalcitrant female employers would be compelled by financial penalties to acknowledge their moral obligations toward their employees. The ensuing reduction in the hours of the apprentices – as well as their increased supervision – would help them, too, to achieve the harmony of body and mind essential to a stable, moral and (above all) Christian femininity.

In exactly the same way that the female bodily economy required regulation by a Christian moral economy, so too did political economy. Tonna and Paget's religious prescription for England's health as a commercial nation was identical to that given for the seamstress, drawing in all men and women of all classes. The body politic also needed the external regulation and intervention provided by Christian values to ensure its harmonious operation and prevent the slide into immorality and corruption – that is, to cure it of Southey's wens, tumours, aneurisms and palsies. In their fiction, social sickness and disorder could indeed be mapped onto the female body, but Tonna and Paget's fundamentalist Christian beliefs meant that this mapping also worked in reverse. Placing the female body at the centre of a critique of commerce, they had traced a direct link from the derangement of the seamstress's uterus through to the derangement of national apocalypse. If the treatment of women was an infallible index of civilization then their unstable bodies told that, without an urgent return to a Christian moral economy, the end of England's body politic was nigh.

Notes

1 Robert Southey, *Letters from England*, ed. by Jack Simmons (London: Cresset, 1951), p. 210.
2 For more on Southey's use of this rhetoric, see David Eastwood, 'Ruinous Prosperity: Robert Southey's Critique of the Commercial System', *Wordsworth Circle* 25 (1994): 72–76; and Philip Connell, *Romanticism, Economics and the Question of 'Culture'* (Oxford: Oxford University Press, 2001), pp. 247–54.
3 Donald Winch, *Riches and Poverty: An Intellectual History of Political Economy in Britain, 1750–1834* (Cambridge: Cambridge University Press, 1996), p. 5.
4 See David Eastwood, 'Robert Southey and the Intellectual Origins of Romantic Conservatism', *English Historical Review* 104 (1989): 308–31.
5 'Milliners and Dress-Makers' was the first of four stories published separately under the umbrella title of *The Wrongs of Woman* (London: Dalton, 1843–1844). The edition used here is Charlotte Elizabeth Tonna, 'Milliners and Dress-Makers', *The Wrongs of Women* [sic] in *The Works of Charlotte Elizabeth Tonna*, 2 vols (New York: Dodd, 1850), vol. 2, pp. 397–417; hereafter referred to in the main text as 'Milliners and Dress-Makers'. The full title of Paget's story is F.E. Paget, *The Pageant; or, Pleasure and Its Price. A Tale for the Upper Ranks of Society* (Rugeley: Walters, 1843); hereafter referred to in the main text as *The Pageant*. R.D. Grainger, 'Report to the Commissioners on the Employment of Children and Young Persons', *Children's Employment Commission: Appendix to the Second Report of the Commissioners. Trades and Manufactures*, Part I (1842), ff. 1–42. The 'Report on Millinery and Dress-Making' is a sub-section on ff. 29–33; the corresponding evidence is supplied in 'Evidence Collected by R. D. Grainger, Esq.', on ff. 204–37.
6 The virulently anti-Catholic Tonna, for example, applauded her fellow pre-Millenarian, Lord Ashley, for having made a 'noble dash' at the 'Puseyites' or 'Jesuits in the Church' in parliament; see Edwin Hodder, *The Life and Work of the Seventh Earl of Shaftesbury, K.G.* (London: Cassell, 1888), p. 209. Boyd Hilton, *The Age of Atonement: The Influence of Evangelicalism on Social and Economic Thought, 1785–1865* (Oxford: Clarendon Press, 1986), pp. 27–8, notes affinities, but also increased antagonism in the 1840s.
7 M[ichael] Ryan, *A Manual of Midwifery, and Diseases of Women and Children*, fourth edn (London: no pub., 1841), p. 73. For details of Grainger's career, see Nick Hervey, 'Grainger, Richard Dugard (1801–1865), *Oxford Dictionary of National Biography*, http://owww.oxforddnb.com.catalogue.ulrls.lon.ac.uk:80/view/article/11236, last accessed 4 March 2007.

8   Sally Shuttleworth, *Charlotte Brontë and Victorian Psychology* (Cambridge: Cambridge University Press, 1996), p. 78. See also chapter 5 entire, which is on the female bodily economy. See also Thomas Laqueur, 'Orgasm, Generation, and the Politics of Reproductive Biology', *Representations* 14 (1986): 1–41 (30).
9   As two examples, see Ralph Grindrod's tract, *The Slaves of the Needle; An Exposure of the Distressed Condition, Moral and Physical, of Dress-makers, Milliners, Embroiderers, Slop-workers, &c.* (Manchester: Irwin, 1844), p. 3 ('The condition of woman, has, in all ages of the world, been an unerring criterion of the existence or extent of civilization'); Samuel S. Scriven on girls working in mines in 'Report to the Commissioners on the Employment of Children and Young Persons in the Collieries of a Part of the West Riding of Yorkshire', *Children's Employment Commission: Appendix to First Report of Commissioners. Mines. Part II* (1842), p. 75 ('The estimation of the sex has ever been held a test of the civilization of a people').
10   *Children's Employment Commission: Second Report of the Commissioners. Trades and Manufactures* (1843), p. 205. £60 is roughly equivalent to £4,250 at the time of writing.
11   See, for example, that given by Miss O'Neil: Grainger, 'Evidence', f. 205.
12   Grainger, 'Evidence', ff. 234, 232, 235.
13   Grainger, 'Evidence', f. 233.
14   For a detailed account of the history of chlorosis, see Helen King, *The Disease of Virgins: Green Sickness, Chlorosis and the Problems of Puberty* (London and New York: Routledge, 2004), passim.
15   Ryan, *Manual of Midwifery*, p. 338; Dr [Samuel] Ashwell, 'Observations on Chlorosis, and its Complications', *Guy's Hospital Reports* 1 (1836): 529–79 (534).
16   This is unsurprising, given that 'hysteria' was derived from the Greek for 'womb'; see Julie-Marie Strange, 'Menstrual Fictions: Languages of Medicine and Menstruation, c. 1850–1930', *Women's History Review* 9 (2000): 607–28 (616).
17   Grainger, 'Evidence', ff. 236, 232, 236.
18   Walter Johnson, *The Morbid Emotions of Women: Their Origin, Tendencies and Treatment* (London: Simpkin, Marshall, 1850), p. 1.
19   Johnson, *Morbid Emotions of Women*, p. 1.
20   Ornella Moscucci, *The Science of Woman: Gynaecology and Gender in England, 1800–1929* (Cambridge: Cambridge University Press, 1990), pp. 15–16.
21   Ryan, *Manual of Midwifery*, p. 73.
22   Dr Charles Waller, 'Lectures on the Function and Diseases of the Womb', *Lancet* 1 (25 January 1840), p. 639.
23   Ashwell, 'Observations on Chlorosis', pp. 533–4, 546–7.
24   Johnson, *Morbid Emotions of Women*, p. 24.
25   Thomas Laycock, *A Treatise on the Nervous Diseases of Women; Comprising an Inquiry into the Nature, Causes, and Treatment of Spinal and Hysterical Disorders* (London: Longman, Orme, Brown, Green and Longmans, 1840), p. 210.
26   Laycock, *Treatise on the Nervous Diseases of Women*, p. 141.
27   Ryan, *Manual of Midwifery*, p. 403.
28   Laycock, *Treatise on the Nervous Diseases of Women*, pp. 76, 83.
29   Grainger, 'Evidence', f. 206.
30   Grainger, 'Evidence', f. 232.
31   Grainger, 'Report', f. 33.
32   See, for example, the testimony of Mr Devonald in Grainger, 'Evidence', f. 236.
33   Grainger, 'Evidence', f. 234. See also, Shuttleworth, *Charlotte Brontë and Victorian Psychology*, pp. 79–81.
34   Beth Harris, 'The Works of Women Are Symbolical: The Victorian Seamstress in

the 1840s', unpublished PhD thesis, City University of New York, 1997, p. 10. I am grateful to Dr Harris for sending me an email copy of her thesis. See also, Lynn M. Alexander, 'Creating a Symbol: The Seamstress in Victorian Literature', *Tulsa Studies in Women's Literature* 18 (1999): 29–38.
35 Ian Haywood, 'The Retailoring of Dickens: *Christmas Shadows*, Radicalism, and the Needlewoman Myth', in *Famine and Fashion: Needlewomen in the Nineteenth Century* (Aldershot: Ashgate, 2005), pp. 67–86 (p. 78).
36 *Second Report*, p. 208.
37 *Second Report*, p. 208.
38 Grainger, 'Report', f. 29. To gain a sense of this moral panic, see *Athenaeum* (4 March 1843): 203–5; *The Times* (21 April 1843): 5–6.
39 Hilton, *Age of Atonement*, p. 27.
40 Hilton, *Age of Atonement*, p. 103. On the social and economic implications of Paget's Tractarian beliefs, see Simon Skinner, *Tractarians and the 'Condition of England': The Social and Political Thought of the Oxford Movement* (Oxford: Clarendon Press, 2004). For those of Tonna's pre-millenarian Evangelicalism, see Hilton, *Age of Atonement*, pp. 95–7, and Ella Dzelzainis, 'Charlotte Elizabeth Tonna, Pre-Millenarianism, and the Formation of Gender Ideology in the Ten Hours Campaign', *Victorian Literature and Culture* 31 (2003): 181–91.
41 Paget, *Pageant*, p. 69, refers to a 'light octavo of 250 pages'.
42 I take 'reed-like' to be a reference to the seamstress's failure to develop the secondary sexual characteristics (breasts, hips) that mark the accomplishment of puberty.
43 See also Laycock, *Treatise on the Nervous Diseases of Women*, p. 210.
44 John Sekora, *Luxury: The Concept in Western Thought, Eden to Smollett* (Baltimore, MD, and London: John Hopkins University Press, 1977), pp. 64–77, 104–5, 111–13.
45 T.R. Malthus, *An Essay on the Principle of Population*, ed. by Donald Winch (Cambridge: Cambridge University Press, 1992), pp. 321–3; Adam Smith, *An Inquiry into the Nature and Causes of the Wealth of Nations*, ed. by Edwin Cannan (Chicago, IL: Chicago University Press, 1976), pp. 87–8.
46 Christopher J. Berry, *The Idea of Luxury: A Conceptual and Historical Investigation* (Cambridge: Cambridge University Press, 1994), pp. 88–9.
47 Sekora, *Luxury*, pp. 39, 41.
48 William C. Lehmann, *John Millar of Glasgow 1735–1801: His Life and Thought and His Contributions to Sociological Analysis* (Cambridge: Cambridge University Press, 1960), p. 225.
49 Lehmann, *John Millar*, pp. 226–8.
50 Grainger, 'Report', f. 33.
51 Grainger, 'Report', f. 33.
52 1 Timothy 3.3, 8. Skinner, *Tractarians*, pp. 222–54.
53 For an example of smugglers as 'the free traders', see Walter Scott's *Guy Mannering* (1815), chapter 5. I am grateful to Ayse Celikkol for this detail and reference.
54 Charlotte Elizabeth Tonna, 'The Lace-Runners', *The Wrongs of Women*, p. 502.
55 Skinner, *Tractarians*, pp. 222, 292.
56 Dzelzainis, 'Charlotte Elizabeth', 181–91. Southey also trusted in the power of the state (see Skinner, *Tractarians*, p. 212).
57 The quotations are from 1 Timothy 2.9, 10.
58 This strategy recalls the earlier boycott by female abolitionists of slave-grown sugar. See Clare Midgley, *Women against Slavery: The British Campaigns, 1780–1870* (London and New York: Routledge, 1992), pp. 60–2.

4. Isaiah and Ezekiel – But What about Charley? An Essay on 'Wanting to Believe'*

Philip Davis

The Prophets Isaiah and Ezekiel dined with me, and I asked them how they dared so roundly to assert that God spake to them; and whether they did not think at the time, that they would be misunderstood, & so be the cause of imposition.

Isaiah answered: I saw no God, nor heard any, in a finite organical perception; but my senses discovered the infinite in every thing, and as I was then persuaded & remain confirmed that the voice of honest indignation is the voice of God, I cared not for consequences but wrote.

Then I asked: does a firm persuasion that a thing is so, make it so?

He replied: All poets believe that it does, & in ages of imagination this firm persuasion removed mountains; but many are not capable of a firm persuasion of any thing.[1]

This is William Blake, from *The Marriage of Heaven and Hell*, speaking in what he wills to be his own age of imagination – an age in which you could naturally *believe* in what you imagined, and not merely think that you *only imagined* it. But the satiric voice of the logical, rational sceptic that is also in Blake may indeed ask: 'Does a firm persuasion that a thing *is* so, *make* it so?' In our emphatically post-Romantic fashion, most of us would agree that the truth of a thought is not to be measured by the subjective intensity with which it is held or asserted. The poet in Blake can find a freer place in his own world where, as he again puts it in *The Marriage of Heaven and Hell*, 'every thing possible to be believed is an image of truth' – where subjective belief can have its own objective power; where everything possible to be believed holds some truth somewhere and in some way. But to a post-Romantic, to think that a belief holds good in it is not the same as being able to have that belief. As John Stuart Mill put it, in the midst of his nervous breakdown, 'Of the truth of this I was convinced, but to know that a feeling would make me happy if I had it, did not give me the feeling.'[2] This is not just to do with helpless-

---

*A version of this essay was published in *The Reader*, issue 21 (Spring 2006), pp. 29–41.

ness: scrupulousness too may mean the necessity of suspecting the good that may come from a belief that is really a comforting illusion.

Thus, you are told that 'firm persuasion' can move mountains. But – say the prophets – many are not capable of that firm persuasion. What do you do if you are not Isaiah or Ezekiel, but one of those many? Take the case where it is not simply that you disbelieve: you believe in belief, its power, its confidence, but you don't seem to *have* any. How do you go about getting belief? And is it a belief at all, if you have to try to get it?

In order to be clear, I am going to call these reluctant non-believers, these sensitive, sincere and vulnerable agnostics, *Charley* – for reasons I will speak of later. Now let's put Charley where actually he or she most belongs – not in Blake's 1790s but in George Eliot's 1850s. And now imagine Charley having to hear this, from Feuerbach's *Essence of Christianity* which George Eliot translated as Marian Evans:

> That which the unreligious man holds in his head merely, the religious man places out of and above himself as an object, and hence recognises in himself the relation of a formal subordination. The religious man has an aim. Only activity with a purpose, which is the union of theoretic and practical activity, gives man a moral basis and support, *i.e.*, character. Every man, therefore, must place before himself a God, *i.e.*, an aim, a purpose. He who has an aim has a law over him; he does not merely guide himself; he is guided. He who has no aim, has no home, no sanctuary; aimlessness is the greatest unhappiness. An aim sets limits; but limits are the mentors of virtue. He who has an aim has a religion.[3]

This is of course a well-nigh secular version of what is a religion, of what is a God. With Feuerbach anything, potentially, can be the object of belief – not just religion, but politics, money, love, private life. It seems as though you could choose your ground. But even so the pressure on Charley is severe. If you do not believe in anything, you are not a real person, your life hasn't a purpose, and you must be fundamentally unhappy. So, Charley, what do *you* believe in and what is *your* ultimate aim? No wonder our Charley believes in the importance of belief. Under such social and historical pressure, what is remarkable is not so much that Charley does not know if he has anything matching up to that belief, but that he dare admit that he may have none. What is more, these Charleys are intelligent people, not least because their intelligence is relatively free of any allegiance. What they see is that which unreligious people know they have made up *inside* their heads, religious people unconsciously place *outside* themselves, as though to make those meanings somehow more real. We do not want to guide ourselves; we want to feel guided. That is why all our religions, all our beliefs may really be subjective and fictional meanings we do not want to discover to be unconsciously fictional and subjective. We do not want to think we have made them up rather than received them as given.

There is an easy way out beckoning here, as I am sure you can see. We could say: this is the trouble with the Victorian age; this is its historical dilemma in the transition towards a more full-blown secularization – namely, that by a vicious circle, the more the conditions for belief became unpropitious, the more the pressure to retain some version of such belief symptomatically increased. The greater the fear of no-belief, the greater is the pressure to produce that fiction of belief. And the greater that pressure to believe, the less chance of believing – in particular among those, like Charley, who wanted most sincerely to do so. For they conscientiously wanted their faith to come from within, when the pressure was also coming from without. Thus they had to fight against what outside forces were demanding, even as inside themselves they wanted the selfsame thing – belief. Charleys want their beliefs to be neither an unconscious form of coerced and dutiful social conformity nor a fiction projected out of their own individual psychological neediness. In the alternations of *In Memoriam* Tennyson feared his desire to believe but still, for all that, did want to believe, and yet not merely as a psychological refuge from despair.

Was not all this to set the bar too high? As Henry Scott Holland puts it, in *Lux Mundi*, looking back at his century from 1889:

> Now faith, under rapid and stormy challenges, is apt to fall into panic. For this, surely, is the very meaning of panic – a fear that feeds upon itself. Men in a panic are frightened at finding themselves afraid. So now with faith: it is terrified at its own alarm. [...] If our faith were real faith (we say), would it ever lose its confidence? To be frightened is to confess itself false: for faith is confidence in God, Who can never fail. How can faith allow of doubt or hesitation.[4]

And so, says Scott Holland, a whole generation has talked itself into distrusting and then abandoning their faith not just because of a crisis of confidence but more because they thought they shouldn't be having any such a crisis at all, if they were true believers. Under the pressure of over-high demands, these Charleys believed that the very fact of *having* a crisis of confidence was incompatible with belief; was already a sign of the inner failure of not believing.

I concede that it is historically true that these Victorian Charleys were placed in the intolerable position of – as Lewis Carroll might put it – having to try to believe three impossible things before breakfast. In this I speak as someone who has tried to write a literary history of the

Victorians which is also, necessarily, a history of feeling in that period.⁵ Only, some of the critics have said that they are not sure how far I actually believe in history. And now I have to say that, in a sense, they are right. That is to say: I don't believe in writing off the Victorian predicament as though it were merely historical – a post-Romantic religious hangover en route to the later haven of secular modernity and postmodernity. The different time-dimension that is literature and not just history means that we should not make it easy for ourselves by putting in a safe historical distance and remaining outside these concerns. To make the thought harder, to get closer to a genuine imaginative experience of the mid-century predicament, let's just suppose, instead, that for all this counter-productive pressure to believe, what the Victorian pressure was signalling might not necessarily be false. In other words, suppose we take seriously the proposition that not to have any belief – if that is possible – is indeed a potential disaster. This is like saying: the Charleys may have been paranoid, but they did also have real enemies at the same time. The best Victorian novels think *both* these things.

I am arguing that we should take seriously the phenomenon of 'wanting to believe' as a position characteristically stuck in between believing and not believing. What is clear is that wanting-to-believe is thus a secondary or second-order condition and one, moreover, which belongs not to an age of imagination so much as an age of self-consciousness. So Carlyle writes in his great essay 'Characteristics', 'The healthy know not of their health, but only the sick.'⁶ That is to say, the sign of health is unconsciousness, a certain primary spontaneity of being and of doing. Ages of action and of heroism and of belief are not ages of moral philosophy, says Carlyle. As soon as something has ceased to be an involuntary part of a whole way of being, has had to become separately aware of itself, and argued over, then, says Carlyle, it is already in decline. Self-consciousness is what comes afterwards, comes second because it is secondary, and is itself the sign of disease, even whilst still seeking for its own cure. Thus wanting-to-believe is of an ironic and fallen condition because there would not be this want-as-desire if there were not, behind it, the want-as-lack.

It is this second-order condition that is occupied above all in the mid-Victorian period by Arthur Hugh Clough, the Claude of *Amours de Voyage* (1858). In one of the poem's drafts his friend Eustace writes to Claude, saying that Claude's doubt is all too much the product of inaction, of living always in the scrupulous beforehand: 'Action involves belief,' writes Eustace, 'Act and all will be clear'.⁷ But in the final version of the poem Claude himself writes (V.ii.20–4):

> *Action will furnish belief,* – but will that belief be the true one?
> That is the point, you know. However, it doesn't much matter.
> What one wants, I suppose, is to predetermine the action,
> So as to make it entail, not a chance-belief, but the true one.

It is the same here as it is in Clough's 'Dipsychus' – both warn that the mid-Victorian stress on the priority of action, on the cold shower of practical duty, may have degenerated into a version of an anti-intellectual PE master at Rugby School. For what Dipsychus insists upon is that action might be a form of giving-up and selling-out; that action might itself be a fear of hesitation and a flight from waiting; and thus, above all, that action ironically might be a form not of belief but of despair, sacrificing a larger hope you cannot seem to realize to a smaller practical gain you immediately can, instead. Get on with it, throw yourself into it. But all too automatically, action *will* furnish belief and you become what you have done, not out of first principles or true belief but through chance belief and knock-on effects – the thought automatically following the action rather than truly producing it. The sheer autonomous rational *intelligence* of Clough is characterized by its no longer being, as it were, in time with time. For intelligence is what steps out of the temporal sequence, and by the sheer force of extraordinary intellect turns the sequence round in one's head to get at what lies behind it:

> *Action will furnish belief,* – but will that belief be the true one?

Thus the intelligent creature tries, even by secondary reflection upon what one *might* do, to produce what one *should* do:

> What one wants, I suppose, is to predetermine the action
> So as to make it entail, not a chance-belief, but the true one.

It is an attempt to re-create within this realm of the secondary the lost world of truth's priority, from back to front. In other words: if you know in advance, as a result of what has happened before in the past, that *x* stimulus will almost automatically produce in you *y* response, and you find yourself in a situation where *y* is what you truly know you need to offer, then this time you may artificially use *x* stimulus to get *y* out of yourself.

Thus, for example, the late-seventeenth-century Anglican divine William Law advocated the use of set and external habits of devotion rather than waiting till the spirit spontaneously moved him to prayer: if we could not always get into the right religious spirit from inside out, because of our fallen infirmities, we would have to get into it more regularly from outside-in. Samuel Johnson admired this tough, determined discipline in Law. Though a fallen way, it was the right way for Law because he was first of all sure that the believing spirit was the true and necessary one – howsoever we fallen creatures by secondary means could get ourselves into it. But, like a Charley, Clough was not so sure, was scared of 'factitiously' creating in himself what he might not otherwise accept. In a notebook of 1849, written partly in Rome but partly in Liverpool, Clough commented upon what he called the wrong doctrine of habits: such that by doing acts *like* those of love, we shall indeed come to love. To Clough this was mechanical habituation – getting soldiers into the way of marching by means of music, schoolboys into the way of thinking by learning off by heart, husbands into the way of loving by giving their wives flowers.[8] The establishment of a virtuous 'hexis' or disposition, by acts of repetitive habit, was the way classically prescribed by Aristotle, but to Clough it increasingly seemed a form of what he called Victorian virtue-manufacture. For Clough was a covert Platonist, a would-be idealist who wanted to re-call, re-create and re-discover in himself in the second place only what he was certain he already believed, secretly or half-forgottenly, in the first.

Yet the first did not seem to be there. 'He does not even love God second-hand', complains a young woman in *Wilfrid Cumbermede*, a novel of 1872 written by that great, uneven and still-neglected genius, George MacDonald. To which another character replies, 'Perhaps because he is very anxious to love him first-hand.'[9] The person they are talking about is called Charley, Charley Osborne. He is the son of a stern, remorseless evangelical. Let's not talk simply of the pressure-to-believe created by 'Victorian Society' – that is all too abstract and easy; let's talk of the more personally confusing form in which that was made felt: the parent–child relationship. As Wilfrid Cumbermede himself says of Charley's father (*Wilfrid Cumbermede*, chapter 16, p. 139):

> A good man I do not doubt he was; but he did the hard parts of his duty to the neglect of his genial parts, and therefore was not a man to help others to be good. His own son revived the moment he took his leave of us – began to open up as the little red flower called the Shepherd's Hour-Glass opens when the cloud withdraws. It is a terrible thing when the father is the cloud, and not the sun, of his child's life.

That is why there is no first base for such children, even as they grow. The father that remains inside Charley himself *wants* to believe, in that fallen derivative of faith; but the son part of Charley cannot simply believe, and cannot even trust the wanting to, in all its mere secondariness. It is easier if you simply ditch the religion with the father; but what if the father is only a confusingly wrong version, the twisted personal form, of what may still be right? 'From his father,' says Cumbermede, Charley 'had inherited a conscience of abnormal sensibility; but he could not inherit the religious dogmas by means of which his father had partly deadened, had partly distorted his' (*Wilfrid Cumbermede*, chapter 16, p. 139). These Victorian challenges deserve to be taken seriously: if you don't believe in anything, if you had a poor relationship with your parents, not only do those two things go together but together they mean you may be a lost person. It is out of something like those hard thoughts that George Eliot writes *Daniel Deronda*.

At any rate, Charley finally cries out to his friend: 'If there *were* a God – that is, if I were sure there was a God, Wilfrid!' Wilfrid has to try to reply (*Wilfrid Cumbermede*, chapter 21, p. 181):

> I could not answer. How could I? *I* had never seen God, as the old story says Moses did on the clouded mountain. All I could return was,
> 'I suppose there should be a God, Charley! – Mightn't there be a God!'
> 'I don't know,' he returned. 'How should *I* know whether there *might* be a God?'
> 'But *may* there not be a *might be*?' I rejoined [...]
> I do not mean this was exactly what he or I said. Unable to recall the words themselves, I put the sense of the thing in as clear a shape as I can.

This is the shaping of belief: 'May there not be a might be?' Are such formulations *always* an easy indulgence, or are they not, on the contrary, sometimes as here a great risk, a wonderful linguistic effort at holding on as by the fingertips of writing? Charley says to Wilfrid that the worst of all possible miseries would be to believe in a lovely thing and then find that, after all, it was not true (*Wilfrid Cumbermede*, chapter 35, p. 298):

> 'You might never find it out, though,' I said. 'You might be able to comfort yourself with it all your life.'
> 'I was wrong,' he cried fiercely, 'Never to find it out would be the hell of all hells.'

The hell of all hells, even while you thought it was heaven. This is Charley's impossible thought – refusing a delusion which you would not know if you had it. It is the other side of the position Clough himself for once achieved by the end of his 'Hymnos ahymnos', saying to God (lines 39–40, Phelan, p. 273):

> Be thou but there, in soul and heart,
> I will not ask to feel thou art.

Here indeed are the two great thoughts in religious dilemma: I don't feel God is there but he is; I think God is there but he is not. And both of them are beyond the limits of thought, are double thoughts we cannot really think nor wholly avoid, and need literature even to imagine. In his respect for a God he cannot believe in but will not falsify, how can it be that this Charley, potentially the most religious of persons, could not be religious at all? Is there something wrong with him or is there something wrong with what religion is taken to be? What do you call Charley's refusal of a comforting fiction which he might never find out to be a fiction? All this is like a preparation for something that may never happen – as if *that* might be what life itself is for such people, left by their own scrupulous intelligence hanging in the realm of unresolvable possibility, without decision or action.

Even in his intelligence, even in his resistance to a practical narrowing down, I call Charley, still, the son of his cruelly dogmatic father. I think that his honourable refusal of easy belief is almost as much a product of that father in him as his signing up for evangelicalism would be: reacting against the father is different from going along with him but not sufficiently so to make a new life. We like to talk of Keats's 'negative capability' a great deal, but I am not sure that we can or should long hold positions of sustained neutrality. There is, I grant, a cruelty involved in forcing the premature taking of sides. But, equally, there is an abuse of intellectual freedom when all it serves is a refusal of what such freedom is for. Everything is a decision at some point. We are, biologically, feeling and believing and doing creatures, with all the risks involved. It is William James who takes on the Victorian heritage in these matters, when in 1895, in a talk at Harvard on W.H. Mallock's book *Is Life Worth Living?*, he writes as follows – speaking of intelligence's neutrality as finally unsustainable:

> This is because, as the psychologists tell us, belief and doubt are living attitudes, and involve conduct on our part. Our only way, for example, of doubting, or refusing to believe, that a certain thing *is*, is continuing to act as if it were *not*. [...] If I doubt that you are worthy of my confidence, I keep you uninformed of all my secrets just as if you were *un*worthy of the same. If I doubt the need of insuring my house, I leave it uninsured as much as if I believed there were no need. And so if I must not believe that the world is divine, I can only express that refusal by declining ever to act distinctively as if it were so, which can only mean acting on certain critical occasions as if it were *not* so, or in an irreligious way. There are, you see, inevitable occasions in life when inaction is a kind of action, and not to be for is to be practically against; and in all such cases strict and consistent neutrality is an unattainable thing.[10]

What William James offers instead of a self-damaging scrupulosity held safe in a world of literary ambiguity is the venturing position of 'as if'.

In lecture 3 of *The Varieties of Religious Experience* (1902) he writes of how 'we can act *as if* there were a God; feel *as if* we were free; consider Nature *as if* she were full of special designs; lay plans *as if* we were to be immortal; and we find then that these words do make a genuine difference in our mortal life'.[11] I call this position a venture because it involves what James calls 'going with ideas upon which we can ride' – ideas that seem to create a vitality in us and make for greater possible movement into a future. They are called thoughts or ideas, because their *as if* dynamically frees them from the pressure of their having to be called static and certain beliefs. For let us be clear about the pragmatism of these *as if*s: like George MacDonald's 'may be a might be', they are instrumental and provisional, essays in the very process of our making ourselves do more and be more and go further than we might dare in advance. 'I am well aware,' says James in 'What Pragmatism Means', 'how odd it must seem to some of you to hear me say that an idea is "true" so long as to believe it is profitable to our lives [...]. Ought we ever not to believe what it is *better for us* to believe?'[12]

That is the bold proposition: if it makes things better, there must be truth in it. But is not this precisely what Clough would dismiss as 'truth' turned merely into comfortable convenience, the sustaining illusion of fiction, the self-deception of fantasy? But I think not: James does not simply choose a belief because it is comfortable. His point is rather this: that if it works, there must be something in it, something literally vital because 'belief and doubt are living attitudes'. And this is why pragmatism is a venture, a narrative that replaces 'thinking before' with 'following through', a testing out of a living future for an idea, because pragmatism is not only to do with results, but with a radical change in orientation. That is to say: pragmatism is 'the attitude of looking away from first things, principles, "categories", supposed necessities; and of looking towards last things, fruits, consequences, facts' (*Selected Writings*, p. 8). There is no going back to check where the thought has come from, but rather a going on with where it may be leading to. It is a route therefore in which one trusts first principles to come into play, eventually, as part of biological or organic development, rather than in anterior abstract planning.

In James's life what this was about was a son's fight against youthful depression. As a young man, on the verge of a breakdown, he had looked at the world and wondered whether he could believe in the life it seemed to offer. The world could look like a mere machine of which we were no more than determined parts. But James himself, evaluating life, knew he was already an element in the equation he was trying to make out in advance. His depression at the very least contributed to his sense of determinism, as well as arising out of it. But the first act of freedom might be to risk believing in freedom itself. He is writing to his past, young self when he later writes in 'Is Life worth Living?': 'Your mistrust of life has removed whatever worth your own enduring existence might have given it' (*The Will to Believe*, p. 60). Think of a train robbery he says in *The Will to Believe*: a whole train of passengers may be robbed by a few highwaymen simply because the highwaymen can count on one another, while each passenger fears that if he makes a movement of resistance he will be shot before anyone backs him up. 'There are, then, cases where a fact cannot come at all unless a preliminary faith exists in its coming [...] *where faith in a fact can create the fact*' (*Selected Writings*, p. 265). That is what is wrong with taking oneself out of the account in apparent neutrality. The subject – what you are and what you make of yourself – has also its part to play in the summing of the objective. This is for James the great moment, the great shift from mere defeated sadness, when suddenly you realize that paradoxical gift of responsibility, that second gear which you can find in yourself. The difference you feel you need, for life to be worthwhile, is already *there* as a nascent element in *you*. Define life but remember that our own reactions upon the world, small as they are in bulk, are themselves 'integral parts of the whole thing, and necessarily help to determine the definition'; 'Believe that life *is* worth living, and your belief will help create the fact' (*The Will to Believe*, p. 62). Above all then, this makes wanting-to-believe not merely secondary, wistful or untrustworthy: it makes wanting-to-believe itself a form of personally risked belief through the route created by 'as if'. It expresses belief in human 'need' not as defeat but as aspiration.

Indeed, James goes so far as to say that this personal sense of want may be how what we call 'God' works, with god coming into being in the world through our flawed personal belief in him. Charley thinks he needs an external or higher validation for a true sense of belief. But it may be we only need the imagination of such a sanction. If that is so, we couldn't at once exercise that imagination *and* be conscious that that *was* what we were doing, without returning to Charley's fear that it was fiction. It may be that it doesn't matter. What we can do for ourselves, even if we have to call that God – even if it *is* God – we must do in whatever ways we find we have to. But I say again, as though to Charley: these aren't thoughts that, in our limitation, we can really think.

This is why I pause briefly to mention and commend two theological works that are written precisely on that very boundary of human understanding: H.L. Mansel's *The Limits of Religious Thought*, the Bampton lectures for 1858 and the book that he acknowledges lies behind it, Bishop Joseph Butler's *Analogy* (1736).

Both these works, for all their ostensibly austere rationality, are secret books, works consisting in two parts, of which only the first part is written. For in each of these works the first part is written, and written on *this* side of our limits, and concerns both the attempt to think and the inability to accomplish that attempt. The first part in Butler and in Mansel is an act of reason to show reason's own limitations. It speaks to the sense that our whole consciousness is compassed about with restrictions which we are ever striving to pass, and ever failing in the effort. But the first part is also clear that the very experience of this limitation implies something on the *other* side of itself, the very inadequacy of reason pointing to some higher truth, of which it indicates the existence but does not make known the substance.

And the second part? The second part if written would be mystical, but is not there. The second part is left secret, implied and unwritten on the other side of the first, with everything left in place there by remaining silent about it.

The secret book might say with James that God himself allows us to create him in our own way; that whatever we creatively believe in is, as with Blake, an image of truth, however distorted or mishandled. But to Feuerbach, of course, it was always we who did it, we who made the difference, even though we have to think it is God who is responsible. We *are* God, says Feuerbach; unconsciously we made him; the divine attributes are really the best of human ones, projected upon a fictive Other. Feuerbach says to Charley or to Claude: why can't we now go onwards, pointing the creativity of our previously religious gifts and values no longer out towards God but back to our own purely secular, human ends?

But I am saying, with William James, that we should not be too sure of what is human and what is religious, or where our best things come from. I started with that deep sentence of Feuerbach's: 'That which the unreligious man holds in his head merely, the religious man places out of and above himself as an object.' To this, William James adds one crucial consideration with which I must end. And it is this: that, after all, the religious person may be right about our essential experience of thinking – that it does not just exist in our heads. Of course, thinking exists in our own heads if it is no more than the putting of thoughts into ready-made names and categories. But James hates *that* kind of thinking which still, I fear, dominates even the study of literature: neat, tamed, uncreative and pigeon-holingly thematic or contextual. He loves instead what he calls 'the unclassified residuum', a literary sort of thinking which in him goes on outside literature itself. To George MacDonald, for example, in his own struggles against Charley, when a new thought arises in the mind, a person is rather *being thought* than thinking. And the best thing that Nature did for Wordsworth, says MacDonald, and that Wordsworth does for us, is to put a human being into that mood or condition or space or shape in which thoughts come of themselves.[13] That is what shaping belief truly might be like, making room and space and place for thought. For to James, our real thinking is that we do not make thoughts, but thoughts in some sense *come* to us, not felt as originating in ourselves, but *as if* constituting a demand or a gift or a necessity from somewhere else. And such thoughts exist in us precisely to refer us towards what they stand for outside ourselves, blurring just that boundary between the person who has them and the things they themselves point to. It is as though we are the bar of iron James describes as follows (*The Varieties of Religious Experience*, lecture 3, pp. 55–6):

> It is as if a bar of iron, without touch or sight, with no representative faculty whatever, might nevertheless be strongly endowed with an inner capacity for magnetic feeling; and as if, through the various arousals of its magnetism by magnets coming and going in its neighbourhood, it might be consciously determined to different attitudes and tendencies. Such a bar of iron could never give you an outward description of the agencies that had the power of stirring it so strongly; yet of their presence, and of their significance for its life, it would be intensely aware through every fibre of its being.

So there we are, like blind and dumb things, sensing a field of forces and energies around us in which we are involved (*The Varieties of Religious Experience*, lecture 9, p. 197):

> We have a thought, or we perform an act, repeatedly, but on a certain day the real meaning of the thought peals through us for the first time, or the act has suddenly turned into a moral impossibility. All we know is that there are dead feelings, dead ideas, and cold beliefs, and there are hot and live ones; and when one grows hot and alive within us, everything has to re-crystallize about it.

When the thoughts that come light up the brain as if they were beliefs, then we are in the process of seeing how important they are, by seeing how far forward they can take us, how far they can work for the making of life, what they do for us in brain and affect. When Thomas Hardy read William James's vitalist dictum, 'Truth is what works', he wrote in his notebook that a worse abuse of language had never been perpetrated: truth to Hardy was all that did *not* work.[14] For such as Hardy, a belief might not make for life, might be reluctantly negative, in the name of a tough truth that goes against the grain of all our warmest human feelings and ignores them. It is not easy but it remains all too possible to believe that life is fallen, and that, despite ourselves, life itself remains intrinsically disappointing. That too was part of James's struggle against depression, to work within and struggle against such considerations, to see what if anything was still resiliently left in us when we tried to accept them. I do not discount those terrible possibilities. Yet at some level, James himself implicitly believed that belief itself always, finally, has to be a faith in an ultimate *good* in the universe which the very belief helps exist. Reading James really does give you just that feeling he describes: the feeling of thoughts generating live excitement, energy, heat, change – whatever the pain or difficulty of their specific content. It is 'as if' those thoughts were a response to something which Doris Lessing in her *Canopus in Argos* series of space fictions calls Need – Need, which includes a sense not only of neediness but also of necessity. These thoughts feel called for: that's the wager.

It is above all writing that is the most genuine form of thinking in terms of trying out what works. And by that I mean writing, like James's own, which does not know beforehand where it is quite going, where it is taking us. James's 'as if' and MacDonald's 'may be a might be' are syntactical instruments which create space for a dynamic form of writing, not knowing in advance the way or shape it is trying out. As one of James's own disciples, John Dewey put it:

> Different ideas have their different 'feels', their immediate qualitative aspect, just as much as anything else. One who is thinking his way through a complicated problem finds direction in his way by means of this property of ideas. Their qualities stop him when he enters the wrong path and send him ahead when he hits the right one. They are signs of an intellectual 'Stop and go'. If a thinker had to work out the meaning of such ideas discursively, he would be lost in a labyrinth that had no end and no centre.[15]

Art teaches us how to think by and through writing, in the thick of biological-mental experience. We have such trusts and trials and intuitive economies deep within those 'feels' of ours that writing works within. Let's not try to work it all out cerebrally in advance, if that is impossible, but, Charley, try instead to follow it all through.

Notes

1. *William Blake*, ed. by M. Mason, Oxford Authors (Oxford: Oxford University Press, 1988), p. 13.
2. John Stuart Mill, *Autobiography*, 1873, ed. by J. Stillinger (Oxford: Oxford University Press, 1971), pp. 83–4 (chapter 5).
3. Ludwig Feuerbach, *The Essence of Christianity*, trans. by Marian Evans (1854) (New York: Harper and Row, 1957), p. 64 (chapter 5).
4. *Lux Mundi*, ed. by Charles Gore (London: Murray, 1889), p. 18.
5. Philip Davis, *The Victorians 1830–1880*, vol. 8 of the new Oxford English Literary History (Oxford: Oxford University Press, 2002).
6. Thomas Carlyle, 'Characteristics' (1831) in his *Critical and Miscellaneous Essays*, 7 vols (London: Chapman and Hall, 1869), vol. 4, p. 1.
7. See *Clough: Selected Poems*, ed. by J.P. Phelan (London: Longman, 1995), p.141. Further references to this edition are hereafter cited after quotation in the text as 'Phelan'.
8. Roma Notebook quoted in Phelan, p. 15.
9. George MacDonald, *Wilfrid Cumbermede* (1872), second edn (London: Strahan & Co, 1873), chapter 42, p. 354. Further references to this edition are hereafter cited in the text as *Wilfrid Cumbermede*.
10. William James, *The Will to Believe and Other Essays* (1897) (London: Longman, 1915), pp. 54–5. Further references to this edition are hereafter cited in the text as *The Will to Believe*.
11. William James, *The Varieties of Religious Experience* (1902), ed. by M.E. Marty (Harmondsworth: Penguin, 1985), p. 55. Further references to this edition are hereafter cited in the text as *The Varieties of Religious Experience*.
12. William James, *Selected Writings*, ed. G.H. Bird (London: Everyman, 1995), pp. 12–18. Further references to this edition are hereafter cited in the text as *Selected Writings*.
13. George MacDonald, *A Dish of Orts* (London: Sampson Low, Marston & Co, 1893), pp. 4, 254.
14. *The Personal Notebooks of Thomas Hardy*, ed. R.H. Taylor (London: Macmillan, 1978), p. 89.
15. John Dewey, *Philosophy and Civilization* (New York: Minton, Blach, 1931), p. 120.

II. Shaping Subjectivities: Belief, Aesthetics and Space

5. 'Repairing Everywhere without Design'? Industry, Revery and Relation in Emily Dickinson's Bee Imagery

Victoria Morgan

'Growing careless': Dickinson and Religious Orthodoxy

Like Victorian Britain, the mid-nineteenth-century New England of Emily Dickinson's lifetime (1830–1886) was marked by religious and social change in which ideas of belief were being challenged and reformulated. This produced a proliferation of various 'unevangelical' religious groups such as Unitarians, who rejected Trinitarian doctrine.[1] The emergence and recognition of formalized divergent religious groups, combined with the popularity of new philosophies such as Transcendentalism, which espoused notions of self-reliance that were not dependent upon a Christian model of salvation, posed an increased challenge to the once deeply held convictions and practices of New England Puritanism. Robert Baird's *Religion in the United States of America* (1844) provides a list of the 'unevangelicals' – the Roman Catholics, Jews, Shakers, Swedenborgians, Unitarians, Mormons, Deists and Atheists, Transcendentalists, Spiritualists and Native Americans – who were rejecting in Baird's view 'true' Christianity, and threatening also the perceived unity of Protestant Christianity.[2] Both Unitarianism and Transcendentalism, and the various ways in which both groups sought to reshape the frameworks and designs placed upon spirituality, no doubt influenced Dickinson's thinking on spirituality.[3] Both Transcendentalism and Unitarianism were popular in literary circles and espoused in the works Dickinson read by Ralph Waldo Emerson and Thomas Wentworth Higginson. The latter, a former Unitarian minister, a writer and critic, also became a literary mentor figure for Dickinson, with whom he corresponded for most of her life as a poet.[4] However, the consideration of poetic identity and the textual connection between the formation of subjectivity and spirituality which Dickinson's poetics persistently forge, is something which sets her work apart from her contemporaries' belief in nature's 'transcendental' design. The externalized *and* inherent 'Unity' across beings which Emerson saw through his constructed notion of the 'Over-Soul;' 'that Unity, that Over-Soul, within which every man's particular being is contained and made one with all other' is also echoed within nature's design in his poem 'The Humble-bee':

> Wiser far than human seer,
> Yellow-breeched philosopher!
> Seeing only what is fair,
> Sipping only what is sweet,
> Thou dost mock fate and care,
> Leave the chaff and take the wheat.[5]

The design that Emerson sees as perfected in the industry of the bee is something to which Dickinson's bee imagery also alludes. However, rather than attempting to fill an absence, or validate the notion of over-arching design and purpose with orthodox beliefs or available philosophies of 'Unity', Dickinson's poems circumnavigate such fixed notions. Thus creating a relational space – instead of a version of static 'Unity', a textual interweaving of poetic spaces in which the self and spirit are re-imagined. Moreover, despite the popularity of Transcendentalism and Unitarianism in the liberal and literary circles of Dickinson's social milieu, she fiercely resisted association or affiliation with any group. Her letters confirm a continuing resistance to the religious revivals which called many of her friends and family into Congregational Protestantism: 'Christ is calling everyone here, all my companions have answered, even my darling Vinnie believes she loves and trusts him, and I am standing alone in my rebellion, and growing very careless' (3 April 1850, to Jane Humphrey);[6] and a disrespect for formal religious 'doctrines': 'Father has called upon Mr S[eelye] but I am waiting for Vinnie to help me do my courtesies. Mr S preached in our church last Sabbath upon "Predestination," but I do not respect "doctrines," and did not listen to him, so I can neither praise, nor blame' (13 February 1859, to Mrs Joseph Haven).[7]

Whilst stating that she could 'neither praise, nor blame' the preacher and his doctrinal assertions, Dickinson's stance against orthodox religion was rather more critical and pro-active than this comment suggests. When asked in 1862 by T.W. Higginson about her family, Dickinson's reply that 'They are religious – except me – and address an Eclipse, every morning – whom they call their "Father"' (25 April 1862)[8] makes her sense of separation clear. This mode of an isolated 'careless[ness]' and increasingly conspicuous 'rebellion' are echoed strongly in poems written during the period of both the Great Awakening and the Civil War, when many of her poems containing bee imagery were written.

Paradoxically, despite the rejection of formalized religion and 'doctrines', the struggle towards a belief in an over-arching design is something that characterizes Dickinson's work most strongly. Although there appears in Dickinson's poems a fragmented sense of self that anticipates postmodernism's rejection of totalizing theories, equally, her poetics incorporate an elaborate and paradoxical attraction towards structure and design. Dickinson's use of bee imagery sustains a triune connection and interplay between the notions of industry, revery and relation. Such a dynamic enforces an implicit challenge to the use of the Protestant notion of salvation through work to support a division between work and pleasure, and between individuality and relationality. The ways in which Dickinson's bee imagery explodes such divisions delineates an ideal space in which the shapes, and shaping, of spirituality are articulated.

The absence of a discernable thematic pattern or shape within Dickinson's poetics has been the subject of some debate.[9] Tracing a particularized use of her metaphors is ultimately perplexing because of their changeability across poems, while searching for textual continuity in Dickinson's poetry is as problematic as trying to locate and capture a continuum of atheism or religiosity in her work. The bee appears frequently with the resonant force of an emblem yet at the same time always ruptures and retreats from the delineations of continuity it teases the reader with. Whilst not arguing for a totalizing theory of Dickinson's use of a particular set of images, this essay will demonstrate how Dickinson's bee imagery conveys her engagement with religious orthodoxy through a reworking of the Protestant notion of salvation through work in which both her position as poet, and the connection between writing and spirituality are evaluated. Dickinson's bee carries implicit notions of industry, revery and relation across each poem in various ways, but this discussion will focus on the progression in Dickinson's uses of and allusions to the industry/idleness diptych of Protestant theology. It will also show that whilst a defiant rejection of religious orthodoxy feeds much of Dickinson's parodies of the Puritan, the connection between industry and revery (in later poetry especially) enables a relational space in which the divine is endlessly re-imagined.

Dickinson's bee imagery is inevitably shaped by her education and reading. Articles in the *Atlantic Monthly* during the 1850s and 1860s, such as one that includes a poem 'Telling the Bees' and one with a prose piece entitled 'Individuality', are contemporary examples of how bees were connected with ideas of industry and community. The latter, which describes the sociability of bees, would not have gone unnoticed by Dickinson, as this same edition of the *Atlantic Monthly* also included T.W. Higginson's article 'Letter to a Young Contributor', to which Dickinson famously responded.[10] Advances in science and interest in natural history also play a part in Dickinson's fashioning of bee imagery in many of her poems. The work of Sir John Lubbock (Lord Avebury) is a likely informative source, as his illustrated *On the Origin and Metamorphoses of Insects* and his study *Ants, Bees and Wasps* were published in 1874 and 1882 respectively. The influence of Edward Hitchcock on Dickinson's interest in natural history has been noted by biographers. Sewall identifies the president of Amherst College as: '[a] man of God and man of Science, who inspired a whole generation with a love of nature that combined a sense of its sublimity with an accurate knowledge of its parts and processes, as far as the natural sciences of the day knew them.'[11]

Dickinson's intimate relationship with nature is reflected in her use of the bee's movements and different noises in her poems, and there are of course moments when her bees are simply that; a favoured insect she chooses to utilize as a metaphor for physical pleasure or the capacity for human interconnectivity. However, the strong resonance in literary history of the bee with the notion of leading a useful life means that the image goes beyond being simply a personal metaphor for pleasure or sociability. Dickinson's bee imagery, more so than any other imagery in her work, illustrates her direct engagement with the idea of the poet.[12] Critics such as Benjamin Lease have argued that Dickinson's life and art were inextricably linked, with Lease arguing that although Dickinson's metaphors should not be taken literally, they are 'rooted in ideas that she took seriously – that we can and should take seriously'.[13] Nowhere is the connection between life and art made more apparent than in Dickinson's bee imagery, which pressurizes and reconfigures a cultural paradigm of usefulness to accommodate experience. Dickinson invests the bee with the power and force of an emblem to symbolize the nature of that experience and the struggle involved in processes of transformation.

Industry and the 'Divine Perdition' of Idleness

> And that ye study to be quiet, and to do your own business, and to work with your own hands, as we commanded you;
> That ye may walk honestly toward them that are without, and ye may have lack of nothing.
>
> I Thessalonians 4.11–12

Whilst Dickinson's rejection of affiliation with religious orthodoxy is clear, the Protestant notion of salvation through work which pervaded nineteenth-century didactic literature proved a useful paradigm for the poet struggling to articulate and simultaneously perform her own sense of vocation and belief through poetry.[14] Dickinson's use of bee imagery is important because it incorporates the Puritan rhetoric on industry and idleness that surrounded mid-nineteenth-century debates on the work ethic in relation to the woman question.[15] Her consideration of her position as poet in relation to spirituality can be seen most clearly through her use of bee imagery that fully exploits cultural anxieties about idleness. Although there are too many poems to cover here (there are at least ninety poems in the Dickinson corpus which include bee imagery and cognate words associated with the bee's movements and noises) a few examples of such poems provide forays into Dickinson's consideration of her own position as a poet and also her series of challenges to 'orthodox' ideas of industry and perfect design in nature which exclude her own experience.

Dickinson's dissent from the traditional modes of religious orthodoxy has been evidenced within criticism on Dickinson by the various deviations from the common hymn metre associated with the eighteenth-century hymns of Isaac Watts.[16] However, it was Watts's famous poem for children, 'Against Idleness and Mischief' which served to eulogize the notion of salvation through work which dominated American Puritan history and which Dickinson's bee imagery often parodies. Lewis Carroll's parody of Watts in *Alice's Adventures in Wonderland* (1865) where Alice's inability to recite correctly 'How doth the little' indicates the change which has taken place in her, and also reveals how familiar Watts's verse was in the mid-1860s.[17] Watts employs the cultural association of bees with industry[18] to depict a memorable model of virtue for children:[19]

> How doth the little busy bee
> Improve each shining hour,
> And gather honey all the day
> From every opening flower!

78   Shaping Belief

and to clarify the opportunity for satanic influence over 'idle hands':

> In works of labour or of skill,
> I would be busy too;
> For Satan finds some mischief still
> For idle hands to do.

However, in Dickinson's poems the paradigmatic connection between industry and idleness is deconstructed. Her bee imagery invites an inversion of the trope's resonance, where idleness is reconfigured as wisdom and virtue. Such idleness, or 'divine perdition' as in the poem below, is for Dickinson an assertion of spiritual growth as it connotes a move away from the organizing structures of religion:

> The Bumble Bee's Religion –
>
> His little Hearse like Figure
> Unto itself a Dirge
> To a delusive Lilac
> The vanity divulge
> Of Industry and Morals
> And every righteous thing
> For the divine Perdition
> Of Idleness and Spring –[20]

The bee in this poem is a caricature of the Puritan going about his business of 'Industry and Morals'. An association of flowers with femininity and of bees with masculinity also operates to separate the active, masculine 'Bumble Bee' from the comparatively passive, 'delusive' feminine Lilac. The slow deadening of life ('Hearse' and 'Dirge') which such an adherence to a design for life imposes is presented as a show for the static, 'delusive Lilac' to observe. 'Delusive' and 'divine Perdition' invoke the Lilac's deviation and separation from conventional access to Christian grace or salvation through business and movement, while, the lesson the Lilac observes in the bee's sombre movements is one of vanity. The flower exists in a comparative state of damnation because of its being a flower, unable to move, whereas the bee's 'design' allows for movement and production. However, the configuration of industry as morality becomes vanity only where choice and capacity are not considered. A doctrine that deems the bee's innate movement (which is also its mode of industry) as a form of morality is not only absurd but vain also in its implicit exclusion of those (like the lilac) who cannot move, or whose 'design' does not include movement. Unable to accommodate difference, the 'Bumble Bee's Religion' (one of the very few titles Dickinson gave to a poem), that is, the Protestant moralizing of work, is a form of enslavement. Therefore, the Lilac's exclusion, the position of 'divine perdition' in this poem, is one of resistance and is constructed as being preferable to the culturally ordained 'Religion' or pattern of the bee's industry. Moreover, the state of grace and ecstatic pleasure that 'divine perdition' of the Lilac connotes is an alternative mode of relation with the world – 'Idleness and Spring' are necessarily made concomitant by renouncing the structures of religion. 'Spring' is already in motion, the immanent, explosive force which can not stop itself. It is the 'Bumble Bee's Religion' which defines 'idleness', but Dickinson's deconstruction of the industry/idleness diptych in this poem renders it not only a redundant exercise, but a vain one too.

The connection of bee imagery with the Puritan can be seen again in an earlier poem, written towards the end of the Civil War in 1865. The Protestant work ethic is referred to explicitly in relation to the bee which here connotes the figure of the Puritan, prepared and ready to defend faith in battle (Fr. 979):

> His feet are shod with Gauze –
> His Helmet, is of Gold,
> His Breast, a single Onyx
> With Chrysophras, inlaid –
>
> His Labour is a Chant –
> His Idleness – a Tune –
> Oh, for a Bee's experience
> Of Clovers, and of Noon!

On one hand the image is a parody of the Puritan and a version of the biblical metaphor of the breastplate as righteousness and the helmet as salvation which extends from the Old Testament in Isaiah (59.17) to the New Testament in Thessalonians: 'But let us, who are of the day, be sober, putting on the breastplate of faith and love; and for an helmet, the hope of salvation' (1.5–8). On the other hand, the poem holds up for scrutiny the effectiveness of the poet's own vocation as a form of such industry. The two stanzas differ in that the first is an attempt on the poet's part to render the bee image, in self-consciously poetic language, into a set of lapidarian, gem-like, and therefore also static images. She uses 'gold', 'onyx' and 'chrysophras' to describe the bee's armour-like body parts. The word 'chrysoprase' can be connected with Christ by the way the word sounds ('chrys' from the Greek 'khrusos' for gold)[21] and is evocative in the poem of Christ as the Puritan's breastplate and spiritual protection. These work well to describe the bee and its colouring, onyx being a precious stone with black and white bands and chrysophras (chrysoprase) being gold with a green sheen – gold and green being colours Dickinson associated with immortality. (In a letter she thanks a friend for the gift of a book, saying, 'Why did you bind it in green and gold? The *immortal* colours. I take it for an emblem.'[22]) Both gold and chrysoprase are chalcedonies and are among many of the precious stones used to describe the foundations of the walls of heaven in the Book of Revelations (21.18–21) which Dickinson cited as a source of inspiration for writing.[23]

The activity of the bee in the poem's second stanza and its casual triumph of experiencing the fullness of life ('clovers' and 'noon') whilst simultaneously producing a 'chant' or 'tune' throws the self-consciously stylized language of the first stanza firmly into focus. Dickinson thus points towards the excessiveness of her own desire to be equally industrious, as she implies that the bee's ability to produce an individual 'tune' (which is simultaneously distinct from, but also only a variant of, the collective chant of labour), whilst at the same time being indulgent and seemingly 'idle', eludes her. Dickinson's poetic vision is secondary to the bee's seemingly effortless 'experience'. The poet's own vocation or 'labour' struggles to capture the experience that the bee's movements delineate. In this poem, as with many of the other poems which carry bee imagery, Dickinson retains the notion of the Puritan way of life and the surety of faith in the structure and design inherent in the bee's life – going to and from the hive in order to produce honey for the collective good. But the bee's movements are always balanced in her poems with a definite lack of restraint and assertion of individuality as it is also defiantly errant and has the freedom of choice which flower to visit and how long to linger. In other words, the bee, like the human, possesses free will, but unlike the human is always working within the overall design of its purpose, and within its relation to the hive. So, whilst requiring isolation as a poet, Dickinson's poetics convey a preoccupation with the idea of interconnectivity that the bee imagery lends. Industry and pleasure are brought together in this poem to represent an ideal experience – the 'Bee's experience' in which every mode is productive. Dickinson's consideration of this ideal is something that permeates poems in which the bee is made a prominent feature.

Dickinson's positioning of her reflections on the role of the poet within the discourse of the Protestant work ethic (both indicated by 'work' and 'idleness' in the poem below) conveys a dialectical response to the discourse of orthodox religion. She offers a detailed, painterly description of the movements of a butterfly emerging from its cocoon that delineates a scene that is laden with existential drama. Dickinson positions herself as the artist, who is at pains to 'trace' the design, the continuity or meaning in the 'scene,' and therefore also in life which ends in death (Fr. 610):

> From Cocoon forth a Butterfly
> As Lady from her Door
> Emerged – a Summer Afternoon –
> Repairing Everywhere –
>
> Without Design – that I could trace
> Except to stray abroad
> On miscellaneous Enterprise
> The Clovers – understood –
>
> Her pretty Parasol be seen
> Contracting in a Field
> Where Men made Hay –
> Then struggling hard
> With an opposing Cloud –
>
> Where Parties – Phantom as Herself –
> To Nowhere – seemed to go
> In purposeless Circumference –
> As 'twere a Tropic Show –
>
> And notwithstanding Bee – that worked –
> And Flower – that zealous blew –
> This Audience of Idleness
> Disdained them, from the Sky –
>
> Till Sundown crept – a steady Tide –
> And Men that made the Hay –
> And Afternoon – and Butterfly –
> Extinguished – in the Sea –

The poem is striking because the butterfly, along with the design or pattern that the butterfly usually represents, that is, God's promise of resurrection, and metamorphosis from human existence into a heavenly one, is 'extinguished' at the end of the poem, along with the 'Men' and the 'Afternoon' in the final stanza. The poem's seemingly more minor characters, both 'Bee' and 'Flower' are, by comparison, stripped of any romantic/artistic livery, and are described simply as the bee 'that worked –' and the flower which 'zealous blew –'. They are ascribed a tenacity which places them in sharp contrast to the 'Audience of Idleness' which 'Distained them, from the Sky.' The activity of the scene, together with the fact of being below the 'sky' or eye of Heaven is something which links each life form in the poem, but particularly the bee and the 'Men who made Hay' in their shared capacity for 'work'. Although nineteenth-century uses of the terms 'labour' and 'work' might have had different associations where the former is manual and the latter cerebral and/or spiritual, Dickinson's use of 'labour' and 'work' as interchangeable throughout the poem suggests a disregard for such divisive distinctions. Her placement of 'notwithstanding' in relation to the bee in this poem is arresting; the tetrameter stretches the word out in order to make it seem adjectival, rather than the qualifier for the poem's final dramatic closure. Initially, Dickinson makes the bee's presence in the poem appear to be less significant than it is, whilst it actually serves to highlight the problematic division in the poem between those who perform an interconnected function and those who appear to be isolated, as the butterfly, in 'purposeless [c]ircumference'. The 'struggle' that the speaker observes appears to be subsumed into a larger, discernable 'design' which is provided by the work involved in daily toil. The bees gathering honey, like the men gathering hay, can be seen as being part of the same process of life which is illuminated briefly, and then pulled back into the inevitable darkness. Dickinson chooses to illuminate the commonality of all life in this poem that stands apart from the darkness, to provide an alternative idea of design and pattern, and goes some way to negate its power to 'extinguish'.

Again, the Puritan abhorrence of 'idleness', as depicted in Watts's 'Against Idleness and Mischief', is reversed in this poem. The sky's comparative vacancy is placed in contrast against the industry and spirit of the bee who simply 'worked'. Implicit in Dickinson's idea of industry is the ability to err, to 'stray abroad/on Miscellaneous Enterprise'. Here, 'work[ing]' and 'enterprise' both point towards Dickinson's notion of her own enterprise as a poet, which is distinct from the decidedly feminine ('Lady'), chaotic, substanceless ('Phantom as Herself') meandering that the butterfly conveys, despite the appearance of design, or promise of fulfilment that its patterned wings symbolize. In this way, the poem also echoes the critique of idle womanhood in novels such as Harriet Beecher Stowe's *My Wife and I* (1871).[24]

Whilst Dickinson's poetic persona challenges and confronts the notion of idle womanhood, the poem conveys, equally, a conflicting attitude towards poetic subjectivity. Dickinson places herself as the poet-onlooker in this poem, but is keen also to play down her part as the scene is revealed casually, with a colloquialism ('her pretty parasol be seen') that has a distancing effect and minimizes poetic agency. She describes her role as being that in which she is able to 'trace' the scene, when what she actually provides is an intense scrutiny of the way in which the 'Sky' controls the movements of the various forms of life and activity below. In this way, she displays a sight that at first declares non-specificity, whilst also conveying a sight of both depth and clarity. The anxieties about poetry evident in this conflicting attitude also echoes anxieties about belief itself. The 'Audience of Idleness' possesses in the poem the weight of God's omniscient judgement, but it also indicates the speaker herself, who, searching for 'Design' before her, finds only a 'Tropic Show', or accepted ways of thinking about nature. The images of the summer day that the poet-onlooker wants to invest with the resonant meaning of 'tropes', by 'tracing' symbols of either resurrection or hope, are emptied of their significance and become merely affectation or 'show'. The symbol of achieved potential which is the emergent butterfly, daubed with the evidence of the design implicit in the cocoon, is usurped in this poem by the bee who, simply by 'working', escapes the disdain from above. Ultimately, it is the butterfly who fails, unable, like the bee, to repair or accommodate for the lack of design apparent in the scene on offer. The poet's own admission of 'trac[ing]' design within the scene outshines the butterfly's journey for design by observing, casually, the design implied in the bee's 'work' and the flower's 'zealous[ness]'. The subjective 'I' in this poem is placed at a remove from the stereotypes on gender that butterfly and bee both connote. Dickinson's persona reaches out in this poem for a sense of purpose and scrutinizes religious certainty; in absence of the latter, she is able only to reveal or expose her own 'work', as conveyed by the industrious role of the worker that the bee in this poem represents.

Dickinson's treatment of the industry/idleness diptych fluctuates between a parody and subversion of the Puritan and his ethics, and becomes also a direct confrontation with ideas of both omnipotent design and the poet's subjective desire to impose design, in which she encounters difficulty and struggle. Whilst the fascination with design remains with Dickinson, the impulse to explode the industry/idleness diptych, and to deconstruct the hierarchies implicit in nineteenth-century assumptions about gender and spirituality that it inevitably includes, is always strong.

'Lost in Balms': Idleness, Sexuality and Revery

And here are Robins – just got home – and giddy Crows – and Jays – and will you trust me – as I live, here's a *bumblebee* – not such as summer brings – John – earnest, manly bees, but a kind of Cockney, dressed in jaunty clothes. Much that is gay – have I to show, if you were with me, John, upon this April grass.

Emily Dickinson, April 1856 to John L. Graves[25]

Another configuration of Dickinson's bees, as the above excerpt from one of her letters conveys, is the excessive, 'jaunty' entrepreneur. Dickinson's description of the 'Cockney' bumblebee invokes the 'drone philosophy' of Mr Skimpole in *Bleak House*.[26] The male (non-industrious) drone bee is connected with the deceptive nature of Mr Skimpole's character, conveying the opposite of the more widely held association of the worker bee with worthwhile industry. It displays not only the prevalence of the notion of the 'busy bee', and the extent to which it had become idiomatic in popular literature during the nineteenth century, but also the distinction between industrious bees and non-industrious drones which Dickinson, having read *Bleak House*, must have been aware of when using bee imagery. The idea of the morally dubious character or the association of the bee's ecstatic nature with criminality is invoked in many of her representations of bees, as for example in poems where bees are; 'Buccaneers of Buzz'(Fr. 1426), 'drunken'(Fr. 207), or dwelling 'a little everywhere / [...]With no Police to follow / Or chase Him [...]' (Fr. 1056). These poems are instances of Dickinson using the bee image to criticize society's expectations and how one must be seen as being productive or face moral reprehension. In them, as in 'The Bumble Bee's Religion', she questions the notion of productivity as well as querying the portrayal of joy, exuberance and ecstasy as being necessarily counter to orthodox religion's ideas on being industrious. Thus, Dickinson's depiction of the bee's industry as 'criminal' challenges both Protestant morality and also political uses and interpretations of scripture.

Dickinson disrupts the industriousness culturally associated with bees by employing bee imagery in her depictions of physical and spiritual excess and pleasure. The depiction of the idle mind as an abandoned castle inhabited by reptiles and birds in Henry Ward Beecher's *Seven Lectures to Young Men* (1844) is cited by Rodgers as being indicative of the 'gathering nervousnesses' about idleness that were particular to the nineteenth century. Conceiving the idle mind as dangerous, the Puritan emphasis on the importance of work and usefulness fed into nineteenth-century anxieties about ungovernable sexuality.[27] Dickinson's excessive bees emulate the 'dangerous' sexuality that is forbidden, but also embody the rhapsodic spiritual pleasure which organized religion attempts to name and own.

Thus in Dickinson's poetics the industrious bee persistently comes up against the excessive bodily bees that connote rhapsodic pleasure, linking both the material and spiritual realms of experience. Whilst presenting a parody and subversion of the Puritan work ethic, such ubiquitous bee imagery also recalls the Puritan emblematic use of language to define a holy life, where 'world and word alike were a shadowing forth of divine things, coherent systems of transcendent meaning'.[28] Preachers such as

Jonathan Edwards often used language like this. The 'field or garden of God', with particular emphasis on the flower, is a favourite image employed by Edwards in his *Personal Narrative* (1743):

> [S]uch a little white Flower, as we see in the Spring of the Year; low and humble on the Ground, opening its Bosom, to receive the pleasant Beams of the Sun's Glory; rejoicing as it were, in a calm Rapture; diffusing around a sweet Fragrancy; standing peacefully and lovingly, in the midst of other Flowers round about; all in like Manner opening their Bosoms, to drink in the Light of the Sun.[29]

The bee in Dickinson's poems provide a counter not only to the stereotypes on gender to which the supplicatory and responsive nature of Edwards' flower image (human) and the penetrative action of the sun beams (God) in *Personal Narratives* correlates, but also the notion of God as being distinctly separate from humans which the hierarchical metaphor of the flower also connotes. As will be discussed further, as much as Dickinson's bee imagery lays the hierarchical design of organized religion open for scrutiny and ridicule, it also places emphasis upon the relationality of the bee's design, that is, its implicit relation to the wider community/collectivity of the hive. If the bee is constantly in relation to the wider body/context of effective and 'moral' work or production within the wider bee community, then so too is the errant, pleasure-seeking behaviour which Dickinson's bees often enact.

In opposition to Edwards's emblematic, static flower, Dickinson's bee operates as a non-static metaphor associated with spiritual transcendence. The bee's freedom, multiplicity and ability to signal a disruption to convention with both noise and bodily excess is also Dickinson's trope for ecstatic pleasure, for revery. Dickinson's construction of excessive 'revery' behaviour delineates a powerful subjectivity which booms and bounces through poems to disrupt the convention which it also signifies and leaves traces of in its wake. The notion of revery and its associations is explored by Dickinson in a group of poems in which the ecstatic bee is in turns 'drunken', 'fainting' and 'lost' in the 'balms' of its flowers. In this way, Dickinson uses the idleness/industry diptych to connect spiritual ecstasy with sexuality and exuberance. This can be seen in the group of closely related poems, of which Fr. 205, Fr. 1562 and Fr. 1630 are examples; depicting the bee as the 'fainting' lover, the philanderer with the 'jaded eye', and the role model for a 'connoisaeur [*sic*] in Liquors'. Dickinson's eroticized bees have divided critics over the matter of the positioning of gender. Judith Farr notes the extent to which Dickinson's use of the bee–flower formulation can be seen as describing excess which borders upon rape, where flowers are ravished and the bee is unruly, drunken, taking his nectars in.[30] Power relations between genders is certainly described in terms of a sexual encounter in many instances of Dickinson's bee imagery, as the bee–flower formulation implies. However, the active/passive binary relation culturally inscribed in gender is also connected with the power relation implicit in organized religion. Both are exploded in Dickinson's configurations. The excessively fuzzy body of the bumblebee and its interruptive noises and movements can be seen as articulating sexual desire in the connection they illustrate between physical pleasure and ecstatic transcendence. This particular configuration of the bee trope allows Dickinson to highlight the sterility and comparative silence of 'official' religious and literary culture. John B. Pickard observes the 'erotic expectations' in poems where Dickinson is 'employing the bee-flower image to convey physical desire' and gives examples of the poems 'Come slowly-Eden!' (Fr. 205) and 'A Bee his burnished Carriage' (Fr. 1351) but also describes these as her 'most sentimental and derivative love poems'.[31] However, the resistance of gender that the bee imagery allows, provides a wider interpretation which takes the poetic imagery beyond such aesthetics of heterosexual procreation. The range of fluctuation with regard to gender which is available within the bee imagery means that it is at different times, and even all at once, the 'manly, earnest bee', the solitary queen bee, the chaste, asexual bee and the delirious rapist.

The 'fainting' bee in poem Fr. 205 is an example of experiential, physical ecstasy and it conveys both fleeting and considered abandon. The speaker's appeal is that paradise should be reached 'slowly'. Although the bee is 'ecstatic' in the sense that it roves from flower to flower, collecting nectars and thus being 'late' getting to the next one, it is the moment of recognition, when transcendence is both anticipated and registered, which is emphasized in this poem. Ecstasy should be experienced 'slowly', like the bee who considers his rosary-like 'nectars' before giving himself up to being 'lost in balms'. Moreover, the experience of life should be savoured before reaching an Edenic unknown (Fr. 205):

> Come slowly – Eden!
> Lips unused to Thee –
> Bashful – sip thy Jessamines –
> As the fainting Bee –
>
> Reaching late his flower,
> Round her chamber hums –
> Counts his nectars –
> Enters – and is lost in Balms.

Connecting spirituality and sexuality, the metaphor of the bee entering the flower extends beyond generative imagery to a congregation member entering a place of worship and considering the moment of spiritual transcendence. The 'nectars' are considered, computed even, and this moment of consideration is emphasized by the poem's initial directive of 'slowly' and the following exclamation mark. Unheeding of both time and production, the bee is detained ('reaching late his flower') by the multiple opportunities for pleasure. In spiritual and physical ecstasy, the bee explodes the idleness/industry paradigm by being both lingering and on course, both aimless and in pursuit. In this way, Dickinson also deconstructs the teleological premises of the Puritan's spiritual journey, where pleasures are postponed for the afterlife.

Ecstatic pleasure is explicitly connected with notions of idleness in poems where Dickinson parodies the rhetoric of temperance literature. Drunkenness (a variant of 'idleness') is often connected with the bee to symbolize ecstatic pleasure or revery. For example, in poem Fr. 1630 the bee is upheld as knowing the right way to 'delight' and 'joy,' and the idea of excess is championed over abstemiousness (Fr. 1630):

> A Drunkard cannot meet a Cork
>   Without a Revery –
>   [...]
> The moderate drinker of Delight
> Does not deserve the Spring –
> Of Juleps, part are in the Jug
> And more are in the Joy –
> Your connois[a]eur in Liquors consults the Bumble Bee –

The bee's innate connection with nature and the dictates of 'Spring' serves to link physical pleasure with spiritual ecstasy. 'Joy' is a necessary element of 'Juleps'; materiality is abstracted and then reshaped into something definite and tangible. The speaker's knowledge of such joy is referred to the bee, which is a model for consultation. However, unlike Emerson's elevated 'yellow-breeched philosopher', Dickinson's bee is the '[d]runkard', instinctive and anarchic. Moderation is frowned upon here as being non-conducive to 'revery'. This expression, which Dickinson uses to convey a state of 'joy' connected with spirituality in this poem, is also inextricably connected with poetry and writing.

If Dickinson's use of the industry/idleness diptych in Protestant doctrine highlights an anxiety about poetic vision as much as a scepticism about religious doctrine, then it also, equally, provides an unexpected trajectory, a design of sorts, for reaching towards and reconfiguring belief through writing. The ecstatic bodily excess that the bee often conveys in Dickinson's poems also delineates a strong subjectivity which negotiates the confines of gender, and which feminist literary theory has connected with the 'horizon' of spirituality. Moreover, the reconfiguration of gender stereotypes and the connection she makes between this and spirituality goes some way to negotiate a powerful alternative to the religious revivals that inspired Dickinson to grow 'careless' and rebel. Luce Irigaray's definition of religion as the 'horizon fulfilment of a gender' is useful:

> Religion marks the place of the absolute for us, its path, the hope of its fulfilment. All too often that fulfilment has been postponed or transferred to some transcendental time and place. It has not been interpreted as the infinite that resides within us and among us, the god in us, the Other for us, becoming with and in us – as yet manifest only through his creation (the Father), present in his form (the son), mediator between the two (spirit). Here the capital letter designates the horizon of fulfilment of a gender, not a transcendent entity that exists outside becoming.[32]

The renegotiation of binary opposition, including that of gender and of human/divine which Dickinson's use of bee imagery allows, also opens up a space for alternative ways of conceiving the divine which transcend both gender and traditional religious ideology. In this way, Dickinson's bee imagery indicates an important trajectory for belief and the unexpected and disruptive ways in which its shaping can be made visible. In an emulation of the bee, Dickinson's subjective play returns repeatedly to the ecstatic 'Inebriate of Air' and 'Debauchee of Dew' (Fr. 207) model that the 'drunken' bee represented for the poet in earlier poems. By constructing a subjectivity though the idleness/industry diptych which her use of bee imagery explodes, Dickinson firmly connects her poetic work with an endless store of spiritual revery.

Shaping Spaces: Revery in Relation

> Mystical would also be the relation of the poem to the religious tradition whose statements it presupposes, but uses in order to make them say the absence of what they designate.[33]

Michel de Certeau's description of the 'mystic' poem could easily be applied to Dickinson's relation to religious tradition. The ability of such a poem to make visible the absences and contradictions apparent in religious tradition by refusing definitions of the divine which constrict and attempt to shape it resonates with Dickinson's most powerful poetic strategy of space and openness. However, any mystical transcendence is held firmly in material terms by the strong connection it retains with industry in Dickinson's poetics. Moreover, rather than representing spiritual transcendence above human, earthly existence, the bee operates to connote a mystical immanence which is always in relation. That is, human relation with the divine in others and nature, as an outwards and horizontal relationality, as opposed to the vertical (God descending from above) and hierarchical (God–man–woman) assertions of spirituality to be found in Puritan theology. Moreover, 'reverie', a term usually connected with dreaming or imagination, is pointedly reconfigured ('revery') by Dickinson as a trope for such mystical immanence, as well as for writing, in its relation with the bee in one of her most compact and yet most complex poems.[34]

Undated, but bearing the economical style of Dickinson's later poetry of the 1880s, the poem below indicates a reconsideration of the bee's relationality. It attempts to present what is almost an emblematic formula for the spiritual dimension that was always present and at work in her bee imagery poems. With its economical display of language, this poem dissects and lays bare the mechanism of 'revery', and effectively encapsulates the interconnection between writing and spirituality that her use of bee imagery implies. Here 'revery' is exposed as being the creative force that exists in relation, as an interconnected element of a trinity (Fr. 1779):

> To make a prairie it takes a clover and one bee,
> One clover, and a bee,
> And revery.
> The revery alone will do,
> If bees are few.

The poem utilizes procreative imagery – one of each (clover and bee) to multiply and produce 'revery'. But the analogy also stretches to a minister and a congregation, that is, the bee who provides the vehicle for worship, and the clover, the receptacle who receives the divine lesson. Her assertion at the end of the poem is to use imagination ('revery') if 'bees are few'. Here, she urges for a worship that is freely accessible to those who employ their own active engagement as the vehicle for spiritual ecstasy. The association of 'revery' with imagination connects spiritual worship with the act of writing, and the production of 'revery' with her own vocation.

Above all, this poem teases the reader with the urge to separate the elements that combine to make a 'prairie' (a pun on 'prayer'). The poem offers in a prescriptive manner the fact that to engage with spiritual worship, one must either have things which are in some way oppositional in their make-up ('bee' and 'clover', male/female, God/human), and an element of imagination, mystery or 'revery'. Or, if this is not possible, imagination, 'revery', must be substituted instead. The poem is problematic because satisfactory substitutions cannot be made adequately, nor can one permutation of the triune connection be rationalized as being preferable to the other. In such a triune pattern, which invokes the Trinity, received notions of religious faith and morality are forever fused together against the flux of human experience that pulls ideology into a space which signifies its contradictions, incompletenesses and absences. This is Dickinson at her perplexing best, teasing the reader with the formulated phrases of religious orthodoxy versus the potentially liberating space of poetry. The triune relation in this poem is indicative of the intimate connection between poetry, subjectivity and spirituality at work in much of Dickinson's bee imagery.

She returns to this again, in another undated poem that similarly bears the short, compacted style of her later work (Fr. 1788):

> Fame is a bee.
> It has a song –
> It has a sting –
> Ah, too, it has a wing.

Concerned with the subject of 'fame', which, by this stage must have been connected in Dickinson's mind with the act of writing poetry, the poem clarifies the link between writing and spirituality by invoking, as in the previous poem, a tripartite relation in the image of the bee. This time it is the bee's elements that are dissected and reassembled in a trinity, again invoking the Trinity of Christian doctrine, thus conveying simultaneously separation and unity. Industry and revery are again intimately connected (both 'sting' and 'song') to indicate the transportive and spiritual effects of writing ('wing'). Ultimately, poetry stands in the place of organized religion to provide access to an unbounded spirituality.

Paradoxically, Dickinson's poetics work towards a 'design' for belief that is in perpetual flight from the constraints of design inherent in the doctrines of organized religion. By connecting the quest for spirituality with the role of the poet through bee imagery, Dickinson goes some way to creating the ideal subjective space which Irigaray argues is central to a woman's conception of her own version of the divine.[35] Whatever shape relationality might take, the poems open up an imaginative space in order for creative thought to occur, without privileging one particular version of that shape. It is this indivisibility for which the bee becomes most emblematic in Dickinson's poems, as it is this which is intimately connected with her own 'industry' as a poet.

To use Certeau's terms, the space which Dickinson's poems generate operates in a 'heterologous' way.³⁶ While utilizing the framework of religious orthodoxy as a reference point for her departures, Dickinson's poems create an alternative space that is both within, but also outside of such a framework. Her use of bee imagery can be seen as an attempt to both critique and utilize the modes of religious orthodoxy which were culturally familiar, and also to offer one way of perceiving the shape or design of her industry and license as a poet, and ultimately, her own intimate connection and relationship with 'revery', and with belief. Just as the bee's relation to the hive allows all activity to be placed within the frame of 'industry and morals', so Dickinson's relation to poetry places her in constant relation to the cognitive spaces which make the divine accessible. The framework of the idleness/industry diptych is not only challenged and destabilized by Dickinson, but is also radically reformulated to incorporate a new mode of relation to the divine. Tracing Dickinson's use of bee imagery, as I have done here, through its connotations with the ideas of industry, revery and relation, not only foregrounds her engaging critique and negotiation of the work ethic prevalent in nineteenth-century culture, but also, highlights the intimately related poetic spaces in which Dickinson connects spirituality firmly to writing. With this in mind, 'tracing everywhere without design' becomes an affirmative action, as to let go of all certainties is perhaps the ultimate sacrifice which re-inscribes itself, paradoxically, as faith.

Notes

1   Both the second Great Awakening (a series of religious revivals in New England from the 1830s onwards) and the Civil War (1861–1865) were contributing factors to such changes. Unitarianism rejects the doctrine of the trinity and the divinity of Christ in favour of the unipersonality of God. See E.A. Livingstone, *Oxford Concise Dictionary of the Christian Church* (Oxford: Oxford University Press, 2000) p. 595.
2   For a discussion of religious plurality in nineteenth-century America, see Catherine A. Brekus, 'Interpreting American Religion', in *A Companion to Nineteenth-Century America* (Oxford: Blackwell Publishing, 2001), ed. by William L. Barney, pp. 317–33. Brekus cites Robert Baird's *Religion in the United States of America* (Glasgow: Blackie, 1844), p. 606.
3   For Dickinson's rejection of Calvinism and the influence of Unitarianism and Emersonian Transcendentalism, see James McIntosh, *Nimble Believing: Dickinson and the Unknown* (Ann Arbor, MI: University of Michigan Press, 2000).
4   Dickinson's reading of Emerson is documented in her letters; 23 January 1850 to Jane Humphrey refers to Emerson's *Poems*. Dickinson's correspondence with T.W. Higginson was initiated by her on 15 April 1862 in response to his article on advice to young writers in the *Atlantic Monthly*. See T.H. Johnson, ed., *The Letters of Emily Dickinson*, 3 vols (Cambridge, MA: Belknap Press, 1958). For

discussion of Emerson as literary influence on Dickinson, see Gary Lee Stonum, 'Dickinson's Literary Background', in *The Emily Dickinson Handbook*, ed. by Gudrun Grabher, Roland Hagenbuchle and Cristanne Miller (Amherst, MA: University of Massachusetts Press, 1998), pp. 44–60. Perhaps to avoid any association with Emerson and Transcendentalism, Dickinson avoided meeting him when he visited her brother's house next-door.

5   Ralph Waldo Emerson, 'The Humble-bee', in *American Poetry: The Nineteenth Century*, ed. by John Hollander (New York: Library of America, 1996), p. 109. For discussion of the Over-Soul, see Ralph Waldo Emerson, *Essays* (1841) (London: Dent, 1904), pp. 197–221 (p. 198).
6   Johnson, ed., *Letters of Emily Dickinson*, vol. 1, p. 94.
7   Johnson, ed., *Letters of Emily Dickinson*, vol. 2, p. 346.
8   Johnson, ed., *Letters of Emily Dickinson*, vol. 2, p. 404.
9   Marietta Messmer briefly surveys the arguments for and against textual cohesion in 'Dickinson's Critical Reception', in *The Emily Dickinson Handbook*, ed. by Grabher *et al.*, pp. 299–321 (pp. 318–19).
10 'Individuality', *Atlantic Monthly* 9:54 (April 1862): 424–30; 'Telling the Bees', *Atlantic Monthly* 1:6 (April 1858): 722–24. For Dickinson's famous response to Higginson's article in 9:54, see T.H. Johnson, ed., *Emily Dickinson: Selected Letters*, eleventh printing, 2002 (Cambridge, Mass: Belknap Press, 1958), pp. 171–2.
11 Richard B. Sewall, *The Life of Emily Dickinson*, vol. 2 (London: Faber and Faber, 1976), pp. 342–3.
12 Dickinson's education which included Classical literature suggests that she would be familiar with the tradition of associating the figure of the poet with the bee because of the ability to produce 'honeyed words'. Plato and Sophocles were known as the 'Athenian Bee' and the 'Attic Bee'. See E. Cobham Brewer, *A Dictionary of Phrase and Fable*, new edn (London: Cassell and Company, 1958), p. 113. For Dickinson's education and reading, see Benjamin Lease, *Emily Dickinson's Readings of Men and Books* (London: Macmillan, 1990).
13 Lease, *Emily Dickinson's Readings*, p. 62.
14 For further discussion of the use of the religious and moral framework of the Protestant work ethic in western capitalism, see Max Weber, *The Protestant Ethic and the Spirit of Capitalism* (1930) (London: Routledge, 2004).
15 Daniel T. Rodgers, *The Work Ethic in Industrial America 1850–1920* (Chicago, IL: University of Chicago Press, 1974), pp. 182–209. In his chapter on feminist versions of the work ethic, Rodgers describes the critique of 'idle womanhood' in feminist works, such as *My Wife and I* (1871) by Harriet Beecher Stowe. In the novel, Stowe criticizes the conventions that forced middle-class women into marriages which fostered and perpetuated idleness and purposelessness in otherwise capable women of 'faculty'.
16 The two most influential essays on the area of Isaac Watts's hymns and Dickinson are Shira Wolosky, 'Rhetoric or Not: Hymnal Tropes in Emily Dickinson and Isaac Watts', *New England Quarterly* 61 (1988): 214–32, and Martha Winburn England's chapter 'Emily Dickinson and Isaac Watts', in Martha Winburn England and John Sparrow, *Hymns Unbidden: Donne, Herbert, Blake, Emily Dickinson and the Hymnographers* (New York: New York Public Library, 1966), pp. 113–48.
17 Lewis Carroll's parody, 'How doth the Crocodile,' appears in chapter 2 of *Alice in Wonderland*. Martin Gardner provides the full text of the Watts poem in his edition *The Annotated Alice* (London: Penguin, 1965; revised edn 1970), pp. 38–39.

18 For discussion of literary and cultural uses of the bee's association with industry see Bee Wilson, *The Hive: The Story of the Honeybee and Us* (London: John Murray, 2004), pp. 17–58.
19 Isaac Watts, *The Poetical Works of Isaac Watts, with a Memoir* (Boston, MA: Little, Brown and Company, 1866), pp. 340–1. From *Divine and Moral Songs for Children* (1715).
20 R.W. Franklin, ed., *The Poems of Emily Dickinson: Reading Edition* (Cambridge, MA: Belknap Press, 1998), pp. 573–4, Fr. 1547. All poems cited hereafter from Franklin's reading edition and appear with the abbreviation 'Fr.' followed by poem number.
21 *Oxford English Dictionary*, vol. 3, second edn (Oxford: Clarendon Press, 1989), p. 192.
22 Johnson, ed., *Letters*, vol. 2, p. 358, 26 December 1859 to Mrs Bowles.
23 Johnson, ed., *Letters*, vol. 2, p. 404. Dickinson includes Revelations in her list of reading material: letter 261, 25 April 1862 to T.W. Higginson. The list of gem stones in Revelations is rich; *Holy Bible: King James Version* Revelations 21.20 'The fifth, sardonyx; the sixth, sardius; the seventh, chrysolyte; the eighth, beryl; the ninth, a topaz; the tenth, a chrysoprasus; the eleventh, a jacinth; the twelfth, an amethyst.'
24 See note 15 above.
25 Johnson, ed., *Letters*, vol. 2, p. 327. Describing the homestead on main street, where they had moved to in November 1885.
26 Charles Dickens, *Bleak House* (1853) (London: Penguin, 2003), p. 116. Evidence that Dickinson read *Bleak House* can be gathered from her letters: 'Vinnie and I had "Bleak House" sent to us the other day – it is like him who wrote it – that is all I can say', Johnson, ed., *Selected Letters*, p. 86, 5 April 1852 to Susan Gilbert.
27 Rodgers, *The Work Ethic*, p. 11.
28 Malcolm Bradbury and Richard Ruland, *From Puritanism to Postmodernism: A History of American Literature* (London: Routledge, 1991), p. 25.
29 Daniel. B. Shea, 'The Art and Instruction of Jonathan Edwards' Personal Narrative', in *The American Puritan Imagination: Essays in Revaluation*, ed. by Sacvan Bercovitch (London: Cambridge University Press, 1974), pp. 159–72 (p. 169). Shea cites Jonathan Edwards' *Personal Narrative*, pp. 29–30.
30 Judith Farr, *The Gardens of Emily Dickinson* (Cambridge, MA: Harvard University Press, 2004), pp. 184–5.
31 John B. Pickard, *Emily Dickinson: An Introduction and Interpretation* (New York: Holt, Rinehart and Winston, 1967), p. 87.
32 Luce Irigaray, 'Divine Women', in *Sexes and Genealogies*, trans. Gillian C. Gill (New York: Columbia University Press, 1993), pp. 57–72 (p. 63).
33 Michel de Certeau, 'Mystic Speech', in *The Certeau Reader*, ed. by Graham Ward (Oxford: Blackwell Publishing, 2000), pp. 188–206 (p. 205).
34 Dickinson's interest in the popular novel both she and her brother had admired, *Reveries of a Bachelor* (1850) by Donald Grant Mitchell (Ik Marvel) might also feed into this reconfiguration of the term. For discussion of Dickinson's responses to it, see Lisa Spiro, 'Reading with a Tender Rapture: "Reveries of a Bachelor" and the Rhetoric of Detached Intimacy', *Book History* 6 (2003): 57–93 (83).
35 Irigaray, 'Divine Women', p. 63.
36 Michel de Certeau, *Heterologies: Discourse on the Other*, trans. by Brian Massumi (Minneapolis, MN: University of Minnesota Press, 1986), p. 20. Certeau's term 'heterologies' refers to the project of examining the interplay between 'the other' and the representational part of discourse.

6. Poetry, Poetic Perception, and Emerson's Spiritual Affirmations

David M. Robinson

The Orphic Poet

Over the course of some four decades Ralph Waldo Emerson made numerous pronouncements about both the qualities and methods of poetry, and offered many descriptions of the poet's crucial role in both the social world and in the spiritual experience of the individual. Consistent throughout this extended discourse was the close identity between poetry and the spiritual life, a closeness that at times transformed 'poetry' into a kind of synonym for religious insight and spiritual fulfilment. Despite his ostensible identity as both a visionary and an optimist, the history of Emerson's religious experience is one of crisis, inner struggle, and a perpetual attempt to find new grounding and stable assurance for his religious outlook. In that effort the poet and his methods were a crucial point of reference, an enduring sign of the accessibility of a dynamic cosmos, rich in significance and energy.

Emerson's first important assertion of the linkage between spiritual renewal and the methods of poetry appears in the concluding pages of his first book *Nature* (1836). There Emerson unexpectedly and dramatically shifts the essay's narrative voice, introducing an 'Orphic Poet', a keeper of ancient and divine wisdom, whose words 'have always been in the world, and perhaps reappear to every bard' (*Collected Works*, vol. 1, p. 42).[1] This late shift in voice and persona allowed Emerson to intensify his already impassioned call for spiritual confidence and self-affirmation, the central strand of his argument in *Nature*. The Orphic Poet proclaims that in ancient times man 'was permeated and dissolved by spirit. He filled nature with his overflowing currents.' Now, however, 'man is the dwarf of himself' (*Collected Works*, vol. 1, p. 42). The spiritual power that is a crucial human legacy has, in the modern world, been lost. The poet, with unbroken access to ancient sources of wisdom, urges that each person reclaim an original vigour and clarity of vision. The loss of that essential power, Emerson argues, is both a spiritual and an aesthetic diminishment, costing us both inner fulfilment and dulling our sense of beauty. 'The problem of restoring to the world original and eternal beauty', he contends, 'is solved by the redemption of the soul. The ruin or the blank, that we see when we look at nature, is in our own eye' (*Collected Works*, vol. 1, p. 43). The Orphic Poet exemplifies the original and undiminished perspective that can restore the lost significance of modern life.

Through his Orphic Poet Emerson connected a theory of creative or poetic expression to his earlier account of the experience of visionary rapture, the much-noted passage in which he describes his transformation into an all-seeing yet transparent eye. 'Standing on the bare ground, – my head bathed by the blithe air, and uplifted into infinite space, – all mean egotism vanishes. I become a transparent eye-ball. I am nothing; I see all. The currents of the Universal Being circulate through me; I am part or particle of God' (*Collected Works*, vol. 1, p. 10).[2] In this moment of mystical transport Emerson offers witness to his experience of a profound merger with the infinite, providing a tangible point of reference for the later proclamations of his Orphic Poet. What the poet enunciates as a lost estate and an aspiration for the future, Emerson's earlier persona has in fact already achieved, though briefly, in the 'transparent eye-ball' experience. The Orphic Poet reanimates this possibility, making it clear that it is through the work of poetry and imaginative expression that 'the redemption of the soul' must be pursued.

In his depictions of mystical experience Emerson posits an aspiration towards wholeness as a fundamental condition of spiritual fulfilment; he characterizes imaginative or poetic perception in these terms as well. In the moment of transparency and mystical illumination, one loses a separate and isolated identity, becoming part of something larger and more significant. The 'currents' that circulate through the self, manifestations of divine energy, are also the currents of the earth's atmosphere and waters, with which the self has merged. The individual becomes dissolved in the vastness of 'infinite space', and in the grandeur of God. This vision of unity, offered early in *Nature*, is countered by the Orphic Poet's later mythos of the flood of human creative power and its long recession into spiritual drought. 'Out from him sprang the sun and moon; from man the sun, from woman the moon', the poet explains. 'But, having made for himself this huge shell, his waters retired; he no longer fills the veins and veinlets; he is shrunk to a drop' (*Collected Works*, vol. 1, p. 42). These receding waters starkly contrast the earlier depiction of the circulating 'currents' of inspiration. What now remains is only a distant memory of spiritual potential, mirrored back to fallen humanity by glimpses of nature's beauty. The poet's role is to preserve and enliven that memory, to reconnect men and women with their lost powers of creativity.

The fallen state of the soul, as Emerson describes it, is a condition of disunity with nature that arises from a deeper self-division. 'At present, man applies to nature but half his force. He works on the world with his understanding alone' (*Collected Works*, vol. 1, pp. 42–3). This partial perception of the natural world blunts the original creative power that the Orphic Poet claimed and that the experience of transparency confirmed. Although Emerson was fascinated with modern science, he refers to the recent explosion of new discoveries, information and modes of classification generated by biologists, geologists and other emerging scientific fields as evidence of the modern failure of perception. He sensed that the naturalists of his day never quite broke through the limits of their limited mode of 'understanding'. 'Empirical science is apt to cloud the sight, and, by the very knowledge of functions and processes, to bereave the student of the manly contemplation of the whole. The savant becomes unpoetic' (*Collected Works*, vol. 1, p. 39). Modern naturalists lack this necessary hunger for the 'whole', which Emerson equates with poetic perception.

The poet corrects the scientists' limitations through an attention not only to particular things, but to their relation and interconnection, and to their impact on the perceiving mind. Emerson's ideal poet has a synthetic intellect, a capability to see the linkages among seemingly different objects and events. 'When I behold a rich landscape', Emerson explains, 'it is less to my purpose to recite correctly the order and super-position of the strata, than to know why all thought of multitude is lost in a tranquil sense of unity.' (*Collected Works*, vol. 1, p. 40). To lose the sense of unity is to lose the essential connection of matter with mind, of nature with the soul (*Collected Works*, vol. 1, p. 40):

> I cannot greatly honor minuteness in details, so long as there is no hint to explain the relation between things and thoughts; no ray upon the *metaphysics* of conchology, of botany, of the arts, to show the relation of the forms of flowers, shells, animals, architecture, to the mind, and build science upon ideas.

The implication here, made more explicit in the Orphic Poet's fable of the creation and the fall, is that the very act of intellection is grounded in an underlying kinship between the observing mind and the thing observed. Thought itself is the constant re-enactment, or rediscovery, of the original unity of nature and the soul. 'In the uttermost meaning of the words, thought is devout, and devotion is thought. Deep calls unto deep' (*Collected Works*, vol. 1, p. 43). Poetic perception is the recognition of this similarity. Poetry is its expression and illustration.

Words and Deeds

While Emerson's depiction of the spiritual authority of poetry in *Nature* was grounded in his own witness to visionary experience, such experiences came to seem increasingly rare to him in the decade after he published *Nature*. They could not sustain his faith or provide the energy that for him was the sign of divinity, and thus he faced a painful divergence between his theory of assurance and wholeness and his experience of doubt and isolation. 'I complain in my own experience of the feeble influence of thought on life, a ray as pale & ineffectual as that of the sun in our cold and bleak spring. They seem to lie – the actual life and the intellectual intervals, in parallel lines & never meet' (*Journals and Miscellaneous Notebooks*, vol. 5, p. 489). Emerson's struggle to make the theory of mystical insight converge with the realities of ordinary life intensified over time. 'After thirty', he ruefully remarked, 'a man wakes up sad every morning excepting perhaps five or six until the day of his death' (*Journals and Miscellaneous Notebooks*, vol. 5, p. 77). Emerson's outlook was surely moulded by his experience of repeated loss of those closest to him emotionally. His wife Ellen, with whom he was deeply in love, died some seventeen months after their marriage; he lost his brother Edward in 1834, and his brother Charles, perhaps his closest male bond, in 1836. In 1842 he faced the added burden of grief in the loss of his five-year-old son, Waldo.

His response to the crisis of experience and of belief was both extended and complex, and his conception of poetry played a central role in his response. He did not completely dismiss the philosophical idealism that underlay his thinking, nor did he change his forward-looking message of self-culture and his affirmation of the importance of the inner life. The tone of his work changed however, as one can best recognize in 'Experience' his riskiest, most profound, and most challenging essay. In 'Experience', particularly in its opening pages, images of isolation and disassociation predominate. 'Souls never touch their objects', he writes. 'An innavigable sea washes with silent waves between us and the things that we aim at and converse with.' Such isolation divorces us from a sense of reality, rendering all our experience dream-like and illusory. 'Nothing is left us now but death. We look to that with a grim satisfaction, saying, there at least is reality that will not dodge us' (*Collected Works*, vol. 3, p. 29).[3] Accompanying this gradual disillusionment with the possibility of inward assurance was, perhaps as a compensating gesture, a growing political awareness – an emphasis on ethics and social justice that resulted in his lecture series on *The Times* in 1842 and a series of antislavery works that began with his 1844 address on 'Emancipation in the British West

Indies'. This political advocacy, in which Emerson took a direct role in the brewing political conflict between the American states, made him a much more visible public figure at mid-century.[4]

Emerson had concluded 'Experience' with a call to a renewed attention to the possibilities of 'practical power', and a declaration of the durable hope that 'there is victory yet for all justice' (*Collected Works*, vol. 3, p. 49). In the absence of mystical vision, he seemed to conclude, ethical purpose might provide an alternative path to spiritual renewal. Emerson was also responding to the exigencies of the historical moment, one marked by deepening sectional division over the continuance and spread of legalized slavery, and by restless discontent over the entrenchment of the market economy with its imbalances and competitive exclusions. It is of significance, however, that 'Experience' was published in the same volume, *Essays: Second Series* (1844), as 'The Poet', a defining text in Emerson's poetics, and a powerful reaffirmation of the significance of the poet and of poetic perception and expression. If political engagement represented, for Emerson, a compensating ethical alternative to the loss of spiritual vision and religious assurance, then poetry, broadly conceived, represented a different means by which that vision might be reclaimed more directly.

Emerson's sense of the importance of poetry in this period may well have been augmented by his reading in ancient religious texts, densely symbolic works that he regarded as an Ur-poetry. He had developed an early interest in Hindu, Buddhist and other Asian religious texts, and with Henry David Thoreau, had published excerpts of them in the *Dial* in the early 1840s.[5] Robert D. Richardson has noted that Emerson's 'steadily growing interest in active protest' in the mid-1840s coincided with expanded reading in Islamic, Zoroastrian and Indian texts, which deepened his interest in and commitment to poetry and poetics. 'Beginning in 1844 and 1845 Islam had a major impact on Emerson', Richardson writes, 'especially but not exclusively through Sufi poetry.' Recognizing a kindred view of both religion and the conception of the symbol in Sufism, Emerson 'soon became enthralled with the work of Hafez, the fourteenth-century Sufi master and greatest of Persian lyric poets.'[6] He had access to the Hafez texts in German translations, and spent considerable energy in rendering them into English. Those efforts clearly stimulated his own poetic work, contributing significantly to the publication of his first volume of verse, *Poems*, in 1847.[7]

In the face of disillusionment and a fading access to moments of visionary enlightenment, Emerson saw creative and poetic expression as an important alternative affirmation of his belief in a holistic unified cosmos. Creative expression was also a form of positive action, like ethical and political engagement. 'Words and deeds are quite indifferent modes of the divine energy', he wrote in 'The Poet'. 'Words are also actions, and actions are a kind of words' (*Collected Works*, vol. 3, p. 6). Emerson elaborates this assertion of the identity of words and deeds in his observation of the interaction of ordinary, non-literary men with nature. 'Who loves nature? Who does not? Is it only poets, and men of leisure and cultivation, who live with her? No; but also hunters, farmers, grooms, and butchers, though they express their affection in their choice of life and not in their choice of words' (*Collected Works*, vol. 3, p. 10). Expression through lived experience is, for Emerson, important testimony of a different kind to the insight that the poet seeks. This is especially true, he notes, when we recognize that such expressions, as part of the fabric of ordinary life, are also pursuits of some finally unnameable source of vitality (*Collected Works*, vol. 3, p. 10):

> The writer wonders what the coachman or hunter values in riding, in horses, and dogs. It is not superficial qualities. When you talk with him, he holds these at as slight a rate as you. His worship is sympathetic; he has no definitions, but he is commanded in nature by the living power that he feels to be there present.

The coachman's 'sympathetic' attraction to animals, the countryside, and the life of nature is thus an equivalent of the poet's mystical sense of unity, and, as Emerson was increasingly inclined to believe, an arguably superior form of the recognition of that unity. It is intuitive and not fully explicable, but it confirms the idea that nature is a network of kinships and affinities that suggests that all things are ultimately interrelated. 'There is no fact in nature that does not carry the whole sense of nature' (*Collected Works*, vol. 3, p. 10).

If every part of nature carries its entire 'sense', if, that is, each constituent part is a microcosm of the whole, then we are warranted to observe with care the details of the world around us, confident that those details will be revelatory. Poetry, as both a way of seeing and a responsive expression to what is seen, is the act of the mind in the process of following the revelatory pattern of the things. 'As the eyes of Lyncæus were said to see through the earth, so the poet turns the world to glass, and shows us things in their right series and procession.' What the poet finds when vision pierces the world is not a fixed or static reality, but an energetic metamorphosis, a 'procession' of things in unending development. 'He stands one step nearer to things, and sees the flowing or metamorphosis; perceives that thought is multiform; that within the form of every creature is a force impelling it to ascend to a higher form'

(*Collected Works*, vol. 3, p. 12).⁸ The poet envisions energy, change itself, and recognizes material reality as the superficial manifestation of an underlying source of ceaseless energy.

Emerson describes, therefore, a poetic and religious drive toward discovery and revelation that is, when rightly understood, less a quest for an ultimate wisdom than an attempt to participate in a process of continuing vitality and empowerment. This is the work of the 'imagination', perhaps the most potent term in the vocabulary of Romanticism. 'This insight, which expresses itself by what is called Imagination, is a very high sort of seeing', he explains. This high seeing 'does not come by study, but by the intellect being where and what it sees, by sharing the path, or circuit of things through forms, and so making them translucid to others' (*Collected Works*, vol. 3, p. 15). So the merger of the self into the encompassing unity of things, the vision of transparency that Emerson offered in *Nature*, is reconsidered through the poet's work as an active sharing of the divine circuits of energy.

The Transition of Things

Emerson's vision is strikingly modern. As in the metaphysics of Alfred North Whitehead, in which 'process' is the ultimate reality, or the theology of Charles Hartshorne, in which 'God' is in a perpetual state of change and self-transcendence, Emerson conceives of a world in perpetual metamorphosis – and of the poet as the translator of these constantly changing forms. 'The very character of what is real is the transition of things, the passage one to another', Whitehead wrote. He described a cosmos that could no longer be conceived as material substance, and termed nature 'a structure of evolving processes. The reality is the process.'⁹ Reality is ultimately defined not by discrete constituent parts that fuse into a whole, but by unending currents of force and energy. In this version of the world, motion is life and stasis, death. Poetry is a crucial medium through which this energy becomes apparent and accessible to us.

While Emerson had emphasized change and transformation in the early phases of his career, his emphasis on the conception of the universe in terms of process, energy, and power took on increasing importance as his confidence in mystical enlightenment waned. He increasingly regarded access to new power, to a source of original and productive vigour as an important antidote to scepticism and the enervation that he so clearly described in 'Experience'.¹⁰ His conception of a dynamic, ceaselessly metamorphic cosmos lent further weight to the significance of poetry as an alternative source of both spiritual affirmation, philosophical wisdom, and creative energy. Disintegration, fragmentation and brokenness are the conditions that signify the malaise of scepticism and listless isolation. The poet's pursuit of aesthetic beauty is both a quest for new energy and vitality, and an attempt to restore wholeness, and is thus a crucial spiritual quest, a fundamental act of healing and reconstruction. The absence of beauty signifies a 'dislocation and detachment from the life of God', Emerson argues. The poet 're-attaches things to nature and the Whole' (*Collected Works*, vol. 3, p. 11).

Emerson's growing tendency to understand ultimate reality in terms of energy rather than substance and stasis was also reinforced by his continuing reading in the modern science of his day.[11] Emerson's longstanding interest in scientific developments was sharpened through his lecture tour of England in 1847–1848, and his direct contacts with several leading British scientists, including the anatomist Richard Owen, whose studies in vertebrate anatomy added weight to the developing conception of the evolutionary history of life, and the physicist Michael Faraday, the pioneering investigator of electricity and magnetism. He also met the geologist Charles Lyell, whose studies had helped extend scientific knowledge of the age of the earth and pointed to the significance of fossil discoveries in establishing a theory of planetary change and evolution. In different but related ways Owen, Faraday and Lyell confirmed Emerson's sense that nature could only be understood as a perpetual process of change and transition.

Faraday played a major role in confirming Emerson's vision of nature as a field of energy or power, rather than as substance or matter. He had been aware of Faraday's work before travelling to London, and while there was able to attend his lectures. As Eric Wilson has shown, Faraday's theories of electromagnetism helped to confirm a change in Emerson's cosmological perspective, in which force and energy transplanted material atoms as the ontological foundation of reality.[12] Lecturing in London in the summer of 1848, Emerson explained that a unified, holistic conception of the cosmos, a principle to which he had long adhered, could be reformulated in terms of process and energy. Faraday was his central example. 'Identity at the base. It need not be atoms: Modern theory sets aside atoms as unphilosophical, and the first of English physical philosophers, Faraday, propounds that we do not arrive at last at atoms, but at spherules of force' (*Later Lectures*, vol. 1, p. 161). The new theories of physics confirmed the vision of the dynamic cosmos that Emerson had developed on speculative and intuitive grounds; physics and poetry seemed to be speaking the same language, and revealing the same fundamental truths.

The Shudder of Joy

Emerson's incorporation of this vision of nature as process into his poetics is made clear in 'Poetry and Imagination', an essay that developed over three decades and brought together much of his later thinking about poetry as a crucial spiritual undertaking. Although 'Poetry and Imagination' has suffered comparative critical neglect because of its relatively late publication, Ronald A. Bosco has characterized it as 'Emerson's most important, definitive statement of poetic theory'.[13] The essay clearly shows the impact of Emerson's encounter with Faraday and other scientific leaders in the 1840s, and extends and amplifies his theory of the poet as the individual who glimpses the original energy at the foundation of reality and attempts to translate that energy into language.

In 'Poetry and Imagination' Emerson argues that nature's power over our perceptions lies ultimately in its capacity to point beyond itself. Admiration of nature, even reverence for it, does not freeze us into appreciative stasis, but jolts us out of the commonplace assumption that the surface of things exhausts their reality and significance. We gain 'early hints' that 'Nature is not final', and if we attend to them, they grow into a certainty 'that nothing stands still in Nature but death; that the creation is on wheels, in transit, always passing into something else, streaming into something higher' (*Complete Works*, vol. 8, p. 4). Through nature we recognize limitless energy, but we do not see finality, the ultimate or absolute nature of reality. We see only the metamorphosis. The striking implication of Emerson's language is that there is, indeed, no fixed or final character of reality, that each glimpse we have reveals something not only new but in a state of change.

But can anything that is constantly in metamorphosis be said to be unified? At times Emerson's embrace of unity seems to be in conflict with his vision of process and energy. The resolution to this continuing tension in his thinking lies in the understanding that the resolution of nature's disparate parts comes through its transitions. If the elements of nature are 'always passing into something else, streaming into something higher' (*Complete Works*, vol. 8, p. 4), they are in a constant process of self-transcendence, leaving their individuated identities for a state beyond their present one. Emerson offered a detailed exposition of this concept in 'Circles', (1841) employing the image of the expanding concentric circle as a metaphor for the growing soul. 'Our life is an apprenticeship to the truth that around every circle another can be drawn; that there is no end in nature, but every end is a beginning.' The 'circle' of the expanding self at first seems a new achievement, but can quickly become a wall which will 'solidify, and hem in the life' (*Collected Works*, vol. 2, p. 181).[14]

One's achievement can thus become one's prison unless it is always being surpassed and transformed.

We might profitably compare Emerson's conception of nature 'on wheels, in transit' to Hartshorne's later explanation of a 'God' that is the embodiment of perfection considered as ever-renewing potentiality. Hartshorne contends that 'all-possibility – which is indeed infinite if anything is – coincides with divine potentiality. Thus, God is infinite in what he could be, not in what he is; he is infinitely capable of actuality, rather than infinitely actual.'[15] Hartshorne's conception of being 'infinitely capable of actuality' captures in different terms Emerson's description of nature as 'always passing into something else, streaming into something higher.' As Hartshorne argues, a conception of a God in change, a 'self-surpassing divinity', can indeed be a powerful religious conception.[16]

Hartshorne's language of potentiality and capability meshes well with Emerson's vision of nature 'in transit'. Nature reveals inexhaustible potentiality. The Emersonian poet responds to the boundless creative energy of nature's ceaseless generation of forms, its striving to surpass itself, with spiritual awe, indeed with an almost erotic passion (*Complete Works*, vol. 8, p. 71):

> The nature of things is flowing, a metamorphosis. The free spirit sympathizes not only with the actual form, but with the power or possible forms; but for obvious municipal or parietal uses God has given us a bias or a rest on today's forms. Hence the shudder of joy with which in each clear moment we recognize the metamorphosis, because it is always a conquest, a surprise from the heart of things.

The 'shudder of joy' is not in the perception of the thing or the material form, but in the recognition of the thing's passing, its perpetual impermanence. Such impermanence is less a cause for apprehension than for celebration, for it signals ever-renewing creation.

What the Elm-Tree Thinks

The act of thinking, especially the intensity of thinking poetically, is itself is a fundamental aspect of this ongoing creative process. Emerson describes the experience of being swept up in the momentum of a compelling sequence of ideas, images and analogies as an instance of 'the metamorphosis' as it manifests itself in our perceptual operations. This view of creative intellectual activity makes it seem quite different from a planned, willed, exercise of the artistic ego, and more akin to a joyful participation in a set of forces much larger than the individual. The processes of nature therefore provide an analogy to the processes of our own thought. In considering the transformations of the forms of nature, the individual is also brought to see as part of these events 'the independent action of the mind; its strange suggestions and laws.' Far from being self-generated, some moments of the deepest thinking seem to be alien and 'strange.' Such thinking even seems to work counter to one's nature or will, becoming for the thinker 'a certain tyranny which springs up in his own thoughts, which have an order, method and beliefs of their own, very different from the order which this common sense uses' (*Complete Works*, vol. 8, p. 6).[17]

Emerson portrays the mind in the grip of such an overarching power as a ship caught in 'certain strong currents' of the ocean 'with a force that no skill of sailing with the best wind, and no strength of oars, or sails, or steam' could overcome. 'Such currents, so tyrannical, exist in thoughts, those finest and subtilest of all waters, that as soon as once thought begins, it refuses to remember whose brain it belongs to; what country, tradition or religion' (*Complete Works*, vol. 8, p. 7). Such images of tyranny, capture and shipwreck are unusual ways of describing what might in other terms be called artistic or philosophical inspiration, but they dramatize effectively Emerson's contention that thought transcends its individual thinker, and operates with imperatives of its own.

Such tyrannical currents are what Emerson would elsewhere investigate as the 'laws and powers of intellect'. He wanted to develop a systematic theory of what we might today classify as psychology, based on an attempt to apply the general method and ethos of 'natural history' to mental processes (*Later Lectures*, vol. 1, p. 137). But either as a theory of poetic inspiration, or of the mind itself, Emerson's goal was to connect the inner and outer worlds, thought and nature, by establishing that each category operates within a set of 'laws' that both affirm and limit natural power. 'Identity of law, perfect order in physics, perfect parallelism between the laws of Nature and the laws of thought exist', he declares (*Complete Works*, vol. 8, p. 8). Central to these 'currents' or 'laws' of thought is what he calls 'the impulse to search resemblance, affinity, identity, in all its objects' (*Complete Works*, vol. 8, p. 7). That he uses the term 'impulse' rather than will or intention is significant in reinforcing the idea that the law of thought itself guides the poet toward a fuller understanding of resemblance, connection and relationship. 'All multiplicity rushes to be resolved into unity', he declares (*Complete Works*, vol. 8, p. 7).

The poet bears witness to this network of likenesses through a command of figurative language, which itself acts as a guarantor of the holistic nature of reality. 'The imagination exists', Emerson writes, 'by sharing the ethereal currents.' The imaginative act is, in this sense, the capacity to be carried along by the energy of metamorphic nature. 'The poet contemplates the central identity, sees it undulate and roll this way and that, with divine flowings, through remotest things; and, following it, can detect essential resemblances in natures never before compared' (*Complete Works*, vol. 8, p. 21). Men and women ordinarily observe only the varied surface of reality and experience; the poet's gift is 'a second sight', an ability to use ordinary perceptions of the world 'as types or words for thoughts which they signify' (*Complete Works*, vol. 8, p. 19). That 'second sight' is not a creative power in the strictest sense, but a power of discovery, or of unlocking that which is present but hidden to ordinary perception. The poet does not add to nature, but sees and reveals its full dimensions.

Language replicates the fundamental qualities of the creation itself, particularly when it becomes figurative or metaphorical. It mirrors to us in words what nature shows us through our senses. The essence of metaphor is the connection of seemingly disparate things, the capacity of one image or idea to conjure other images or ideas that superficially do not seem to be related. The metaphoric poet is thus constantly connecting things, or, as Emerson believes, uncovering the always already existing relationships among separate things. Figurative language is in this sense a revelation of new relations, but also an affirmation of the essential unity of the cosmos. 'Nature itself is a vast trope, and all particular natures are tropes', Emerson writes. 'God himself does not speak in prose' (*Complete Works*, vol. 8, p. 15, 12).

The role of the poet is thus to use the metaphoric quality of language to recover the lost or unrecognized traces of unity, the 'central identity', at the root of human experience. The metaphoric quality of language is ultimately a reflection of the metamorphic character of nature, a never-ending transformation of the parts of reality into new versions of each other. Emerson locates the pleasure of poetry, its aesthetic stimulation and satisfaction, in the recognitions of these constant transformations of identity, in which each particular part of nature is the antecedent of some new version of itself (*Complete Works*, vol. 8, p. 15):

> All thinking is analogizing, and it is the use of life to learn metonymy. The endless passing of one element into new forms, the incessant metamorphosis, explains the rank which the imagination holds in our catalogue of mental powers. The imagination is the reader of these forms. The poet accounts all productions and changes of Nature as the nouns of language, uses them representatively, too well pleased with their ulterior to value much their primary meaning. Every new object so seen gives a shock of agreeable surprise.

This description of aesthetic 'surprise' parallels his more impassioned description, quoted earlier, of the 'shudder of joy with which in each clear moment we recognize the metamorphosis' (*Complete Works*, vol. 8, p. 71). In these passages Emerson provides a physical, almost visceral, description of aesthetic experience.

But the stimulation of poetic perception, however intense, was rooted in the recognition that materiality itself was not final. The material world, when fully understood, always drove perception beyond it, always functioned as a sign. The ancient Asian texts that fascinated Emerson seemed to him to derive their power from their symbolic or representative qualities. 'The Vedas, the Edda, the Koran, are each remembered by their happiest figure. There is no more welcome gift to men than a new symbol' (*Complete Works*, vol. 7, p. 13). Emerson maintains that the Hindus carried symbolic expression 'to its logical extreme' in texts that employ 'the higher use of the material world [...] to furnish us types or pictures to express the thoughts of mind'. In such texts the material world is rendered 'phenomenal', or illusory. 'Youth, age, property, condition, events, persons, – self, even, – are successive <u>maias</u> (deceptions) through which Vishnu mocks and instructs the soul' (*Complete Works*, vol. 8, p. 14–15). Deception, or illusion, is the initial stage of a process that leads to deeper enlightenment when one recognizes the false or incomplete nature of materiality, and searches beyond it. The Hindu scriptures employed material experience to suggest its limitations, and to point the way beyond it.

One of the principal powers of poetry, therefore, is its capacity to expand the dimensions of the physical universe, to pierce the world's powerful illusion that materiality is fixed, unchanging, and all-encompassing. Such power constituted a crucial philosophical and spiritual affirmation. The mystical transport of the 'transparent eye-ball' experience became increasingly inaccessible for Emerson over the years, but something of its power, and of its assurance, was preserved in the workings of figurative language and in the realization of the larger philosophical implications of metaphor, analogy and symbol. Emerson's poetic theory therefore served a dual purpose in that it not only explained the powers and methods of the poet, but also reaffirmed a vision of the world that made poetic language is possible. 'This power is in the image because this power is in Nature. It so affects, because it so is' (*Complete Works*, vol. 8, p. 20).

The poetic use of language is thus always an act of affirmation, always a gesture toward certitude, always a confirmation of a faith in the order of the world. 'A happy symbol is a sort of evidence that your thought is just', Emerson writes, illustrating his point with a series of such symbols (*Complete Works*, vol. 8, p. 13):

> I had rather have a good symbol of my thought, or a good analogy, than the suffrage of Kant or Plato. If you agree with me, or if Locke and Montesquieu agree, I may yet be wrong; but if the elm-tree thinks the same thing, if running water, if burning coal, if crystals, if alkalies, in their several fashions say what I say, it must be true. Thus a good symbol is the best argument, and is a missionary to persuade thousands.

The poet taps into the existing energies of nature to formulate and communicate a truth. Language can serve as the medium for this effort because of its capacity to link superficially disparate things. Figurative and symbolic language demonstrates that apparent differences and separations can be resolved, and is therefore a confirmation that the seemingly chaotic world is finally coherent and interrelated.

Poetry and Social Transformation

In unravelling the complicated metaphysics of aesthetic experience, Emerson also clarified the importance of the poet's role in society. He concludes 'Poetry and Imagination' with a depiction of the poet as an educator and liberator, who plays a potentially prophetic role in history and culture. In a world marked by constant metamorphosis and renewal, poetry is a vehicle for progressive change for both the individual and society. The poet's essential role is to force men and women to think in new ways, to 'sing all our old ideas out of our heads, and new ones in'. Such poetry 'like the verses inscribed on Balder's columns in Breidablik, is capable of restoring the dead to life' (*Complete Works*, vol. 8, p. 64).

By setting the mind's energies in motion, poetry causes all settled things to be reconsidered. Poetry drives us out of complacency; its 'supreme value' is 'to educate us to a height beyond itself' (*Complete Works*, vol. 8, p. 65). Emerson validates the revolutionary potential of poetry by describing the impact of Romanticism in establishing nature as the central subject of poetry, an achievement of immense importance in all aspects of European culture (*Complete Works*, vol. 8, p. 66):

> I count the genius of Swedenborg and Wordsworth as the agents of reform in philosophy, the bringing poetry back to Nature, – to the marrying of Nature and mind, undoing the old divorce in which poetry had been famished and false, and Nature had been suspected and pagan. The philosophy which a nation receives, rules its religion, poetry, politics, arts, trades and whole history.

While 'much that we call poetry is but polite verse' (*Complete Works*, vol. 8, p. 73), poetry of a higher order can be epoch-making, bringing changes in social understanding and experience that seem far removed from the merely artistic or literary.

Emerson's deepening involvement in reform politics and antislavery work in the 1840s and 1850s seems at first divorced from his engagement with poetry, poetry translation and poetic theory during the same period, as if he is being drawn in two quite opposite directions. But these apparently disparate commitments were for Emerson actually complementary activities, pragmatic responses to the ethical challenges of modern society. The activist, like the poet, convinced others to see beyond the apparent and resist in the name of principle the pressures of immediacy and expediency. Such resistance entailed deeper thinking and a longer view of social progress. In such a view hope resides. The fact that the poets were the bearers of new ways of seeing and thinking, 'agents of a reform in philosophy', placed them in a socially vulnerable position. Poetry is 'a lonely faith' (*Complete Works*, vol. 8, p. 74), and the poet is one who often goes unrecognized and unrewarded. While poetry may not appear to have immediacy in the day's political events, it provides a sharpening of consciousness and a refinement of sensibility that has wide-ranging and positive ethical and political results. The practice of creative perception and expression shapes men and women to see experience as continuously new, always bearing potential for transformation (*Complete Works*, vol. 8, p. 31):

> To the poet the world is virgin soil; all is practicable; the men are ready for virtue; it is always time to do right. He is the true re-commencer, or Adam in the garden again. He affirms the applicability of the ideal law to this moment and the present knot of affairs.

The poet sees possibility in men and women, recognizes that they are 'hungry for poetry, starving for symbols', and are instead 'indemnifying themselves with the false wine of alcohol, of politics or of money' (*Complete Works*, vol. 8, p. 70). Emerson's assertion of the poet's role as a mythically compelling, empowering figure who experiences a world that is perennially new, remained, through many iterations the focal point of both his aesthetic theory and of what we might term his spiritual vision.

Notes

1 The following editions of Emerson's works will be cited by shortened titles, followed by volume and page number in the text: *Collected Works*: *The Collected Works of Ralph Waldo Emerson*, ed. by Alfred R. Ferguson *et al.*, 6 vols to date (Cambridge, MA: Harvard University Press, 1971–); *Journals and Miscellaneous Notebooks*: *The Journals and Miscellaneous Notebooks of Ralph Waldo*

Emerson, ed. by William H. Gilman *et al.*, 16 vols (Cambridge, MA: Harvard University Press, 1960–1982); *Later Lectures: The Later Lectures of Ralph Waldo Emerson*, ed. by Ronald A. Bosco and Joel Myerson (Athens, GA: University of Georgia Press, 2001); *Complete Works: The Complete Works of Ralph Waldo Emerson* [Centenary Edition], ed. by Edward Waldo Emerson, 12 vols (Boston, MA: Houghton Mifflin, 1903–1904).

2 For information on the development of *Nature*, with a selection of key critical perspectives, see Merton M. Sealts, Jr, and Alfred R. Ferguson, *Emerson's Nature: Origin, Growth, Meaning* (1969; rpt Carbondale, IL: Southern Illinois University Press, 1979). For informative readings of the 'transparent eye-ball' passage, see Jonathan Bishop, *Emerson on the Soul* (Cambridge, MA: Harvard University Press, 1964), pp. 9–15; Merton M. Sealts, Jr, *Emerson on the Scholar* (Columbia, MO: University of Missouri Press, 1992), pp. 67–73; Lee Rust Brown, *The Emerson Museum: Practical Romanticism and the Pursuit of the Whole* (Cambridge, MA: Harvard University Press, 1997), pp. 43–58; and Laura Dassow Walls, *Emerson's Life in Science: The Culture of Truth* (Ithaca, NY: Cornell University Press, 2003), pp. 98–101. The fame of Emerson's metaphor has been augmented by the publication of a manuscript cartoon version of the image – a barefoot eyeball in top hat and tails – by Emerson's friend and disciple Christopher Pearse Cranch, a poet and landscape painter. See F. DeWolfe Miller, *Christopher Pearse Cranch and his Caricatures of New England Transcendentalism* (Cambridge, MA: Harvard University Press, 1951). See in particular illustration 3, following p. 36.

3 On the significance of 'Experience' see Stephen E. Whicher, *Freedom and Fate: An Inner Life of Ralph Waldo Emerson* (Philadelphia, PA: University of Pennsylvania Press, 1953), pp. 109–22; Barbara Packer, *Emerson's Fall: New Interpretations of the Major Essays* (New York: Continuum, 1982), pp. 148–211; David Van Leer, *Emerson's Epistemology: The Argument of the Essays* (Cambridge: Cambridge University Press, 1986), pp. 143–87; David M. Robinson, *Emerson and the Conduct of Life: Pragmatism and Ethical Purpose in the Later Work* (Cambridge and New York: Cambridge University Press, 1993), pp. 54–70; and Robinson, 'Experience, Instinct, and Emerson's Philosophical Reorientation', *Emerson Bicentennial Essays*, ed. by Ronald A. Bosco and Joel Myerson (Boston, MA: Massachusetts Historical Society and University Press of Virginia, 2006), pp. 391–404.

4 On Emerson's commitment to the antislavery cause, see Len Gougeon, *Virtue's Hero: Emerson, Antislavery, and Reform* (Athens, GA: University of Georgia Press, 1989); Len Gougeon and Joel Myerson, eds, *Emerson's Antislavery Writings* (New Haven, CT: Yale University Press, 1985); Eduardo Cadava, *Emerson and the Climates of History* (Stanford, CA: Stanford University Press, 1997); Gary Collison, 'Emerson and Antislavery', in Joel Myerson, ed., *Historical Guide to Ralph Waldo Emerson* (New York and Oxford: Oxford University Press, 2000), pp. 179–209; T. Gregory Garvey, ed., *The Emerson Dilemma: Essays on Emerson and Social Reform* (Athens, GA: University of Georgia Press, 2001); and David M. Robinson, ed., *The Political Emerson: Essential Essays on Politics and Social Reform* (Boston, MA: Beacon Press, 2004).

5 See Arthur Versluis, *American Transcendentalism and Asian Religions* (Oxford: Oxford University Press, 1993), pp. 187–91. Further discussions of Thoreau's engagement with Hinduism can be found in Alan D. Hodder, *Thoreau's Ecstatic Witness* (New Haven, CT: Yale University Press, 2001).

6 Robert D. Richardson, Jr, *Emerson: The Mind on Fire* (Berkeley, CA: University

of California Press, 1995).
7   On background of *Poems* see Joseph M. Thomas, '"The Property of my Own Book": Emerson's *Poems* (1847) and the Literary Marketplace', *New England Quarterly* 69 (1996): 406–25; and Saundra Morris, 'The Threshold Poem, Emerson, and "The Sphinx"', *American Literature* 69 (1997): 547–70. Readers should be aware of the edited and annotated collection of Emerson's complete poems and poem translations: Ralph Waldo Emerson, *Collected Poems and Translations*, ed. by Harold Bloom and Paul Kane (New York: Library of America, 1994).
8   The idea of metamorphosis, flux, or process is central to Emerson's philosophical conception of reality, and plays an important role in both his aesthetics and his ethics. For further exploration of this concept see Richard Poirier, *The Renewal of Literature: Emersonian Reflections* (New Haven, CT: Yale University Press, 1987), pp. 47–52; Robinson, *Emerson and the Conduct of Life*, pp. 192–5; and Jonathan Levin, *The Poetics of Transition: Emerson, Pragmatism, and American Literary Modernism* (Durham, NC: Duke University Press, 1999), pp. 1–44.
9   Alfred North Whitehead, *Science and the Modern World* (1925; rpt New York: Free Press, 1967), pp. 93, 72. On Hartshorne's theology, see Charles Hartshorne, *The Divine Relativity: A Social Conception of God* (New Haven, CT: Yale University Press, 1948; rpt 1964); and *A Natural Theology for Our Time* (La Salle, IL: Open Court, 1967).
10 Emerson's identity as a philosopher of 'power' has been explored by Michael Lopez in *Emerson and Power: Creative Antagonism in the Nineteenth Century* (De Kalb, IL: Northern Illinois University Press, 1996); and the special 'Emerson/Nietzsche' issue of *ESQ: A Journal of the American Renaissance* 43: 1–4 (1997), ed. by Lopez.
11 Emerson's interest in science has been a topic of growing scholarly interest. See David M. Robinson, 'Emerson's Natural Theology and the Paris Naturalists: Toward a "Theory of Animated Nature"', *Journal of the History of Ideas* 41 (1980): 69–88; Robinson, 'Fields of Investigation: Emerson and Natural History', in *American Literature and Science*, ed. by Robert Scholnick (Lexington, KY: University of Kentucky Press, 1992), pp. 94–109; Brown, *The Emerson Museum*, pp. 49–168; Eric Wilson, *Emerson's Sublime Science* (New York: St Martin's, 1999); Walls, *Emerson's Life in Science*; and Laura Dassow Walls, '"If a Body Can Sing": Emerson and Victorian Science', *Emerson Bicentennial Essays*, ed. by Bosco and Myerson, pp. 334–66.
12 For a thorough discussion of Emerson's knowledge of Faraday's work, and of Emerson's recognition of the philosophical implications of experiments in electricity, see Wilson, *Emerson's Sublime Science*, pp. 87–97.
13 On the development and significance of 'Poetry and Imagination', see Ronald A. Bosco, '"Poetry for the World of Readers" and "Poetry for Bards Proper": Theory and Textual Integrity in Emerson's Parnassus', *Studies in the American Renaissance 1989*, ed. by Joel Myerson (Charlottesville, VA: University Press of Virginia, 1989), pp. 257–312 (p. 311). Bosco describes the close connection between this essay and Emerson's late poetry anthology, *Parnassus*.
14 For further commentary on 'Circles', see Harold Bloom, *Figures of Capable Imagination* (New York: Seabury, 1976), pp. 53–64; Barbara Packer, *Emerson's Fall*, pp. 14–19; David Van Leer, *Emerson's Epistemology*, pp. 106–14; and Robinson, *Emerson and the Conduct of Life*, pp. 24–9.
15 Charles Hartshorne, *A Natural Theology for our Time* (La Salle, IL: Open Court Publishing, 1967), p. 21.
16 Hartshorne, *A Natural Theology for our Time*, p. 25.

17 As Joseph M. Thomas has recently pointed out, Emerson is not entirely consistent in his poetic theory, and also articulates at various points in his career 'a skeptical poetics, which undercuts his countervailing emphasis on self abandonment and "vital authority"'. See 'Poverty and Power: Revisiting Emerson's Poetics', *Emerson Bicentennial Essays*, ed. by Bosco and Myerson, pp. 213–46.

7. Sacrificial Exchange and the Gothic Double in *Melmoth the Wanderer* and *The Picture of Dorian Gray*

Alison Milbank

It is a commonplace of the history of the gothic novel that the castles and haunted abbeys of its eighteenth-century beginnings give way to the human being as site for haunting in the Victorian period. Similarly, terror and awe at the unknown and supernatural are held to be replaced by the horror of the unrecognized self, represented by Freud's theory of the uncanny and evidenced either in a self that splits into dual or multiple selves, or in the apparition of a doppelgänger.[1] Nineteenth-century attention to the fissured and doubled self is held up as primarily a secular phenomenon, and a radical questioning of the unitary subjectivity that upholds social and religious order.[2] This essay gives a very different reading of the gothic double as potentially a mode of social and political critique, taking texts from either end of the nineteenth century by Charles Maturin, a cleric of the Church of Ireland, who published *Melmoth the Wanderer* in 1820, and his great-nephew Oscar Wilde, whose *Picture of Dorian Gray* appeared in serial form seventy years later. In arguing for a religious reading of the fissured self, I shall have recourse to the theories of mimetic desire by the contemporary theorist, René Girard, who has offered a universal theory of the origins of sacrifice and the doubling mechanism in his *Violence and the Sacred* (1972) and its many sequels. This association of sacrificial violence with the double is, as we shall see, central to the two texts under discussion, while sacrifice itself becomes a way of understanding social and national identity in nineteenth-century social theory.

Something new enters the gothic novel with the publication of Rev. Charles Maturin's sprawling epic, *Melmoth the Wanderer* in 1820. No longer is the gothic threat located in a place such as a fortress in the Apennines or a tyrannical monastery, so that the heroine can flee from the dungeon out to safety beyond the castle walls. Instead, Maturin suggests that gothic tyranny is to be encountered in the very structures of societal and familial relations themselves. Like the Catholic faith in

Augustine's formulation, coercive power in Maturin's fictional world is 'ubique, ab omnibus et semper' – eternal, ubiquitous and believed by all. For a novel that spreads temporally across centuries, and spatially spans the globe from India to Spain, Maturin is ambitiously attempting a universal history to rival those Enlightenment projects of Vico, Hume and Montesquieu. Like the post-Revolutionary French writer, Joseph de Maistre, Maturin reads the whole of human society, past and present, in terms of sacrifice. In his essay, 'Enlightenment on Sacrifices', Maistre argues that pagans were straining after the truth in their understanding that redemption comes by blood, although they distorted this understanding by acts of substitutionary sacrifice of captives and even, on occasion, their own children. Sacrifice then becomes a way to interpret and unite a range of religious practices. For Maistre, on this point the whole of history does not show a dissenting voice. The entire theory rests on the dogma of substitution. It was believed (as was and always will be the case) 'that the innocent could pay for the guilty'; from which it was concluded that, life being guilty, 'a less precious life could be offered and accepted in place of another'.[3]

Maturin had already shown an interest in the subject of sacrifice in his novel, *The Milesian Chief* of 1812, a romance about Irish independence in which the hero, Connal, gives his life for a free Ireland: 'I will offer this last sacrifice for my country', he exclaims, 'Though the temple is in ruins, and the priest himself the victim.'[4] The attitude to Connal's heroism is ambiguous but broadly positive, but by the time of his greatest novel, *Melmoth the Wanderer*, Maturin uses sacrifice much more negatively.[5] The narrative is framed by the arrival of one John Melmoth at his uncle's deathbed in the nineteenth century. There he encounters the mysterious figure of the seemingly immortal Melmoth the Wanderer, the common element to a number of embedded narratives, including the incarceration of Stanton in 1677 in a lunatic asylum, the tale of a Spaniard, who is confined to a monastery by his mother, escapes only to be taken to the Inquisition, takes refuge underground with a Jew, and finally arrives on the shores of Ireland. Other important strands are the account of a complicated cross-party love affair in the English Civil War, and the tale of Guzman's family who are so impoverished through disinheritance that one daughter sells her body and a son his blood. A whole range of minor sub-plots explore cannibalism and every imaginable permutation of gothic horror and blood-letting. Each major character, at the apex of his or her suffering and despair is offered an exchange of places by Melmoth the Wanderer, who is fated to immortality unless he can find someone with whom to change places. None of the characters accepts the offer.

Maturin's historical pretensions are most strongly evident in the Indian section of the novel, in which Melmoth courts and deceives an innocent shipwrecked Spanish girl, who lives an Edenic existence on an Indian island. He follows William Robertson in tracing a religious development from animism (represented by the musings of Immalee on her participation in the life of the flowers and animals around her), through the polytheism of Hindu worship to the monotheism of Judaism and Christianity. Melmoth gives Immalee a telescope, through which she can observe religion on mainland India. Maturin is careful, however, to demonstrate that each of these stages of religious development is marked by sacrifice, whether it be the human hearts inserted in the idol on Immalee's island, or the fearful excesses of Juggernaut worship. Unlike the Enlightenment tendency to see sacrifice as left behind, Maturin draws attention to a sacrificial residue in post-diaspora Judaism, in the ritual killing of a cock on the Day of Atonement that startles Alonzo in the Jewish home that gives him refuge from the auto-da-fé. And Catholicism, most of all, is portrayed as a monstrous engine of sacrificial substitution in which its adherents endlessly expiate their own sins by putting the penalty and guilt onto others. The Catholic parricide taunts Alonzo with this logic in his cell at the Inquisition: 'Mine is the best theology, – the theology of utter hostility to all beings whose sufferings may mitigate mine. In this flattering theory, your crimes become my virtues – I need not any of my own [...]. I have literally worked out *my* salvation by *your* fear and trembling' (*Melmoth the Wanderer*, p. 225). The Calvinists in the novel, however, are just as concerned with sacrificial bloodshed. A puritan weaver in the lunatic asylum, who should as a good protestant believe only in the one sacrifice of Christ to remove sin, calls for an expiatory holy war in the manner of de Maistre: 'Blood! Blood! The saints call for it, earth gapes to swallow it' (p. 50).

As one of the most important and influential early-nineteenth-century gothic novels, *Melmoth the Wanderer* presents – even more extremely than *Frankenstein* – for the first time a wholly gothicized universe, which is characterized not so much by natural suffering as by substitutionary violence. Indeed, one of the most impressive features of the novel is the way in which its use of dualist structures works to unmask social and religious modes of operation as mirror images of each other in their violent underpinnings. Royalist and puritan are united all too closely in their bloodthirsty railings in the asylum, and Calvinism and Catholicism work to deconstruct each other. Self-sacrifice also is revealed as but another will-to-power: one telling example is the perverted way in which Alonzo Monçada's mother turns the sacrificial tables on her son by claiming the role of victim when she is his sacrificer, by lying prostrate in the convent doorway, her body the price of his obduracy in refusing the religious life. This is in accord with Maturin's own sermon on the atonement, which takes Micah for its text: God 'will not be appeased by outward service, though we sacrificed all that is precious to nature, though we gave our firstborn for our transgression'.[6] *Melmoth the Wanderer* presents a sorry picture of child sacrifice in the tales of Walberg, Monçada and the young Immalee whose very name suggests the Latin *immolare*, to sacrifice. Child sacrifice is nicely poised between sacrifice of the other and sacrifice of the self in one's own flesh, as is also the marital cannibalism of the young man walled up with his wife in the Madrid convent, since in Christian marriage, following Genesis 2.24, the couple become 'one flesh'.

Although Maturin's stress on the universality of sacrifice links him with Maistre, who views it as 'rooted in the furthest depths of human nature', unlike Maistre he seeks to show that these sacrifices are ineffectual.[7] As Monçada says, '*How false is a treaty made with God which we ratify with our own blood,* when he has declared that there is but one sacrifice he will accept, even that of the lamb slain from the foundation of the world' (p. 95). The language echoes the Pauline text also quoted in Maturin's sermon but also Archbishop Magee's *Disquisitions on the Atonement*, originally given as sermons during Maturin's time at Trinity College Dublin.[8] Magee is important to Maturin because unlike earlier Anglican theologians who viewed Jewish sacrifice as gift or symbol, Magee saw it as expiatory. He stressed the expiatory element to argue against the Deists the effectual nature of Christ's redemptive death. Maturin's novel shows that without this reliance on the one sacrifice of Christ one gets instead a bloodbath of scapegoating. So in the monastery Alonzo is called 'the Judas among the brethren; a branded Cain amid a primitive family; a scapegoat that struggles to burst from the hands of the congregation into the wilderness' (p. 161). The reference here is to the ceremonies of the Jewish Day of Atonement as laid out in Leviticus 16, in which Aaron as priest casts lots over two goats, one of which is to be offered as a sin offering, while the other is sent out to the wilderness, with the sins of the people literally on its head, since Aaron is to whisper their confession into its ear (Leviticus 16.21). After the fire at the Inquisition the novel presents both Alonzo and the parricide as analogues of the two goats used for the Day of Atonement. The parricide is the first goat killed in the temple because he is torn apart in a quasi-Dionysiac *sparagmos* by the mob, while Alonzo is the actual 'scapegoat' who is driven out to bear away the sins of the people. He is actually addressed as such by the Jew to whose house he escapes, and who is caught in the act of performing his own sacrifice of a cock on that same holy day.

René Girard, in a series of studies, including one entitled *The Scapegoat*, similarly reads all social and religious order as based on sacrificial substitution and scapegoating.[9] Reworking Freud's myth of the parricides who kill the patriarch to gain access to his power and women in *Totem and Taboo*, Girard puts the emphasis instead on rivalry within the group of brothers.[10] For him all desire is mimetic: one desires not so much an object such as the women but rather the desire of the other. It is the rival's desire that renders the object desirable and means that one does not so much desire the object craved by another so much as want his desire itself, causing one to imitate his rival as if in a game of 'Simon Says'. This competition then leads to a crisis only resolvable by means of the emergence of a scapegoat who is both like but regarded as unlike the sacrificers. This association of desire and mimicry makes sense of the way in which the characters of *Melmoth the Wanderer* are so fascinated by Melmoth and seek him out, since they are being drawn into his desire. Mimetic contagion, indeed, permeates the world of the novel so that Alonzo, for example, watching from a window the dismemberment of the parricide by the crowd, finds himself 'mimicking, in my horrid trance, the shouts of the multitude' (pp. 256–7). In mimetic contagion the desire of the other forms the subject's desire so that they become mirror images of each other.

Melmoth himself is an embodiment of mimetic contagion as he seeks to draw close to his victims and infect them with his desire, so that they can become the bearer of his sin and burden of longevity and thus his scapegoat. He longs to create his own double, a true doppelgänger who will precipitate his death and allow him release. This is why we encounter him at the deathbed of old Melmoth and the accession of his namesake, John Melmoth, and why he chooses the tabula rasa of the isolated Immalee for his attentions. But it is noticeable that every feverish search for Melmoth by those to whom he has made his offer is accompanied by an act of repudiation of him, in the strongest of terms. This contradiction can also be explained by what Girard calls the 'monstrous double'. Incited by Melmoth's own original desire – curiosity – which was how he came to make his bargain with the devil, the characters become more and more isolated and thus like him in such a way that antagonism and identification become dialectically related.

But the monstrous double as a means of denying the rivalry of desire does not fully account for what happens in *Melmoth the Wanderer*. Girard assumes that texts (with some important exceptions) and the societies that produce them occlude the similarities that render scapegoating the way out of an unacknowledged doubling and competitive desire. Recourse to violence is justified by threats to social order or religious sanction. In contrast, *Melmoth* makes mimetic contagion, doubles and scapegoating its subject: these themes do not have to be detected but are deliberately drawn to the reader's notice. And the novel draws our attention constantly to rivalrous brothers, yoking Juan and Alonzo as Cain and Abel, and naming its Jewish brothers Solomon and Adonijah after the Biblical king and the brother he had put to death in I Kings 2, following a dispute about which of them should succeed David. In this way *Melmoth the Wanderer* both acknowledges the tendencies to murderous imitation in the human psyche and seeks a way to deal with them.

The answer to sacrificial violence offered in the novel is to suggest that one can transform the scapegoat mechanism by an acceptance of the doubled self and exchanges of stories and acts of generosity that embody a positive mimesis. Readers have noted the bizarre way in which the so-called incommunicability of Melmoth's offer of an exchange of fates is actually obliquely yet frequently revealed and narrated by various characters in the novel. Although all the sufferers refuse the exchange of their souls to end their pain, the protagonists *do* bear the offer as narrative, and in so doing become like the scapegoat in being a double figure: the one who escapes but the one who carries the knowledge of the sins, which was whispered into their ears by Melmoth. Protagonists who encounter Melmoth find and acknowledge a double in others (Alonzo in the atheist monk, the parricide, the old Jew Adonijah and his own brother) but also in the self (Immalee in India is also Isidora the Spanish gentlewoman once back with her family). Indeed suffering opens even minor characters to 'the agony of consciousness' that opens a fissure in the self and forces a duality upon them. The point here is that each character becomes aware of their likeness to another, as Alonzo is horrified at his own similarity to the parricide monk who guides him out of the monastery passages, but that the choice offered by Melmoth forces a sense of the self as fissured by that knowledge. Alonzo, for example, is sent dreams by Melmoth: '"I saw *myself*; and this horrid tracing of yourself by your own spectre, while you still live, is perhaps a curse almost equal to your crimes visiting you in the punishments of eternity"' (p. 236).

Critics such as Richard Haslam and Chris Baldick have noted the central importance of Calvinism to *Melmoth the Wanderer* and its tendency towards dualism, evident in that same puritan weaver whose creed 'retaliates upon him' at night when he pours out execrations upon the beliefs he holds dear.[11] It is no accident that tales of the double are frequent in Calvinist cultures since a belief in double predestination – that one is destined either for salvation or damnation from the beginning – opens a space of anxiety about one's own election. In Luther's theology this terror – *Anfechtung* – can be beautiful and spiritually helpful, since it presages the operation of grace but in Calvinism it must be followed by a sense of assurance or it can itself be a sign of damnation, as in the 'ineffectual calling' of James Hogg's Robert Wringham in *Memoirs and Confessions of a Justified Sinner*, in which the anti-hero's experience of election calls forth the devil as his doppelgänger.[12] Since puritan piety also decreed constant self-examination by the believer, a duality of subjectivity marks its experience, even into sanctification. Maturin, perhaps because of his Huguenot background, described himself as a 'high Calvinist' in a letter to Sir Walter Scott but it is usually assumed that he was no longer a Calvinist by the time he wrote *Melmoth*. But there is nothing in the novel to preclude Calvinism's five points: double predestination, the irresistibility of grace, the total depravity of humanity, particular redemption and the final perseverance of the saints. This last point is held in conscious opposition to the Arminian doctrine that the elect could fail, and it seems clear that only this position makes sense of the fact that, despite the appalling murderous character of human society presented in the novel, each character tempted to exchange suffering for immortality successfully resists.

My reason for stressing the Calvinist basis for the doubled self in the novel is to argue that it allows a move from a 'bad' duality of anxiety about election to a 'good' duality in which conscience becomes a second self that helps to build up sanctification in the believer. This is precisely what the encounters with Melmoth effect. In the offer of an exchange of fates the monstrosity of Melmoth as the character's own desire for escape from time and the sufferings of mortality is revealed. Afterwards, this knowledge as deictic narration is borne by the tempted protagonist who thereby turns his bad duality into a productive one, in which the narration operates as a sort of conscience. Indeed, it is by virtue of a mutual exchange of narratives about Melmoth's offer that what non-violent society there is in the novel is re-established, most notably in the friendship between young John Melmoth and Alonzo Monçada, who is shipwrecked on the Wicklow coast. It is begun in acts of mutual self-sacrifice and rescue, since not only does young Melmoth try to save the drowning crew but the Spaniard rescues him after he falls off the rock into the raging waters. This reciprocity is later cemented by the exchange of narratives and the novel ends with the pair exchanging 'looks of silent and unutterable horror' as they trace the path of the doomed Melmoth up the cliff to his final end (p. 542). This society is a brotherhood of scapegoats, of those who acknowledge the fact that, as Maistre puts it, paraphrasing St James, 'man is double in all his ways', whereas Melmoth is always single and isolated.[13] Unsuccessful in his attempts to recreate doubleness by substitution his only recourse is to laughter which, as Baudelaire perceptively noted, is implicitly Satanic in that it separates the one who laughs both from the creatures below and the God above.[14] Melmoth is often found laughing at scenes of suffering and violence, such as the storm that causes death of two young lovers struck by lightning: 'and after looking on them for some time [he] burst into a laugh so loud, wild and protracted, that the peasants, starting with as much horror at the sound as at that of the storm, hurried away, bearing the corpse with them' (p. 30). Although Melmoth is accompanied to his death by young Melmoth and Monçada, his laughter reveals his isolation and despite the allusions to Byron's Satanic overreacher protagonist, Manfred, who like Melmoth had a comet for his soul, Melmoth does not die holding the hand of a holy man, as does Manfred.[15] The only positive aspect to his demise, after 150 extra years of life, is that same gaze of horror exchanged by the two friends. It marks the awareness that Melmoth brought of the horror of sacrificial substitution, and its replacement by mutuality and an acknowledged doubleness of self. Melmoth's victims *know* their own propensity to mimetic contagion and violence, as Alonzo was aware of his mimicry of the mob's violence in Madrid.

Although Oscar Wilde was writing well after the end of the traditional gothic novel, he was very aware of the tradition, and took the name of his great-uncle's protagonist when he left Britain for France following his prison sentence. He called himself Sebastian Melmoth, uniting the celebrated Christian martyr to the doomed gothic anti-hero in such a way as to show his understanding of the sacrificial basis of Maturin's novel. The near-naked figure of Sebastian struck by arrows became a favourite Renaissance subject for artistic representation of the masculine body, and thus an aesthetic and homosexual icon in Wilde's day. Sebastian, however, stands insouciant amid the archers because it is not the arrows that kill him: he is wounded yet untouched just as Melmoth's victims resist the arrows of temptation he lets fly in their direction. Wilde explored the duality of the self and its relation to sacrificial violence in his gothic story, *The Picture of Dorian Gray*, a text that is not only indebted to *Melmoth* for a number of plot features but also for a way of engendering a productive duality.[16] It is a famously dualist text that begins with a series of epigrams that invert conventional wisdom, such as 'those who find ugly meanings in beautiful things are corrupt' while 'those who find beautiful meanings in beautiful things are the cultivated. For these there is hope. They are the elect...' (*The Picture of Dorian Gray*, p. 3). The technique of reversal, however, that allies sanctity and religious value with the 'cultivated' aesthete locks the terms in to a binary structure of antagonism and substitution – a sort of murderous metonymy. The circularity and entrapment of this linguistic universe is made evident in the frequent resort to the language of mirrors in the epigram section: 'it is the spectator, and not life, that art really mirrors' (p. 4). Mimetic contagion, in which the reader is caught up in mimicry of the mirrored text, becomes the privileged mode of art, culminating in the celebrated pair of aphorisms, 'the nineteenth century dislike of Realism is the rage of Caliban seeing his own face in a glass. The nineteenth century dislike of Romanticism is the rage of Caliban not seeing his own face in a glass' (p. 3). The fact that the character Caliban from *The Tempest* is himself a kind of monstrous double of humanity in his desire to possess Miranda and the island makes the Girardian point all the stronger. *The Picture of Dorian Gray* describes a society more mutedly but decidedly characterized by consumption and violence as Maturin's, as the little duchess notes. 'You would sacrifice anybody', she accuses Lord Henry Wooton, 'for the sake of an epigram' (p. 195). As in *Melmoth the Wanderer* characters are engaged in a pass-the-parcel game of substitution, as the intelligent Lord Henry admits: 'to influence a person is to give him one's soul. He does not think his natural thoughts, or burn with his natural passions. His virtues are not real to him. His sins, if there are such things as sins, are borrowed' (p. 20). These words of Lord Henry to the beautiful youth, Dorian Gray, precipitate his auditor into a world of self-consciousness and dualist modes of thought akin to that of the sufferers of Maturin's gothic universe. Lord Henry even couches his initiation in terms of a parodic version of Calvinist elective anxiety, beginning by plunging the young man into an awareness of sin by telling him 'you have passions that have made you afraid, thoughts that have filled you with terror, day-dreams and sleeping-dreams whose mere memory might stain your cheek with shame...' (p. 21). The call here is not to salvation but 'self-development' and it succeeds as Dorian has 'a look of joy, as if he had recognized himself for the first time' (p. 22). This moment is often interpreted in terms of Freud's stage of primary narcissism but again, a Girardian reading gives a more precise sense of the social formation of desire. For Dorian's self-love is the mimicry of Lord Henry's. It is the older man's desire that awakens his own self-consciousness, but that too had its origin in Basil Hallward's desire for Dorian as expressed in the portrait of the young man. Before that came Hallward's first encounter with Gray, which began with the feeling that someone was staring at *him*, and his fear that the stranger's personality was so strong that 'if I allowed it to do so, it would absorb my whole nature, my whole soul, my very art itself' (p. 10). The language is very close to that used about Melmoth by his victims and the interesting development made by Wilde to Maturin's conception is to make all his main characters potential Melmoths in their desire to influence each other, and to draw them into the cycle of mimetic desire. So the Dorian who makes the fatal wish to exchange roles with the portrait is the creation of the rivalrous desires of the little group of aesthetes whose totem he becomes. With this choice of immortality, however, Dorian moves from victim to perpetrator, in a manner all too common in those abused sexually as children, who learn to imitate their abusers and internalize their desire.

The agent of mimetic contagion like Melmoth, Wooton more successfully infects him with mimetic desire and the double cathexis of fascination and repulsion that renders the adjective 'monstrous' the password of their social circle.[17] Where Basil Hallward truly believes in the power of love as he does in that of art, Wooton dismisses them both as 'simply forms of imitation' (p. 82). The reason why Wooton desires to influence Gray is so that he may act as scapegoat for his own sense of duality. Like his mentor, however, Gray too finds duality unbearable and seeks to offload it onto the portrait (p. 28):

> Why should it keep what I must lose? Every moment takes something from me, and gives something to it. Oh, if it were only the other way! If the picture could change, and I could be always what I am now! Why did you paint it? It will mock me some day – mock me horribly!

The picture has here become Dorian's double and his rival but after his fateful wish it changes its role. Like Melmoth's portrait, which was signed with the date of its painting, 1646, as an indicator of his longevity, its life is bound up with its subject. Melmoth leaves legal instructions to his heirs not to destroy his portrait and when young Melmoth tears it in pieces it appears to reanimate as if it had life of its own. Dorian Gray's portrait is even more central to his identity. As his substitute victim, the painting bears alive like a scapegoat the narrative of Dorian's sins, with not just the effects of ageing but those of every cruel act leaving their mark on the painted countenance. Hallward's vermilion signature then becomes an analogue for the red ribbon tied to the horn of the biblical scapegoat.[18]

There is, however, a model of productive duality in Wilde's novel in the painter Basil Hallward who seeks to hold together in creative tension the ideal and the real in his art. Unlike Dorian, he does not use the painting as his scapegoat for the duality of self but bears within himself also the 'terror' of Dorian's influence upon him in the manner of John Melmoth and Alonzo Monçada, who similarly bear the 'horror' of Melmoth's demise. Hallward is prepared to destroy his own work to prevent the spread of mimetic contagion that follows Dorian's awakening, and later he offers an exchange of narratives with Dorian that might have been his salvation. He then urges Dorian to repent: 'it is never too late, Dorian. Let us kneel down and try if we cannot remember a prayer. Isn't there a verse somewhere, "Though your sins be as scarlet, yet I will make them as white as snow?"' (p. 151). The verse in Isaiah quoted here by Hallward is that used in Isaiah 1.18 to justify the custom of tying the red ribbon to the goat's horn, to see if it will turn white, although Hallward's red signature that parallels the scapegoat ribbon as suggested above, remains here 'bright vermillion' (p. 149). For instead of confessing his sin, Dorian Gray kills Hallward along with a host of other surrogate victims who bear the weight of Dorian's murderous unitariness including the woman who loved him, who commits suicide after her rejection by Gray. The reason for his throwing her off is her failure at mimetic representation. An accomplished actress, her real love for Dorian makes her acting falter: 'I might mimic a passion that I do not feel, but I cannot mimic one that burns me like fire' (p. 84).[19]

Towards the end of the novel Dorian Gray actually comes to look like Melmoth with his eyes 'like discs of blue fire' (p. 108) imitating Melmoth's 'fiery orbs', and his nightmarish visions imitate the last dream of Melmoth in imagining himself being blown or dragged up a precipice to be hurled off to hell. Unlike Melmoth, however, Dorian is more successful in arousing mimetic desire: 'I wish I could change places with you', is said by more than one character, including Lord Henry himself but the irony of Dorian's secret life is that he is locked into an awful self-consciousness by the existence of his 'double', and every attempt to escape fails. Having spent most of his life resisting duality, at length Dorian learns its value and seeks to gain a good conscience by his refusal to ruin a young village girl in the same way that Melmoth 'spares' Immalee. This essay at what he calls 'self-sacrifice' only rebounds back as hypocrisy for he lacks the 'final perseverance' of Calvin's saints and Maturin's protagonists. The portrait does not improve but adds only a look of cunning and hypocrisy.

In a final attempt to escape the second self, Dorian sets about destroying the painting and with it 'this monstrous soul-life' (p. 212). In destroying his portrait he hopes to lose the sense of another self that judges his actions: his conscience. Ironically, in seeking to remove his soul he attacks his body instead, and lies on the floor as an unrecognisable corpse: 'withered, wrinkled and loathsome of visage' (p. 213) just as the dying Melmoth declined suddenly into 'hoary decrepid debility' (p. 540). All that remains of Melmoth is his handkerchief, and all that remains to identify Dorian Gray are his rings. The productive duality of real and ideal is however, restored in Wilde's novel in the form of the 'splendid portrait' that survives in all its original glory and asserts the relative immortality of the realm of art. Wilde's novel ends more tragically than Maturin's in that the cycle of mimetic desire is not broken and the possibility of productive duality represented by Basil Hallward fails.

My interpretation of *The Picture of Dorian Gray* as seeking a way out of bad duality through a union of real and ideal, spirit and matter, is strengthened by the evidence of Wilde's later writing from prison. The two titles for versions of the essay/letter, *In Carcere et Vinculis* ('in prison and in chains', which imitates the titles of two feast days of St Peter and St Paul) and *De Profundis* ('out of the depths', psalm 130), emphasize Wilde's gothic imprisonment but also give his sufferings a religious significance. The whole of Wilde's long letter from prison addressed to his lover, Lord Alfred Douglas, is a self-justification that presents Wilde as a victim of the tempter Bosie and his murderously violent father, the Marquess of Queensberry. Like Maturin's Alonzo, the victim of his family's urge to expiate their sins through his life, Wilde believes that the Douglas family has tried to make him its scapegoat:

> I was arrested and your father became the hero of the hour [...] your family now ranks strangely enough with the Immortals: for with the grotesqueness of effect that is as it were a gothic element in history, and makes Clio the least serious of all the Muses, your father will always live among the kind pure-minded parents of Sunday School literature; your place is with the infant Samuel; and in the lowest mire of Malebolge I sit between Gilles de Retz and the Marquis de Sade.[20]

Gilles de Retz may have come to Wilde's thought here because of Huysmans' novel about Satanic practices, *Là-Bas*, published in 1891, in which the protagonist describes in great detail the appalling crimes of the French bluebeard, who tortured, sodomized and murdered large numbers of small children, all of them sacrificed in his desire to discover the secrets of life and death.[21] Douglas too is presented by Wilde as similarly making his own self-transcendence the god to whom all others must be subsumed: 'your meanest motive, your lowest appetite, your most common passion, became to you laws by which the lives of others were to be guided always, and to which, if necessary, they were to be without scruple sacrificed.'[22] This casts Lord Alfred Douglas as a Dorian Gray figure and Wilde as Basil Hallward. *De Profundis / In Carcere et Vinculis* is an attempt to reverse this cycle of what Wilde believes to be substitutionary sacrifice of himself through showing Douglas his own violent culpability:

> I could have held up a mirror to you, and shown you such an image of yourself that you would not have recognized it as your own till you found it mimicking back your gestures of horror, and then you would have known whose shape it was, and hated it and yourself for ever.[23]

Douglas's unitary selfhood needs to be broken, so that through knowledge and self-examination, he can, as Wilde himself has done, find his productive second self in his soul, which Wilde has already found 'waiting for me as a friend'.[24]

Through suffering and sorrow, Wilde learns a new life that involves a certain separation of the self for self-awareness and development, like the Lutheran conscience, and he uses Christ's passion and acceptance of suffering as the model for himself and Douglas. So Wilde is like Maturin in so far as his text seeks to reveal the way in which Douglas's father has cast Wilde himself in the role of a monstrous double in the Girardian sense, as a cover for his own violence and child-abuse, and he calls Bosie too to open his self up to examination, to reveal his own duality and then turn that productively towards self-development. It is interesting that Wilde turns to Christ as the key to this opening up of productive duality for that is what Girard himself does. For Girard, Christ, who voluntarily accepts the unjustness of his scapegoating, thereby reveals the violent basis of the sacrificial mechanism.[25] In embracing Christ-like sorrow, Wilde seeks to turn his suffering into a similar exposure of substitutionary violence, although his rancour at Douglas's exploitation of him often renders this project unstable.

Both the beginning and the end of the nineteenth century were characterized by attention to the second self or doppelgänger figure, and there has been a tendency in literary studies to read this attention as a symptom of a range of cultural anxieties. Instead I have tried to show that the double instead is a *pharmakos*: a redemptive trope in a society of rampant capitalism and materialism, and one which produces instead a spiritual reality. Maturin's text is proleptic in its siting sacrifice at the heart of the modern social order as well as in the remote past because the nineteenth century was marked by the rise of modern nationalism, which itself demanded sacrifice, as in the Cathleen ni Hoolihan of Yeats's play who sent men out to live for her and die.[26] It is no accident that my two authors are, like Yeats, both Anglo-Irish and nationalist sympathizers. We tend to read Anglo-Irish gothic in terms of guilt and paranoia but in its very instability and duality of cultural identity it offers a less murderously unitary model on which a sense of nationhood might be built. For the problem even for the most famous literary double self, Henry Jekyll, in Stevenson's tale, *The Strange Case of Dr Jekyll and Mr Hyde*, was not having a double but being unable to cope with his own duality and the 'perennial war among my members'.[27] There was so great a gulf between his moral and immoral impulses that he sought to do away with the latter altogether by his medical discovery. The horror that followed the successful division of his dual selves was that separated, the evil part took on a monstrously and disproportionately greater existence than it had enjoyed when it was about one-tenth of Jekyll's personality. In the final statement of the case by Henry Jekyll he looks to a time when 'man will be ultimately known for a mere polity of multifarious, incongruous and independent denizens' (p. 76). Although the selves within may be many and different, even incommensurable, the key word here is 'polity', which implies a social and political organisation that requires nurture, protection and law like any city-state. In the language of social Darwinism, nationalism and imperialism of the late nineteenth century, there was an assumption of sacrificial logic: sacrifice of the weak for the strong in the first, of the individual to the nation or empire in the latter two ideologies. In stressing the duality or multifariousness of the self, Stevenson is questioning the sacrificial logic of offering up the part for the whole, and he is resting upon a religious conception of the self as dual or myriad that is as ancient as religious practice itself. As Otto Rank wrote in his psychological study of the double in 1914: 'the first double is the soul.'[28] As early as St Augustine's *De Trinitate* there was an attempt to find the Trinitarian relations themselves within the self, and to see the soul itself as consisting of memory, understanding and will. Maistre quotes from Augustine's *Confessions* in locating a Christian basis for the doubled subject: '*How much difference there is between* MYSELF *and* MYSELF.'[29] The gothic novel's turn inwards therefore, takes it back into traditional theological understandings of the self as well as anticipations of Freudian psychology. And it finds there models of exchange and the positive double that can offer resistance to the ideological gothic castles of its own time.

Notes

1 Sigmund Freud, 'On the Uncanny', *Standard Edition of the Complete Psychological Works of Sigmund Freud,* ed. James Strachey, vol. 17 (1917–1919) (London: Hogarth Press, 1955), pp. 217–52.
2 See Fred Botting, *Gothic* (London: Routledge, 1996), pp. 140–6; Glenis Byrom, 'Gothic in the 1890s', in *A Companion to the Gothic,* ed. David Punter (Oxford: Blackwell Publishing, 2000), pp. 132–42; Astrid Schmid, *The Fear of the Other: Approaches to English Stories of the Double* (Bern and New York: Peter Lang, 1996). The most sophisticated studies of the gothic double are Karl Miller, *Doubles: Studies in Literary History* (Oxford: Oxford University Press, 1985) and Carl Keppler, *The Literature of the Second Self* (Tucson, AZ: University of Arizona, 1972). Keppler does discuss the positive salvific nature of a second self in relation to Poe's tale of William Wilson and Conrad's *Lord Jim.*
3 Joseph de Maistre, 'Enlightenment on Sacrifices', in *The Works of Joseph de Maistre,* trans. by Jack Lively (London: George Allen and Unwin, 1965), pp. 291–98 (p. 294).
4 Charles Maturin, *The Milesian Chief: A Romance,* 4 vols (London: Henry Colbourn, 1812), vol. 4, p. 94.
5 Charles Maturin, *Melmoth the Wanderer,* ed. by Douglas Grant, intro. by Chris Baldick (Oxford: Oxford University Press, 1989). All further references are to this edition and are noted in the text.
6 Charles Maturin, *Sermons* (Edinburgh: Constable, 1819), pp. 337–8.
7 Maistre, 'Enlightenment on Sacrifices', p. 294.
8 William Magee, *Discourses on the Scriptural Doctrines of Atonement and Sacrifice: With Additional Remarks on the Principal Arguments* (Dublin: Graisberry & Campbell, 1801).
9 René Girard, *The Scapegoat,* trans. by Yvonne Freccero (London: Athlone, 1986).
10 René Girard, *Violence and the Sacred,* trans. by Patrick Gregory (Baltimore, MD: Johns Hopkins University Press, 1977), pp. 143–68, has the clearest outline of the monstrous double and its relation to the sacrificial crisis.
11 Baldick's introduction to *Melmoth,* p. xii. See also Richard Haslam, 'Melmoth and the Calvinist Sublime', in *Gothic Origins and Innovations,* ed. by Allan Lloyd Smith and Victor Sage, Costerus New Series 91 (Amsterdam: Rodopi, 1994), pp. 44–56.
12 On Luther see David Scaer, 'The Concept of *Anfechtung* in Luther's Thought', *Concordia Theological Quarterly* 47 (1983): 28. On the anxiety of double election in Calvinism, see Barbara Lewalski, *Protestant Poetics and the Seventeenth-Century Religious Lyric* (Princeton, NJ: Princeton University Press, 1979).
13 Maistre, 'Enlightenment on Sacrifices', p. 288.
14 Charles Baudelaire, 'On the Essence of Laughter, and the Generation of the Comic

in the Plastic Arts', in *Selected Writings on Art and Literature*, trans. by P.E. Chavret (Harmondsworth: Penguin, 1972), pp. 140–61 (p. 145). Baudelaire actually uses Melmoth as an illustration of the way in which laughter marks a chasm in social relations, and separates one from another.
15 *The Complete Poetical Works of Lord Byron*, ed. by Jerome J. McGann (Oxford: Oxford University Press, 1983), vol. 4, p. 102.
16 Oscar Wilde, *The Picture of Dorian Gray*, ed. by Robert Mighall (Harmondsworth: Penguin, 2000). All further references are to this edition and are given in the text. Paradoxically, Wilde's eventual lover, Lord Alfred Douglas, otherwise known as Bosie, read the novel 'fourteen times running' and it was the reason for his desire to meet Wilde. See Richard Ellmann, *Oscar Wilde* (Harmondsworth: Penguin, 1988), p. 306.
17 The word is in constant use, for example on pp. 21, 56, 86, 124, 126, 137, 149, 152, 159, 211. On p. 159 it is linked to the dragging up a precipice for destruction that is another echo of the fate of Melmoth.
18 A part of the ribbon was attached to a rock before the goat was thrown down a ravine. The people waited to see if it would turn white, showing that their sins had been forgiven. See Yoma 6.6 in Jacob Neusner, *The Mishnah: A New Translation* (New Haven, CT: Yale University Press, 1988), p. 275.
19 Even this plot motif has its origin in Maturin. Armida in *The Milesian Chief*, vol. 2, p. 52, has this same problem. When she falls in love she can no longer perform in public with her former passion.
20 *Epistola: In Carcere et Vinculis* in *The Complete Works of Oscar Wilde*, ed. by Ian Small (Oxford: Oxford University Press: 2003–), vol. 2, p. 44. This edition gives separate titles to the original version of *De Profundis* as a letter to Douglas entitled, *In Carcere et Vinculis* and the essay, *De Profundis*, which other editions subsume under the latter title.
21 Joris-Karl Huysmans, *The Damned (Là-Bas)*, trans. by Terry Hale (Harmondsworth: Penguin, 2001), especially pp. 45–6 on Retz's motivation.
22 Wilde, *Epistola*, p. 43.
23 Wilde, *In Carcere*, pp. 73–4. Alonzo's mimicry of the violent actions of the Madrid crowd seems to be a source for this figure.
24 Wilde, *In Carcere*, p. 113.
25 This is the whole argument of *I See Satan Falling like Lightning*, trans. by James G. Williams (New York: Orbis, 2001).
26 William Butler Yeats, *Cathleen ni Hoolihan: A Play in One Act and in Prose* (London: Caradoc Press, 1902).
27 Robert Louis Stevenson, *The Strange Case of Dr Jekyll and Mr Hyde*, ed. by Martin A. Danahay (Peterborough, Ontario: Broadview Press, 1999), p. 76.
28 Quoted by Freud in 'On the Uncanny', p. 219.
29 Maistre, 'Enlightenment on Sacrifices', p. 291.

8. Church Architecture, Tractarian Poetry and the Forms of Faith

Kirstie Blair

In the introduction to his 1844 volume, *The Baptistery*, a work that was to become one of the most successful and widely disseminated collections of Tractarian poetry, Isaac Williams noted the impact that a decade of activism and excitement had had on the Church of England:

> The Church, 'tis thought, is wakening through the land,
> And seeking vent for the o'erloaded hearts
> Which she has kindled – pours her forth anew –
> Breathes life in ancient worship, – from their graves
> Summons the slumbering Arts to wait on her,
> Music and Architecture, varied forms
> Of Painting, Sculpture and of Poetry.[1]

Williams' suggestion that the 'o'erloaded hearts' of worshippers require 'vent' through the medium of art borrows directly from John Keble's analysis, as aired in his lectures as Oxford Professor of Poetry, of poetry as a 'safety-valve' for the release of dangerously overloaded feelings.[2] The varied forms of Art here allow agitated worshippers to find a productive outlet for their newfound engagement with the Church. In classing music, architecture, painting, sculpture and poetry together, Williams reminds his readers of the innovative developments in church music, such as the increasing use of surpliced lay choirs; the new focus on proper ornamentation and decoration of churches; the interest in religious art fostered by the German Nazarene painters and about to be taken up by the Pre-Raphaelites; and the impact of poetry such as Keble's *The Christian Year* (1827), already well established as a classic by 1844. Perhaps most importantly, he hints at the architectural revival that was underway, and that was to change decisively not only the appearance of churches but the nature of the worship that took place within them. Few writers engaged in the gothic revival would have disputed that architecture, at least in relation to religion, 'slumbered' before the twin powers of the Cambridge Camden Society and the Oxford Movement, assisted by the writings of Pugin and, later, Ruskin, awakened it. In the 1830s and 1840s, church architecture came to be seen as a major power in shaping belief. But it gained this status precisely because it was not perceived as separate from the other arts. Architecture, poetry, music, painting and sculpture were all formal ways of representing, creating and channelling faith. The first three in particular relied upon formal structures, whether of poetic or musical metre or of the geometrical harmonies of lines and arches, to create their effects. As this chapter will argue, several fundamental issues linked religious poetry and architecture in particular as key sites for forming belief. The importance of regulated structures, the use or abuse of symbolism and the centrality of reserve as a theological principle were intensively discussed by writers in both fields and were to prove hugely controversial. Works such as Isaac Williams' *The Cathedral* (1838), a series of poems taking the reader on a guided tour of a cathedral that is both a material building and a spiritual concept, or John Ruskin's *Seven Lamps of Architecture* (1849), may come from very different theological perspectives, but they both fundamentally uphold the view that poetry is architectural just as architecture is poetical.

The revival of church architecture can be roughly dated from the publication of Augustus Pugin's *Contrasts* in 1836 and the foundation of the Cambridge Camden Society in 1839. Pugin's volume created 'something entirely new: a link between an architectural style and a moral obligation', and it did so with particular regard to religious architecture, arguing that the finest aspects of gothic architecture would be pointless, like the 'scattered leaves of a precious volume that have been bound up by an unskilful hand, without connexion or relation to their meaning', unless they were incorporated in a Catholic church and designed to enhance Catholic worship.[3] Such comments were to transform 'architectural practice and criticism into a battleground and [...] each building into a political or theological manifesto.'[4] All Christian architecture, Pugin argued in his opening gambit, represents '*the faith of Christianity embodied, and its properties illustrated*' (*Contrasts*, p. 2). His Roman Catholicism (he converted in 1835) created difficulties for High Church Anglicans, but he was nonetheless deeply influential on their writings. The Cambridge Camden Society, founded by enthusiastic undergraduates with the purpose of drawing attention to neglected churches and aiding in their restoration, embraced Pugin's passion for medieval gothic wholeheartedly and shared his views on the vital purpose of symbolism in religious architecture. The society and its periodical, *The Ecclesiologist*, founded in 1841, rapidly became authorities and arbiters in a growing field. Its de facto leaders and founders, John Mason Neale and Benjamin Webb, reached an extremely wide audience through Neale's tracts *A Few Words to Churchwardens* and *A Few Words to Church Builders*.[5] The Camdenites' views on church architecture, based on what they conceived as the purest gothic ideal, were founded on the notion that, as Pugin wrote in *The True Principles of Pointed or Christian Architecture*, 'the smallest detail should *have a meaning or serve a purpose*': every aspect of church architecture, no matter how small, had its part to play in the symbolism of the building as a whole.[6] While this led to enormously detailed arguments over minor architectural features or points of arrangement and decoration, the society – or at least Neale as its leading publicist – also advocated some central principles, primarily that every church should have a separate chancel, dividing the priest and the altar from the body of the church, and that ideally churches should have rood-screens to preserve the sense of holy mystery connected with the performance of the sacraments. In addition, the Camden Society fought (and largely won) a prolonged battle over enclosed pews and galleries, preferring the more democratic use of open benches.

What Neale, Webb and their associates gave to the early Victorian church was a sense of the building itself as a site for devotion and reverence, which should be treated with awe and respect. Neale wrote of his horror in one church 'when the Churchwarden, wanting to open the east window, got up on the Altar!'[7] Reports by members of the society, who 'took' churches by completing a detailed architectural scheme, followed Pugin in emphasizing the decay and neglect of parish churches and the cavalier treatment of religious and historical artefacts by their guardians. For the Camden Society, architecture and church ornamentation were not adjuncts to faith but essential components of it, possessed of mystical and symbolical importance in leading the mind to God. As Neale's daughter wrote in her memoir of him, they sought 'once more to discover the angel in the stone'.[8] An 1840 report from the society, for instance, warns that neglecting to arrange churches properly will lead 'in some degree to a disregard of ordinances or devotional feelings which such arrangements were calculated to consecrate and promote'.[9] 'Calculated' is the key word here, since it incorporates the Camdenites' primary belief that every aspect of a church was designed to work in harmony with the services performed within it and to promote faith. Building a church without central and side aisles, for instance, would deny the worshipper the chance to gain instruction, since: 'In the symbolical system before adverted to the doctrine of the MOST HOLY AND UNDIVIDED TRINITY was set forth by the three parallel divisions meeting the worshipper as he entered the church at the west.'[10] Failing to install stained-glass windows, or to place the baptismal font at the entrance to the church, or to include gothic arches (popularly understood as symbols of the resurrection), would represent a loss of the 'deep symbolism' essential to the management of faith.[11] The proper affect could only be created by the proper architecture, by the correct integration of form and feeling. In this regard as well as in the use of symbolism, Neale and Webb argued, 'Architecture [...] *is* a branch of poesy.'[12]

The Cambridge ecclesiologists traced their inspiration in part to the ferment caused by *Tracts for the Times* (1833–1841) and to the general enthusiasm for the new ideals proposed by Oxford churchmen. Patrick concludes in his excellent study of Newman and Pugin that between the Oxford and Cambridge movements there was 'if not a causal link, at least deep sympathy', and James F. White notes that Webb was an immense fan of Keble's poetry and that A.J.B. Hope, who later became chairman and then president of the Camden Society in the 1840s and 1850s and was one of its leading lights, hero-worshipped Newman and the poet Frederick Faber.[13] Neale, while he expressed some doubts about the Oxford Movement, was happy to discuss his work on William Durandus (a well-known medieval liturgical writer) and church symbolism with Pusey in 1844 and knew, or knew of, Isaac Williams enough to express anxiety about his near-fatal illness in 1846. He also later collaborated with Keble in compiling a hymn-book.[14] When he stated to Webb that 'It is clear to me that the Tract writers missed one great principle, namely the influence of Aestheticks', Neale evidently saw the Oxford leaders as focused on theological precedent and tradition and the examination of internal justification for faith to the detriment of external, aesthetic, aids to faith.[15] But this is slightly disingenuous. Critics at the time clearly linked the two movements, seeing the church restorations of the Cambridge group as embodiments of the theological tenets of Oxford.[16] Keble's contribution to *Tracts for the Times* on symbolism – one of the most controversial topics – for instance, and Williams' two contributions entitled 'On Reserve in Communicating Religious Knowledge', both argued for the importance of concepts that Neale and Webb were championing with application to architecture. Moreover, some of the most important works associated with the Tractarian movement, particularly poetry by Keble,

Church Architecture, Poetry and the Forms of Faith 133

Williams and Faber, argue implicitly for the vital importance of religious aesthetics not only in their content but through their very existence. This poetry enacted theological principles and helped to produce the appropriate 'sober state of feeling' in a Christian reader, thus acting in precisely the same way as Neale's ideal church.[17] Moreover, these writers and Newman, if not perhaps devoting the level of attention to ecclesiological detail and church-building that Neale desired, were still very much involved with it.

Williams' *The Cathedral*, which, as G.B. Tennyson noted in his foundational work on Tractarian poetry, 'makes unmistakably clear the connection between a Gothic church and devotional feeling' is undoubtedly the most important work with respect to poetry and church architecture, but it is by no means an isolated example.[18] In poetry, Keble is Williams' most important contemporary, since *The Christian Year* not only became a manual for devoted Anglican clergymen, but Keble's personal life as vicar of Hursley also came to serve as a model of how the perfect country pastor would behave. *The Christian Year* is considerably more concerned with the state of the Church in an era of political uncertainty and doubt than it is about the state of church-buildings. In poems such as 'Trinity Sunday', however, Keble's vision of security within the church is associated with the apprehension of a building that is both actual and material and charged with mysticism and spirituality. 'Trinity Sunday', the poem which closed the first volume of *The Christian Year* and thus was placed in a central position in relation to the work as a whole, opens with the speaker pausing to look back over the past year ('Trinity Sunday', *The Christian Year*, vol. 1, p. 198):

> Along the Church's central space
> The sacred weeks, with unfelt pace,
> Have borne us on from grace to grace.

Movement through time (*The Christian Year* requires the reader to read its poems in order, as they follow the sequence of the church year) is here elided with movement through space, as the progress of the Christian year becomes metaphorically linked to the progress of a worshipper in a church towards the shrine. That 'central space', which produces an odd effect of displacement and dislocation if read as an imaginative space of time inhabited by the Church of England, makes sense as a physical space, the central aisle of a church. Keble extends the metaphor in succeeding stanzas, where the soul draws 'nearer to Thy shrine', before the poem seems to shift decisively into the representation of a physical church ('Trinity Sunday, pp. 199–200):

> And now before the choir we pause.
>
> The door is clos'd – but soft and deep
> Around the awful arches sweep
> Such airs as soothe a hermit's sleep.
>
> From each carv'd nook and fretted bend
> Cornice and gallery seem to send
> Tones that with seraph hymns might blend.
>
> Three solemn parts together twine
> In harmony's mysterious line;
> Three solemn aisles approach the shrine:
>
> Yet all are One – together all,
> In thoughts that awe but not appal,
> Teach the adoring heart to fall.
>
> Within these walls each fluttering guest
> Is gently lur'd to one safe nest –
> Without, 'tis moaning and unrest.

Keble's worshipper is apparently located outside the sanctuary, reverently hesitant to enter the chancel and approach the altar. As such, he conforms to the ecclesiologists' later emphasis on preserving a sense of holy mystery by screening or enclosing the most sacred spaces of the church. The symbolical structure of this mystical building is evident both in the three aisles, which, as in Neale's comments, clearly recall the Trinity, and in the 'three parts' which form one line – a line of music, but also suggestively the poetic line and the line of gothic architecture, as the sweeping arches and ornamentation seem to produce and blend with this music. These tripartite forms are of course confirmed and embodied in the three-line stanzas with their confident end-rhymes. Music, architecture and poetry join forces here to create a distinctly aesthetic effect that is also deeply spiritual.

As always in Keble's poetry, the forms and rituals of the church offer a means to soothe the worshipper and provide respite from the world outside. Other Tractarian poetry follows a similar line in representing churches as almost organic beings. Frederick Faber's 'St Mary's At Night' from his book of Oxford poems, *The Cherwell Water-Lily* (1840), for instance, includes the description:

> Steeped in the shades of night thou art unseen,
> All save thy fretted tower, and airy spire
> That travels upwards to yon blue serene,
> Like a mighty altar-fire;
>
> For wavy streams of moonlight creep and move
> Through little arches and o'er sculptures rare,

> So lifelike one might deem that Angels love
> To come and cluster there.[19]

The trope of angels clustering in silent churches was, according to Williams, a received notion, and appears in Keble's sequence of poems on church-going in *Lyra Innocentium* (1846).[20] The tower of St Mary's here, reaching to the heavens, again symbolizes man's aspiration, and as the moonlight streams through the church, the sculptures seem almost alive.

Keble's sense of the importance of proper church architecture, layout and ornamentation was strong enough that when he became the incumbent at Hursley in 1836, he found the eighteenth-century arrangements of the parish church 'painfully unsatisfactory' to the extent of causing 'irreverence and other mischiefs', and promptly set about a decade-long project of rebuilding financed by the proceeds from *The Christian Year* and its successor, *Lyra Innocentium*.[21] Keble used an architect recommended by the Camden Society, J.P. Harrison, and eventually called in William Butterfield to help with the designs for the stained-glass windows, producing a church that was a model of what a dedicated (and wealthy) Anglican clergyman could achieve. As J.T. Coleridge, Keble's friend and biographer, observed: 'Everything, from the first materials to the last finish even of the minutest article in the ornamentation, had his personal care bestowed upon it.'[22] Meanwhile, in the nearby parish of Bisley, John Keble's brother Thomas had also been engaged in various church-building projects along with his close friend and sometime curate Isaac Williams. Williams' twentieth-century biographer notes, 'he was never too busy to take an interest in the building or restoring of a church, and he was frequently consulted in such matters by his friends, among whom he had some reputation as an ecclesiologist'.[23] In their home parish in Wales, Williams' brother built a church lavishly praised by *The Ecclesiologist* as 'one of the most complete and successful imitations of ancient models that the present age has produced', while Williams assisted in church-building at Bussage (with Harrison as architect) and materially supported and befriended the curate of that parish, Robert Suckling, who was censured by his bishop for his activities in the Camden Society.[24] Most significantly, Williams was one of the founders of the Oxford Architectural Society in February 1839. Although it did not share the Cambridge Camden Society's specific interest in church architecture, it nonetheless 'wielded considerable power' in the field, and was often mentioned in the same context by admirers or critics.[25]

Williams had also, of course, served as Newman's curate at Littlemore, another new model church characterized by Patrick as 'the building in which Tractarian theology, the Gothic revival, and Pugin's theorizing were first conjoined.'[26] Newman denied an interest in church restoration after his 1845 conversion and, as Patrick has brilliantly examined, entered into a bitter controversy with Pugin. Yet his earlier sermons, preached in Oxford in the late 1830s and 1840s, as well as articles published in the *British Critic* under his editorship, reveal a clear interest in the ongoing excitement about church architecture and the gothic. In 'The Visible Church an Encouragement to Faith', Newman observes that 'The very disposition of the building, the subdued light, the aisles, the Altar, with its pious adornments, are figures of things unseen, and stimulate our fainting faith.'[27] 'The Visible Temple', preached several years later, comments strongly on how neglecting the visible church damages faith:

> When we go into certain Churches and see the neglected state in which they are left, the font cast aside, or, if not, used as a place to keep any sort of litter in; and the holy Table mean and unsightly [...] I say, when these and such like sights meet us, perhaps, for an instant, we are tempted to say 'Can Christ be here?'[28]

This is very reminiscent of Pugin's disgust at such neglect in his works.[29] Whatever Newman came to believe in later years, his sermons from this period uphold the idea that the proper 'disposition' of churches is essential to create a proper disposition towards faith in the worshipper, that churches should be read symbolically, and that by taking part in building a new church 'ye have been admitted to the truest symbol of God's eternity'.[30]

When Williams published *The Cathedral* in 1838, then, he and his contemporaries were already part of the dynamic revival of interest in church architecture, and the collection could hardly have failed to be read in the light of the events and publications immediately succeeding it. Williams' later status as something of an expert on architectural matters, indeed, no doubt owes a good deal to this work. The subtitle, *The Catholic and Apostolic Church in England*, would have immediately made Williams' alliance to the Tractarians and their take on church tradition clear, and thus deliberately invites controversy. In the only recent critical discussion of *The Cathedral*, Rodney Stenning Edgecombe provides an excellent assessment of its relation to George Herbert's *The Temple* (which Williams cites as an influence along with Wordsworth's famous comment on *The Recluse* as a cathedral in his preface to *The Excursion*), arguing that Williams creates a 'compound familiar ghost', a cathedral that is both solid and etherealized, patched together out of fragments of real buildings.³¹ This is highlighted by the inclusion of a detailed floor-plan at the start of the volume and plates depicting interior and exterior views of a cathedral throughout; illustrations that give the illusion that Williams is describing a real place (and are pictures of actual English and French cathedrals) but do not include any identifications. Williams notes somewhat anxiously at one point:

> The exact uniformity and correspondence with which the two sides of the Nave have been constructed [...] may appear to be beyond the precision required from the example of any of our Cathedrals. But [...] the regularity at which Architecture aims might be more conducive to bring before the mind the end proposed by these associations.³²

This imaginary cathedral, this suggests, represents an ideal that real church-builders could only hope partially to achieve. Although, as Edgecombe observes, Williams seems to miss the point that the attraction to gothic lay partly in its *irregularity*, his desire to claim 'regularity' as the chief aim of architecture is a deliberate move to link architecture, as we will see, with his theological (and poetic) principles. Williams escorts the reader around the cathedral, but rather than attaching a descriptive poem to each feature, he reads the building itself in terms of church texts – hence the three aisles correspond to the Lord's Prayer, the Scripture and the Creed, the cloisters are represented by a series of ecclesiastical sonnets and the transepts become the Psalms. Williams thus clearly signals that the architectural features and the linguistic features of church worship are inseparable. While he does not attempt the kind of patterned verse of Herbert's 'The Altar', where the verse form mimics the shape of the object described, form in *The Cathedral* does have a strong relation to content and the verse, like the building, embodies the ideas it represents. 'The Doxology', for example, which opens with a paean to the 'threefold heavens [...] made One' (p. 67), is divided into three sections with three stanzas in each section, and each stanza, as in Keble's 'Trinity Sunday', has three rhyming lines. The octagonal shape of the Chapter House is mirrored by the eight poems on episcopacy Williams attaches to it, and he justifies this topic by suggesting that chapter houses are 'often supported by a single pillar, springing up in the centre, which might be taken as an emblem of the one Bishop' (p. 302). 'The North Porch' uses a regular iambic rhythm and ABBA rhyming stanzas to create a sense of enclosure, a small, carefully constructed space (p. 53). Williams lacks the skill of Tennyson or Browning in manipulating form to serve the poem's purposes, but the effort to do so is apparent throughout.

The Cathedral opens with a set of poems on 'The Approach' to the cathedral and on its right-hand and central doors, representing Repentance and Obedience. As the speaker enters through the central door, the awe-inspiring building itself seems to inspire obedience (p. 8):

> Ye cloistral shades and angel-haunted cells,
> Chantries, and tuneful roofs, and altars old,
> Where incommunicable Godhead dwells!
> Let your dread spirit fill me, my hand hold,
> And every thought to your obedience mould!
> While through the avenue of numbered years,
> As through a pillar'd vista, I behold,
> Where Christ for me the bleeding burden bears
> Till all my heart be love, and soul-constraining fears.

Writers on church architecture and its affect tended to focus in on the moment when the worshipper first enters a gothic cathedral and is overcome by sensory overload. Pugin opened *Contrasts* with this scene:

> What a burst of glory meets the eye, on entering a long majestic line of pillars rising into lofty and fretted vaulting. The eye is lost in the intricacies of the aisles and lateral chapels; each window beams with sacred instruction and sparkles with glowing and sacred tints [...]. Every capital and base are fashioned to represent some holy mystery.[33]

Neale and Webb closed their introduction to Durandus's work on symbolism with a similarly poetic passage: 'We enter. The triple breadth of Nave and Aisles, the triple height of Pier arch, Triforium, and Clerestory, the triple length of Choir, Transepts and Nave, again set forth the Holy Trinity. And what besides is there that does not tell of our Blessed Saviour?'[34]

Both studies, not to mention Ruskin's later use of the same imaginative trope, seek to make their reader imagine himself or herself seeing the interior of the cathedral from the entrance and immediately being affected, consciously or unconsciously, by the operation of its symbolism. Williams' account follows this pattern in that the atmosphere and structure of the cathedral communicate a sense of mingled dread and reassurance, but he differs somewhat in emphasizing the 'incommunicable' aspects of the cathedral and moving away from straightforward description of the scene. Time and space are elided as the actual 'pillar'd vista' stretching before the speaker as he looks towards the altar becomes a simile ('as through') for the acres of time between him and either the Crucifixion or the final resurrection of the dead. This 'Middle Door' is the place (p. 6):

> Where ancient Discipline
> Keeps watch, amid her treasures manifold,
> And welcomes to stern walls and dim cathedrals old.

II.
At her command the Apostolic key
Opens the solemn doors, in speaking stone
Her glories far withdraw, where none can see,
Seeking the Infinite in secret known,
And tell of wonders which surround his throne;
Her carved embroideries, which retire aloof,
Are ancient virtues, seen by God alone,
And his good Angels, mysteries learned by proof,
And prayers which hide from man o'er Heav'n's embowering roof.

No sooner are aspects of the cathedral called to our vision here than they recede from sight. The 'glories' of discipline incarnated in 'speaking stone' withdraw into secrecy; carvings tantalizingly 'retire' and prayers 'hide'. Williams is perhaps thinking of the fact that the 'speaking stone' of the cathedral often speaks where no-one can hear it. The 'carved embroideries' on the roof, for instance, are too high to be seen by man, just as man is also blind to the roof of Heaven. These hints of wonders which cannot be accessed by man's senses are part of the stern *disciplina arcani*, the notion that the most intimate secrets of faith should be hidden from those who have not yet attained the ability to understand them. This is the doctrine of Reserve, popularized (and made controversial) by Williams' Tracts on the subject.[35] The cathedral's symbolism, and the way in which only part of its glories are visible, make it evident that Williams represents the gothic church as reserve made manifest. His poems are often hesitant or evasive about actually describing what they see, focusing instead on the need to be subjected to 'duteous discipline' ('North Transept', p. 89), and to learn to read both ancient buildings and the traditional texts of the Church as 'embryo forms in secret' ('The North Aisle: The Lord's Prayer', p. 110) of God's grace. The real cathedral fades in and out of view. In 'The South Aisle: The Creed', Williams exhorts the reader ('The South Aisle: The Creed', pp. 142–3):

Go, stand beneath some minster tall,
Stretching in aisles majestical;
In branchings of embowering length,
And avenues of pillar'd strength,
Mid arch and pile aloft arrayed,
And clustering reach of vaulted shade
Dwarf'd to a speck man there doth stand,
Mid the colossal mountain band.
[...]
Thus, in Christ's holy Creed displayed,
Truth on eternal pillars laid,
World beyond world, end without end,
Doth over man her vastness bend.
[...]

> II.
> What is the long Cathedral glade,
> But Faith that in the structured shade,
> Herself embroiders to the sense.

At many points in *The Cathedral* (and in other writing on gothic architecture) the building becomes part of a sublime landscape: a mountain, a tree-lined glade. Again, the pillars here start as the literal pillars of the church and then slide into metaphors for the Creed. The first lines come closer than most poems in *The Cathedral* to describing the interior of the church, but halfway through this stanza the sense of physical location dissipates as the poem moves into a meditation on a text. The idea of '*structured* shade' in part II, and of faith as manifest to the sense in these structures, sums up Williams' argument. The indefinable faith of the worshipper is simultaneously given structure by participation in church rituals and traditions (such as reciting the Creed), by the sense of an overarching history, represented by Williams' poems on leading figures of the Anglican church, and by the structured setting in which it takes place. Each of these structures acts as a material representation of and container for immaterial faith. And since reading Williams' carefully patterned poems, with their strict adherence to form and metre, offers another way of participating in a structured activity, then the poems themselves work in the same way as the cathedral, drawing the reader into Christian obedience.

The Cathedral repeatedly returns to the importance of form. In the second of the ecclesiastical sonnets linked to the cloisters, 'Forms', Williams argues that the soul 'bound' by church traditions should 'her chain above all freedom prize' (p. 12), while in 'The Athanasian Creed' the reader is advised that the church's 'barriers' offer 'best liberty': only in the submission and acceptance of forms and rites passed down through generations can true freedom be found. Yet in *The Baptistery*, a collection considerably more anxious about how Williams' work might savour of Rome, he introduces a less confident analysis of the importance of forms through a prefatory dialogue between two voices:

> A. The Church with her deep mysteries and rites
> Portray'd in semblance of Cathedral aisles
> With pillar'd shades of stone, and cloistral walks
> Deadens and stiffens our expansive thoughts
> Of her ethereal essence, casing them
> In dead cold marble, every finite form
> That would set forth a nature infinite
> Must circumscribe it.

> B.   Yes, in that design
> Your argument was straiten'd to that mould,
> But so the Church is oft disclos'd to man,
> As a material Temple wrought of stones:
> Yet often as a glorious living Form.[36]

Looking back to *The Cathedral*, the first speaker worries that structuring meditations on faith round the form of the cathedral proved limiting and restrictive. In response, the second speaker argues that the 'glorious living Form' of the church is inevitably portrayed through narrow earthly forms, and that the concept of a church as a solid material building does not cancel out the idea of it as also an expansive, living spiritual body. Placing these lines in the context of the architectural debates of Williams' day, what is most striking about them is how much they echo a recurring concern about the relation between form and freedom, or life and law, in gothic architecture. This ongoing argument, moreover, was rehearsed in exactly the same terms with regard to poetics. As I have examined elsewhere, Tractarian poets were very interested in poetic form as containment or law, a 'straiten'd' mould for dangerously expansive emotions.[37] This was as much a theological tenet as a poetic one, and it was inherited to different degrees by later poets influenced by the Anglo-Catholic tradition, notably Matthew Arnold, Christina Rossetti and Gerard Manley Hopkins. If we add Coventry Patmore (another convert from Anglicanism to Roman Catholicism) to this list, then the way in which poetic form and architectural form remained intimately linked in writings on one or the other is clear, given that Patmore was a highly influential writer on both poetic metre – through his much-discussed 'Essay on English Metrical Law' – and on architecture, through his numerous periodical reviews.

Although the importance (or otherwise) of formal laws in gothic architecture was discussed by many writers, it was Ruskin who was to prove most influential. Ruskin's religious opinions were far removed from those of the Tractarians, and his work in the late 1840s and 1850s can be belligerently anti-Catholic, particularly in his somewhat disingenuous repudiation of Pugin's influence. But although Tim Hilton suggests that 'Ruskin […] had no interest whatsoever in the Tractarian debate', he evidently did have a strong interest in the revival of church architecture and was one of the early members of the Oxford Architectural Society.[38] *Seven Lamps of Architecture* is not far removed from High Church literature in its argument that 'Living Architecture' relies on the kind of variation within fixed limits evident in organic forms, an argument later expanded upon in *The Stones of Venice*

(1851–1853).[39] Ruskin comments on the importance of submitting to 'restraints' several times in *Seven Lamps*, and concludes that in architecture as in the natural world 'if there be any one principle more widely [...] than another imprinted on every atom [...] that principle is not Liberty, but Law'(*Seven Lamps*, p. 249).

Simply following rigid laws, however, is not enough – good architecture relies upon the ability to work within necessary constraints to create a vital organic whole infused with truth and beauty. For Ruskin, an analogy with poetic form seems the natural way to convey this idea. He argues that admiration of the workmanship of a building, for example, is false because mere skill in assembly: 'no more constitutes the true power of an architect, than the possession of a good ear for metre constitutes a poet; and every building whose excellence consists merely in the proportion of masses is to be considered as nothing more than an architectural doggerel' (*Seven Lamps*, p. 10). He uses the example of poetic metre again in writing to William White in 1868, when the latter had objected to Ruskin's apparent disdain for the laws of architectural proportion: 'What I mean is, that *cela va sans dire*. Get your poet, and of course he will make laws of metre [...] but the thing to be done is to get your nation into a musical or poetical mind, and no teaching of laws will help that.'[40] Metrical laws, Ruskin argues, underpin a poem just as fundamental laws of structure and proportion underpin the excesses of gothic. But the kind of awestruck emotional response he has in mind can only be created by a poem or building in which these laws are felt as natural restraints upon the vigorous life within.

It was left to Ruskin's close friend Coventry Patmore to elaborate on these principles in his reviews of Ruskin and others. Patmore's writings display a fascination with the question of 'the reconciliation of life and law' in gothic, arguing in an 1849 review of *Seven Lamps* and Neale and Webb's *Symbolism of Churches* that the crucial principle in ornamentation is 'THE GRACEFUL UNION OF A SPONTANEOUS ENERGY AND A RESTRAINING LAW'.[41] Patmore's emphasis on the need for 'regular forms' to check the 'natural energy' of gothic, and, most importantly, his acceptance of this as a religious principle in the case of gothic churches, symbolizing 'the infinite bounded and peacefully bounded by the finite' is profoundly Anglo-Catholic.[42] And like the Tractarian writers, he sees little difference between the formal constraints of architecture and of poetry. If, in a church 'Gothic foliage, again, always feels the law; though, so far from suffering thereby, it is, in its place, far more beautiful than nature'[43], then similarly, in a poem:

> The language should always seem to *feel*, though not to *suffer from* the bonds of verse. The very deformities produced [...] by the confinement of metre, are beautiful, exactly for the same reasons that in architecture justify the bossy Gothic foliage, so unlike Nature, and yet, indeed [...] so much more beautiful than Nature.[44]

Confinement to law in both cases produces more beautiful and meaningful results due to the tension produced by the interaction of energetic, expansive life and the laws which restrain it, a tension that frequently seems to lurk behind earlier Tractarian poems on church architecture.

Ruskin and Patmore's writings demonstrate how ecclesiological debates that had their roots in the specific theological and political contexts of the 1830s and 1840s, at the time when both these writers were starting their careers, could be broadened to hold implications for architecture, poetry and art more generally. Both authors, in their discussions of the gothic here and elsewhere, pick up on issues that can easily be perceived as extensions of theories common in Tractarian theology and poetics. From the late 1830s onwards, a curious undercurrent of religious thought linking church architecture and poetics runs beneath the architectonics of Victorian poetry, while the role of near-forgotten poets such as Isaac Williams in the later gothic revival in architecture deserves further recognition. The focus on the relation between form, content and affect in both kinds of art provides a microcosm for examining how early Victorian writers perceived the shaping of belief, and the shapes they made to create and sustain it.

Notes

1 Isaac Williams, *The Baptistery, or, The Way of Eternal Life* (Oxford: J.H. Parker, 1842), p. x.
2 *Keble's Lectures on Poetry, 1832–1841*, 2 vols, trans. by E.K. Francis (Oxford: Clarendon Press, 1912), vol. 1, p. 55.
3 A.W.N. Pugin, *Contrasts*, second edn (1841), in *Contrasts and the True Principles of Pointed or Christian Architecture*, intro. by Timothy Brittain-Catlin (Reading: Spire Books and the Pugin Society, 2003), pp. vii, 57. Further references to *Contrasts* are given in the text.
4 James Patrick, 'Newman, Pugin and Gothic', *Victorian Studies* 24 (1981): 185–207 (186).
5 James F. White, the leading historian of the Camden Society, notes that the first part of *A Few Words to Church Builders* sold 5000 copies in six weeks. See *The Cambridge Movement: The Ecclesiologists and the Gothic Revival* (Cambridge: Cambridge University Press, 1962), p. 115.
6 Pugin, *The True Principles of Pointed or Christian Architecture* (London: John Weale, 1841), p. 1.
7 Neale to his fiancée, 1842, in *Letters of John Mason Neale*, ed. by Mary Sackville Lawson (London: Longman, 1910), p. 37.

8   Eleanor A. Towle, *John Mason Neale D. D.: A Memoir* (London: Longman, 1906), p. 42
9   *Report of the Cambridge Camden Society for 1840, together with the Address Delivered by the President on Saturday March 28, 1840* (Cambridge: Camden Society, 1840), p. 7.
10   John Mason Neale, *A Few Words to Church Builders* (Cambridge: Cambridge University Press, 1842), p. 7.
11   Neale, *A Few Words to Church Builders*, p. 15.
12   Neale and Benjamin Webb, *The Symbolism of Churches and Church Ornaments: A Translation of the First Book of the Rationale Divinorum Officiorium by William Durandus* (Leeds: T.W. Green, 1843), p. xxiv.
13   Patrick, 'Newman, Pugin and Gothic', p. 816, and White, *The Cambridge Movement*, p. 27.
14   See *Letters of John Mason Neale*, p. 75, and Towle, *John Mason Neale D. D.: A Memoir*, pp. 135, 213.
15   To Benjamin Webb, 1844, *Letters of John Mason Neale*, p. 70.
16   A well-known example of this criticism is found in Francis Close's widely circulated pamphlet, *The Restoration of Popery* (1844): 'as Romanism is taught *Analytically* at Oxford, it is taught *Artistically* at Cambridge' (cited White, *The Cambridge Movement*, p. 142).
17   John Keble, *The Christian Year*, 2 vols (Oxford: J.H. Parker, 1827), Preface, vol. 1, p. i. All further references are given in the text.
18   G.B. Tennyson, *Victorian Devotional Poetry: The Tractarian Mode* (Cambridge, MA: Harvard University Press, 1981), p. 170. Tennyson's excellent chapter on Williams remains the best general critical discussion of his poetry.
19   Frederick Faber, *Poems*, seventh edn (New York: John Murphy, 1856), p. 155.
20   Isaac Williams, *The Cathedral, or the Catholic and Apostolic Church in England* (Oxford: John Henry Parker, 1838), p. 306. See Keble's 'The Empty Church and 'Carved Angels', in which he argues that angel carvings in the rafters of churches symbolize the real presence of child-like angels who help to lift worship towards heaven. *Lyra Innocentium* (Oxford: J.H. Parker, 1851), pp. 158, 162-4.
21   J.T. Coleridge, *Memoir of the Reverend John Keble*, 2 vols, third edn (Oxford: James Parker, 1870), vol. 2, pp. 285-8.
22   Coleridge, *Memoir of the Reverend John Keble*, p. 347.
23   O.W. Jones, *Isaac Williams and his Circle* (London: SPCK, 1971), p. 137.
24   Cited in Jones, *Isaac Williams and his Circle*, p. 96. See also pp. 80-1, 115-18.
25   See W.A. Pantin 'The Oxford Architectural and Historical Society, 1839-1939', read before the Society on 17 May 1939. Reprinted at http://www.oahs.org.uk/historyf.htm, last accessed 28 November 2007.
26   Patrick, 'Newman, Pugin and Gothic', p. 187.
27   J.H. Newman, *Parochial and Plain Sermons*, 8 vols (London: Rivington's, 1868), vol. 3, p. 251.
28   Newman, *Parochial and Plain Sermons*, vol. 6, p. 292.
29   See, for instance, *Contrasts*, p. 75: 'The state of fonts require particular investigation. In the parish church of St Helen's, York, on the 1st of May 1841, the contents of the font were as follows: three dusters, a sponge, a hammer, several pieces of old rope, some portions of old books, a hand broom, several tin candle sockets and candle ends, besides a large deposit of dirt.'
30   Newman, 'The Gospel Palaces', *Parochial and Plain Sermons*, vol. 6, p. 273.
31   Rodney Stenning Edgecombe, 'Allegorical Topography and the Experience of Space in Isaac Williams's Cathedral', *English Studies* 80 (1999): 224-38 (230).
32   Concluding notes, *The Cathedral*, p. 304. All further references given in the text.

33 *Contrasts*, p. 4.
34 Neale and Webb, *Symbolism of Churches*, p. cxxx.
35 Williams' argument was controversial because it implied that the truths of Christianity should be kept hidden from those who were not capable of appreciating them, rather than being accessible to all. In terms of poetry, 'reserve' came to stand for the practice of concealing or avoiding the revelation of personal feeling. On the theory of Reserve and Williams' use of it in *The Cathedral*, see Tennyson, *Victorian Devotional Poetry*, pp. 142–8 and 162–3.
36 'Prefatory Thoughts: A Dialogue', *The Baptistery*, p. vii.
37 See Kirstie Blair, 'John Keble and the Rhythm of Faith', *Essays in Criticism* 53 (2003): 129–51.
38 Tim Hilton, *John Ruskin: The Early Years* (New Haven, CT: Yale University Press, 1985), p. 50. See also Michael W. Brooks, *John Ruskin and Victorian Architecture* (New Brunswick, NJ: Rutgers University Press, 1987), p. 13. Brooks notes that Ruskin's claim never to have read any Pugin, for instance, is belied by his ownership of an annotated copy of *True Principles* (p. 49).
39 John Ruskin, *Seven Lamps of Architecture*, in *The Works of John Ruskin*, 39 vols, ed. by E.T. Cook and Alexander Wedderburn (London: George Allen, 1909), vol. 8, p. 203.
40 Cited Brooks, *John Ruskin and Victorian Architecture*, p. 31.
41 Coventry Patmore, 'Architectural Styles', in *Principle in Art*, second edn (London: George Bell, 1890), pp. 160–201 (p. 192), and 'The Aesthetics of Gothic Architecture', *British Quarterly Review* 10 (1849): 46–74 (66). Patmore notes that 'Architectural Styles' is an elaboration of the ideas expressed in his early periodical articles. On these articles and Patmore's contribution to architectural criticism in general, see J. Mordaunt Crook, 'Coventry Patmore and the Aesthetics of Architecture', *Victorian Studies* 34 (1996): 519–43.
42 'Aesthetics of Gothic Architecture', p. 65 and 'Architectural Styles', p. 186.
43 Patmore, 'Architectural Styles', p. 193.
44 *Coventry Patmore's 'Essay on English Metrical Law': A Critical Edition with a Commentary*, ed. by Mary Augustine Roth (Washington, DC: Catholic University of America Press, 1961), p. 8.

III. Mediating Culture: Inscribing Democracy, Class and Social Identity

9. Caricature and Social Change 1820–1840: The March of Intellect Revisited

Brian Maidment

This essay is concerned with the representation in graphic satire of that complex of socio-cultural upheavals from the first forty years of the nineteenth century which were often summarized under the convenient abbreviation of the 'March of Intellect'. The March of Intellect was, and still is, a convenient shorthand term for a whole range of social and cultural shifts in the first half of the nineteenth century, centrally concerned with evolving technology, the growth of mass literacy and widening access to print culture, through which class structure, as much as the economic order, was being re-defined by education, invention and social aspiration. As well as a generalized term for change during this period, a kind of sceptical or doubting equivalent for 'progress', the March of Intellect both revealed itself in, and was substantially constructed by, a number of specific and discrete discourses.[1]

Such a far-reaching set of social changes fascinated caricaturists in the 1820s and 1830s. The social complexity of the March of Intellect coincided with, or perhaps required, a new visual language that focused on social interaction and diversity rather than on the failings of statesmen and the formulation of single-joke political caricatures that had characterized the mainstream of late-eighteenth-century caricature, and come to a natural halt in the lithographed work of John Doyle in the reign of William IV.

All the best known and established caricaturists of the 1820s and 1830s drew spectacular, engraved or etched large plate March of Intellect images.[2] William Heath, Henry Heath, George Cruikshank and Robert Seymour all produced large crowded images of the March of Intellect on large format etched or engraved single sheets. The importance of these images has long been acknowledged by social and art historians.[3] They are of widely acknowledged significance both in capturing a moment of profound social change and in marking the shift from single-joke political caricature aimed at a relatively exclusive clientele to a broader appeal to anyone who might enjoy the vagaries and inversions of a 'world turned upside down'.⁴ Many of these images are crowded with detail, with emblematic micro-narratives, forming street dramas played out by artisans, tradesmen, working people – here a dustman, wandering into a genteel charity bazaar, tries to stuff a pineapple into his mouth whole, there a coachman engrossed in reading a periodical allows his horses to cause traffic chaos, echoing the careless trampling of a baby in another print due to a pedestrian's absorption in reading a self-improving book. These prints offer chaotic images of anxious energy and freakish innovation, of strange air-ships, of pneumatic transport, of luxurious commodities consumed even by the most vulgar, of even the most socially marginal attempting to enter, however ludicrously, mainstream print culture and civility. Many of the images used the central symptoms of the March of Intellect as a focus for their comedy, especially the generally assumed close connection between the growth of periodical literature such as *The Penny Magazine* and the more general political, economic and cultural aspirations of working people.⁵ Often structured through tropes of reversal (working people adopting the manners and practices of their social 'betters') and irruption (the trespass of the vulgar into the public and commercial spaces traditionally occupied only by the genteel or the aristocratic), these prints invoked the potential threat of a world turned upside down in which working people were neglecting their traditional economic and social deference in pursuit of a travestied version of genteel values and comforts. The central aim of these prints was, of course, to manage this sense of threatening change and reversal, acted out largely in public spaces, through recourse to a cathartic comic vision that drew heavily on the graphic and emblematic vocabulary of eighteenth century caricature. Along the way, in characteristically double-edged fashion, the parodic version of genteel culture being enacted amongst the vulgar also offered humorous comment on the pretensions and affectations of the middle classes.

But if these prints essentially represent the carnivalesque working out of middlebrow social anxieties about literacy and class mobility, something more ambiguous was also represented – a recognition of the need to incorporate and accommodate working people, however dirty, threatening and alien they might appear to be, into civility and productivity. The twin potentials of cultural attainment and economic success within the vulgar and socially liminal workforce could be seen as a necessary, progressive, even heroic 'march' towards a better society. If even the dustman, degraded and sullied by his trade, might be redeemed into civility and 'culture', then surely society was making considerable progress.

In this essay I want to step beyond these relatively well known images to look briefly and selectively at a mass of more obscure caricatures and comic images produced in new graphic forms, largely derived from wood engraving and lithography, and aimed more firmly at a new middlebrow audience. Such forms often used inventive new sub-genres (the mocking title page, the song book or the caricature magazine) and modes of publication/distribution (the series of 'jokes'), and focused attention away from public spaces and spectacular street occasions, drawing attention instead to domestic interiors, shops and the family occasions of urban tradesmen and working people. Caricature was a discourse that was itself going through major changes between 1820 and 1850, with traditionally genteel and elite discourses opening themselves up to a broader and less educated audience and shifting into mass-produced commodity culture. These proliferating new kinds of images, while often crudely drawn and simplistic one-joke prints, nonetheless offer a complex gloss on social change in the 1830s and 1840s.[6] Different in scale (comprising either single-octavo sheets or vignettes), in mode of production (wood engraving and lithography rather than etching or metal engraving, and often associated with texts like songbooks or comic magazines), and, perhaps and more difficult to evidence, in intended audience and readership, such images have largely been subjected to the scorn of cultural historians.[7]

The biggest cultural shift represented by these new kinds of prints however was a move away from the depiction of social change as essentially spectacular, acted out on the streets and in public events and manifestations, to a version of the March of Intellect that situated its manifestations primarily within the domestic interiors of urban tradespeople, in shops, or in the casual social activities of working men and women as they went about their daily routines. Indeed, it is possible to argue that the repeated representation of the March of Intellect, a product of the social anxieties of the new urban professions and the emergent middle classes, was a major factor in hastening the shift of focus in comic image making at this time from public to private, from the political to the socio-economic, from the ruling elite to the 'ordinary' citizen. In the many images of the March of Intellect embedded in the new comic print making genres of the period between 1820 and 1840 the domestic lives of the urban workforce – shopkeepers, sweeps, butchers, dustmen and their like – are fantasized out as a carnivalesque inquiry into the lives and ways of thinking among the previously mute and hidden working classes.

152 Shaping Belief

Such an inquiry pre-dated, but was in many ways parallel to, the emergent genres of urban reportage – the 'sketch' in particular – that characterized a shift towards urban investigation in the journalism and fiction of the 1830s and 1840s. Despite the use of a graphic vocabulary and a series of narrative tropes drawn from eighteenth century caricature conventions, nonetheless the countless lithographs and wood engravings produced between 1820 and 1840 for a broadly middlebrow marketplace represent a major shift in both how to picture and how to manage social change.

Such claims need evidence. To begin with a typical example of the new style March of Intellect images: 'I wont's summut what's sweeping in its hargyment' comprises a poem and a wood-engraved illustration, both small in scale and ambition, and taken from *The Comic Magazine*, a short-lived middlebrow comic journal from the 1830s (Fig. 9.1).[8] The level of the implied audience for this double page is difficult to assess. The image, despite the magazine's (almost certainly spurious) claims to printing 'numerous comic engravings by R. Cruikshank, etc.', is a crudely drawn if vigorous wood engraving filling the entire octavo page. At first glance the heaviness of the lines, the simplified body postures and the sketchily drawn, simplified background seem to allude more to a broadside or vernacular tradition of illustration. But, despite the large-scale and thickly linear drawing, this kind of image could be found in a refined form over and over again in the comic annuals, yearbooks and comic poems released by publishers such as William Kidd in the early 1830s. The most celebrated of these kinds of publications, which sought to broaden the market for visual culture, were Robert Cruikshank's collected *Facetiae* (a gathering of humorous poems with wood-engraved vignette illustrations, one of which, W.T. Moncrieff's mock-heroic *The March of Intellect*, is particularly relevant here)[9] and Thomas Hood's *Comic Annual*, which was successfully published right through the 1830s. The market for these kinds of publications, despite their apparent simplicity, appears to have been, if not genteel, then at least relatively sophisticated – presumably the tradespeople, professionals and middling classes (including women) who had never been able to afford the expensive single plate caricatures.

Here, some evidence of the implied audience for this image can be found in the interplay between the image and the accompanying verses, which contextualized, as well as supplying the tag-line for, the caricature. Under the deliberately ironized title of 'Sapphic', the verses dramatized and then moralized an exchange between a sweep and the

Caricature and Social Change 1820–1840   153

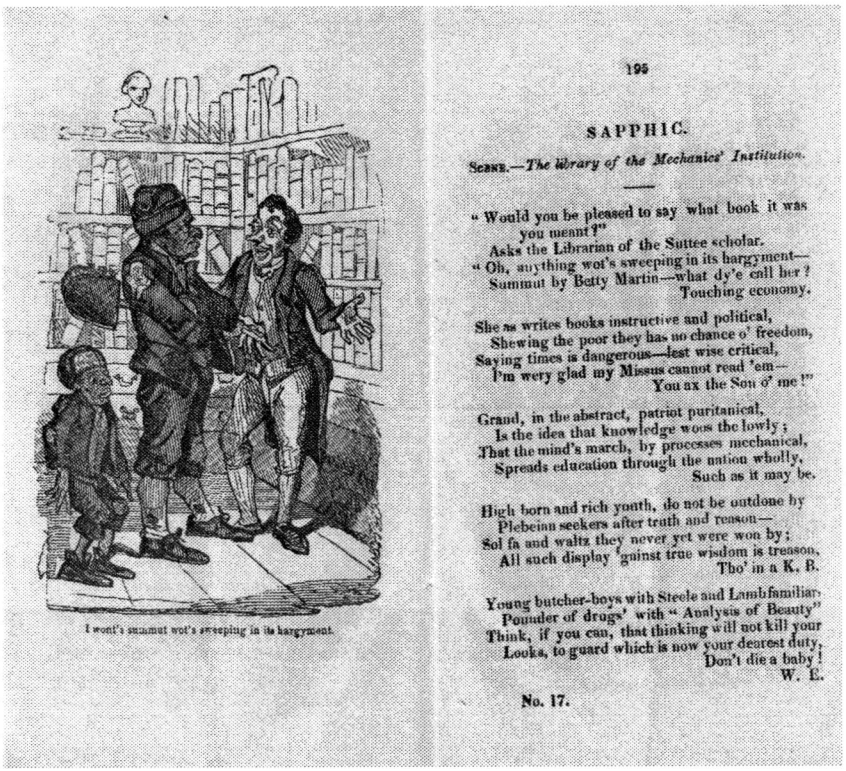

Figure 9.1. Anonymous wood engraving and accompanying poem by 'W.E.', in *The Comic Magazine* (London: W. Marshall, n.d.), no. 19, pp. 194–5

Librarian of a Mechanic's Institute. The sweep, accompanied by an apprehensive apprentice, who seems aghast at the temerity of his master and the grandeur of his surroundings, was in search of Harriet Martineau's work on political economy, although, in his ignorance, he could only muster 'Betty Martin' as the author's name. But if the sweep is unsure of whom he wants to read, he is pretty clear about the author's message – that in 'dangerous' or 'critical' times 'the poor they has no chance of freedom'. The first two verses of the poem dramatize the sweep's quest for book-learning in largely dismissive if humorous terms, underlined by the representation of his speech through the conventions always used after Pierce Egan's *Life in London* to suggest the plebeian Cockney.[10] The sweep is described, in the kind of elaborate pun entirely characteristic of Regency concepts of humour, as a 'Suttee scholar', thus combining the 'learned' meaning of Suttee (Indian suicide) with the derogatory vernacular – the sweep's appearance, and thus by implication, his understanding of the world, is 'sooty'. With unconscious humour, the sweep declares his interest in reading 'anything wot's sweeping in its hargyment', thus unknowingly entering a verbal play on his own occupation, a verbal play that became the punning caption to the image.

But the sustained, if relatively gentle, mockery of the sweep's ignorance and foolishly grand ambitions as a reader were quickly turned into another direction by both poem and image. The wood engraving defined the sweep in stereotypical gestures brought over from many similar caricature images of sweeps and dustmen. Both the sweep and his boy are, even given the representational limitations imposed by the blend of white page and black line of the wood engraving, clearly covered in soot, and thus not to be rubbed up against or, indeed, to be rubbed up the wrong way. The shovel, tucked under his arm, is a reminder of the secondary function of sweeps as night soil collectors. Combined with the solidity of his body, the folded arms, the inquisitive stare, and the aggressiveness of his stance with one foot firmly thrust forward, the sweep's dirtiness speaks of his presence in the Mechanic's Institute as to some extent an act of trespass, even an irruption. The Librarian, with his emollient spread-handed gesture, curly hair, cut-away coat and turned out feet, clearly represents the cultural values of the literate classes. Standing between the chimney-sweep and the shelves of books for loan, the Librarian is shown here as a gate-keeper to genteel book-learning.

But, as the poem made clear by a sudden turn in its argument, there is also something heroic as well as something threatening about the sweep's attempted engagement with Harriet Martineau's political economy. 'Grand, in the abstract [...]. Is the idea that knowledge woos the lowly' the poem declares in verse 3, thus giving the sweep's presence in the Mechanic's Institute a much wider socio-economic context and value. Admittedly, this heroic vision was partly undercut by the rhetorical appeal to the 'patriot puritanical' who has objected not just to the sweep's presence but more widely to the uppity ways of working men. The 'processes Mechanical', a further punning allusion to the diffusionist ideas of the SDUK and other propagandists for cultural change through the education of the working man, offered an ambiguous evaluation of the changes likely to be wrought by the March of Intellect. At this point the argument of the poem veers off again and addresses itself specifically to 'high born and rich youth' who were firmly told to abandon facile if fashionable accomplishments like dancing and singing for fear of being 'outdone' (an interesting choice of words) by 'plebeian seekers after truth and reason'. The rhyme word for 'reason' – 'treason' – reverberates with an echo of the discourses of philosophical radicalism, invoking the 'patriot puritanical' to fulfil his social obligations or to suffer the consequences. Suddenly, then, this becomes a debate about patriotic responsibility. For the 'high born' to neglect the pursuit of knowledge and 'true wisdom' is to cede the socio-political power to the sweep and his ilk, with all the social consequences that such a world turned upside down implied. Tradespeople, too, need to show a similar commitment to 'thinking'. Again using the carnivalesque pun as a medium – the butcher-boys' acquaintance with Steele and Lamb was not only a literary one – the poem concluded by authenticating the central project of the March of Intellect as one proper for, and indeed incumbent upon, all ranks of society. If the depicted chimney sweep's search for economic understanding looked more like a threat than a request, the wider quest for a more literate, more knowledgeable society run by 'wisdom' and 'thinking' remained an entirely worthy, patriotic and necessary one.

Many of the ideas worked through in this poem and illustration were used to structure a widespread debate about the March of Intellect within comic prints, songs and verses in the 1830s – the potential threat, yet heroic trajectory of the pursuit of knowledge within the traditionally illiterate urban working classes; the use of the visual/verbal pun as a central mode of negotiating between these polarities of threat and triumph; the situating of the contest over knowledge within the interiors of shops and houses rather than, as Seymour and his contemporaries had done, in highly scrutinizable public spaces; the centrality of particularly menial and contaminated tradespeople such as sweeps, draymen and dustmen to the pursuit of knowledge; the recognition that print culture was central to the wider aspirations of emergent artisans and workmen. Many prints concentrated on the most iconic symptoms of self-improvement culture as a matrix for their humour, especially the popular novel, the theatre, and, above all, the cheap illustrated periodical, a genre most obviously represented by *The Penny Magazine*. Images that worked through this complex of ideas can be found widely in all the available modes and genres of printmaking – in the albums that drew together the output of caricaturists into collections like Henry Heath's *Caricaturist's Scrapbook* or Robert Seymour's much reprinted *Sketches by Seymour* (Fig. 9.2);[11] in the early lithographed caricature periodicals like C.J. Grant's *Everybody's Album* (Figs 9.3 and 9.4);[12] in the short-lived burst of lithographed parodies of the title pages of contemporary periodicals,

156 *Shaping Belief*

Figure 9.2. Robert Seymour, 'Look Papa', from *Sketches by Seymour*, 5 vols (London: Robert Carlile, 1836), vol. 5, no. 36, 14 April 1836. Etching

especially *The Penny Magazine* (Figs 9.5 and 9.6); in the large-scale lithographed images of street life that had overtaken engraved single-plate political caricature in the 1830s as the most glamorous form of comic printmaking (Fig. 9.7); and in the remnants of the single-plate tradition, often reduced in size (Fig. 9.8) or shifted from etching to lithography as in Seymour's 'Rival Mags' (1832).[13]

Figure 9.3. C.J. Grant, a cut-down page from *Everybody's Album and Caricature Magazine* (London: Kendrick, 1834). Lithograph

158 *Shaping Belief*

Figure 9.4. A scrap from an unidentified album cut out from Grant, *Everybody's Album and Caricature Magazine*. Lithograph

Figure 9.5. Cut-down title page from C.J. Grant, *The Penny Magazine* 1 (London: Edward Lacey, n.d. [*c.* October 1832]). Lithograph

In a brief essay of this kind, it is possible only to offer some symptomatic moments from the prints. There were a number of images constructed very much along the pattern of the *Comic Magazine* illustration, discussed in detail above, where working men ventured into bookshops in pursuit of their cultural aspirations. All these images used dramatized class differences to be found in the dress, posture and formal

Figure 9.6. Anon. [C.J. Grant?], *Arithmetical Terms Being a Frontispiece to 'The Tutor's Assistant'* (London: no pub., n.d.). Lithograph

Figure 9.7. H.K., 'Reading and Understanding' (London: G.S. Tregear, n.d.). Lithograph

Figure 9.8. J.L. Marks, 'The march of Interlect or a Sweep & Family of the 19th Century' (London: J.L. Marks, n.d.). Engraving

structure of the image to construct ideas of threat.[14] Such threat was somewhat more complex than it seemed, incorporating the physical (burly, slouching labourers confronting effete, angular, overdressed and almost unanimously bespectacled), the cultural (self-educating labourers in lowly trades seeking the cultural appurtenances traditionally the preserve of the genteel) and, less obviously, the economic. These images suggested that the urban labour-force had become an important source of *consumers*, with even workers in the most degraded and socially undesirable trades able to afford luxury goods. Their role as consumers gave these assorted dustmen, sweeps, shoemakers and tailors an obvious power over the shopkeepers – their tastes and preferences, however philistine, had to be given respect if only for reasons to do with profit and loss. Even as the images mocked the tastes of the proletarian customer they acknowledged that the shopkeepers and sales assistants were bound to deference by the rules of commerce.

The shortcomings of proletarian reading habits formed an easy subject for satire. In one image a dustman and his boy responded to the punctiliously courteous request of the bookseller ('What shall I have the honor Gentlemen of selecting for your Evening studies?') with the blunt reply 'Let's have any thing wot's short and not werry dry'.[15] In another print a tearful dustman apologetically returns a half-finished novel with the unexpected comment that 'I'm wery sorry Sir to be so werry troublesom, but this 'ere Novel is to [sic] cutting, it as such afect on our nurves, so I vonts you to change it for something more Mild for I and my Sal can't stand it'.[16] An anonymous lithograph published by Thomas Lewis showed a tailor in a bookshop in quest of a 'book o' some sort for my boy' turning down helpfully offered volumes of travels, ancient history and geography in the hope of a *Pickwick*.[17] Yet if the lowbrow tastes of workmen readers were being satirized here, the images proved equally adept at mocking the pseudo-gentility of the shopkeepers in their exaggeratedly fashionable cut-away coats, absurdly high stocks and their coloured spectacles. Against the genteel affectations and cultural pretensions of the shopkeepers the honest vulgarity and lowbrow tastes of the workmen comes across as endearingly sincere, even heroic. Characteristically, satire of the cultural ambitions of working people here becomes implicated in an equally sustained critique of the supposedly genteel or polite manners manifested by those the workmen sought to emulate. Fig. 9.4 shows a shoemaker, tired of work at three in the afternoon, rehearsing his improving options – 'shall I go hear a lecture on physiology, astronomy or the Belles Lettres? Or shall I take a lesson in Dancing or the Piano Forte?'[18] At one level mocked for the absurdly ambitious and inappropriate activities available, not least through his physically unprepossessing appearance, nonetheless the shoemaker's dedication to self-betterment is ascribed a modicum of respect.

If bookshops provided one major site for the comic irruption of the proletariat into genteel culture in pursuit of self-improvement, other images were constructed round a variety of other cultural occasions. The Robert Cruikshank wood engraved frontispiece to W.T. Moncrieff's mock-heroic poem *The March of Intellect* showed a musing pipe-smoking dustman and a belligerent sweep's boy in the foreground of a sceptical crowd listening to a vigorous street oration on the philosophical radicalism of Paine and Cobbett.[19] Attendance at the theatre seemed to be even less conducive to workmen's self education. An 1835 lithograph showed a gormless-looking dustman leaning out of his theatre box to interrupt a dramatic performance with a bellowed request of the cast for something more to his taste – 'I say my fine uns, give us "All round my hat I vears a green Viller".'[20] A characteristically scathing small wood engraving, *The March of Knowledge* from the radical *Penny Satirist* suggested that, far from learning useful or improving lessons from attending the theatre, the audience, especially if young and impressionable, were rather taught the pleasures of criminality. In plays like the immensely popular *Jack Shepherd*, as one knowing juvenile notes 'only see how such coves are handled down to posterity, I thinks it's called, by means of books, and plays, and pictures'.[21] Seen from another perspective, then, entry into print culture could be seen as a mechanism for handing down all that was corrupting and vicious in society rather than a sign of socio-political progress.

In showing a group of roughneck children on their way home from the theatre, the *Penny Satirist* evoked a popular theme with comic artists of the time – how properly to educate children drawn from relatively vulgar backgrounds in the era of the March of Intellect. As suggested above, one dustman found his way into a bookshop to find suitable reading for his son, while another had his son with him, dressed as a perfect simulacrum of his father. Such a concern with the handing on of the cultural and educational ambitions of the urban workforce, however misconceived, took caricaturists into the domestic interior and assumed an interest in the politics of family life. Satirical formulations of this issue occur several times in *Seymour's Sketches*. In one plate (Fig. 9.2) a complacent lounging dustman, at ease with pipe and ale, is asked by his daughter, dressed in her dancing finery, to admire her latest balletic accomplishments. Generational shifts towards gentility, with all the potential contrasts between proletarian vulgarity and nouveau-riche ostentation that they offered, proved an excellent subject for caricaturists. The best known of these images, printed by Louis James in *Print and the People* alongside the text of Moncrieff's song 'The Literary Dustman' and cited by both Hancher and Maidment, offers a richly allusive version of this idea. An unreconstituted dustman, reading *The Penny Magazine* as an accompaniment to a quiet smoke, inhabits an overwrought and pretentious interior that includes such embellishment as an enormous silver monteith for cooling wine, a picture of the stage version of Pierce Egan's novel *Life in London* that showed Dusty Bob dancing with his black common-law wife, and a fortepiano on which his son is bashing out versions of contemporary opera tunes.[22] An even more spectacularly 'fashionable' proletarian interior is shown in 'The March of Interlect or a Sweep and Family', one of a pair of plates published by J.L. Marks (Fig. 9.8). In an absurd travesty of middle-class 'good taste', a dustman and his wife offer advice on good manners and proper conduct to their sons and daughters. It seems as if, for some travellers on the March of Intellect, only the absurd affectations and mannerisms of the wealthy classes are to be learnt. In a telling critique of experiential education, the sweep lolls smoking and reading a scientific treatise on cleaning chimneys while advising his two sons and apprentices to get on with the dirty work of sweeping flues without giving in to the contaminating pleasures of 'smutty' caricature shop windows. Once again, this is a print that suggests that reading and learning are, for tradespeople and workmen at least, a dereliction of their 'proper' duties. Characteristically, Marks' caricature mocks both the cultural pretensions engendered by the March of Intellect at the same time as satirising the tastes of just those social classes that working men aspire to join.

It has already been suggested that print culture, especially periodicals, formed a central site for the negotiation of the politics of the March of Intellect. Drawing on Seymour's original sketch of urban workmen in a coffee-house waiting, with some impatience, for copies of the newspapers to become available, several other caricaturists re-worked the same theme, in one instance abandoning the studious politeness of Seymour's image for a more disputatious scene in which an enfeebled gentleman's polite request of 'I'll thank you for the Times after you sir' is made in front of another smoulderingly ruffianly aspirant.[23] The March of Intellect clearly had its more fractious moments. One favourite joke, repeated in various ways, was the literalism of the newly literate, and the problems caused through failure to understand the complexity of double meanings. In 'Reading and Understanding' (Fig. 9.7) a ragged figure is confounded by the unrecognized distinction between 'whales' and 'Wales', and is thus rendered astonished by the idea of a 95-foot-long Prince of Wales. A more elaborate version of the same joke depicts two dustmen who have managed to penetrate into the realms of the political establishment in order to quiz Lord Brougham, the Whig Lord Chancellor who had been the driving force behind The Society for the Diffusion of Useful Knowledge and hence *The Penny Magazine*. The two grotesquely ingratiating dustmen explain that 've're a studying the Nat-ral history of the Seal in the Penny-Mag – vy ve just popp'd in d'ye see to ax your permission for to give us leave for to take a sight of the hanimal and to make a drawing of it for our private folios!'[24] The print also contains in its densely crowded captions some personal mockery of Brougham, but the substantial, and not unkindly drawn, interest is the ways in which the pursuit of knowledge can often lead to misunderstanding rather than enlightenment.

Apart from the large emblematic caricatures like Seymour's 1832 lithograph 'The March of Literature or The Rival Mags', or the same artist's violent critique of Brougham's cultural interventions in 'Penny Patent Knowledge Mill',[25] the most sustained critique of periodicals as engines of mass instruction was formed by a series of parodic title pages which enjoyed a brief but energetic popularity in the wake of the launch of *The Penny Magazine* in 1832. The sub-genre was initiated by the inventive and protean caricaturist C.J. Grant, never a man to be impressed with the cultural achievements of the urban working classes despite his radical political leanings.[26] Grant's particular scorn was reserved for *The Penny Magazine* not just because of the miscellaneity of its account of the understood world but also because it represented a diversionary ideological intervention by powers that Grant saw to have a vested interest in the political status quo. In the cultural battles over 'useful knowledge' Grant took the view of many of his progressive contemporaries that information could not necessarily be equated with understanding, and that 'really useful knowledge' might well result in a liberating form of social discontent. Grant drew and lithographed three pastiche title pages for *The Penny Magazine* (Fig. 9.6),[27] as well as a 'Frontispiece to Chambers's Information for the People'[28] and a 'Pictorial Companion to the Newspapers'.[29] Thus Grant established a briefly popular vogue (1832–1836) for comic title pages laid out as a grid of small usually lithographed images, an innovatory format that emphasized the miscellaneous accumulation of snippets that had come to characterize the new illustrated journals aimed at an artisan readership. In several places, these parodies directly mocked Brougham and his cultural polemics – 'vol. 1' of Grant's three images has as its centrepiece 'The Penny Trumpeter', a caricature of Lord Brougham in full Lord Chancellor dress, trumpeting the virtues of *The Penny Magazine* in the guise of a street ballad-seller. Elsewhere, the same plate offers mocking commentary on the cultural attainments of the working classes in the form of pointed contrasts between categories of knowledge and their joking manifestation in the everyday life of potential participants in the March of Intellect – a gardener pores over a treatise on botany to find out how to water his plants, the steersman of a rowing boat, absorbed in a book on navigation, steers his crew into a collision, and a delivery boy, careless of his surroundings due to his absorption in a book on physics, is about to prove the laws of gravity by falling down an entry. Several of the small images from Fig. 9.6 proved popular enough to be reprinted separately – Grant issued 'The Penny Trumpeter' as a separate political caricature, and the rather more genial image of a sweep's boy reading an improving magazine while perched on a chimney turned up, entirely unattributed, in *The Mirror of Literature and Amusement*.[30]

But if *The Penny Magazine* proved the easiest target,[31] other informative or improving periodicals were nearly as vulnerable to the caricaturist's ridicule. Grant moved on to *The Comic Almanac* (first published by T. Dawson in 1833 but reissued yearly with a changed date up to 1836) in which his satire was directed at a literary genre which has a particularly important place in the history of popular literacy. One key project of the Society for Diffusion of Useful Knowledge and its publisher Charles Knight had been the suppression of the immensely popular predictive and superstitious almanac in favour of an 'informative' publication, and Grant again seized on a controversial publication, caught between popular pleasure and rational reformist re-invention, in this image. The format caught on and proved amenable to caricature versions of a wide variety of 'informative' publications, not all of them aimed at working men and women. Orlando Hodgson published an undated 'Frontispiece to the Toastmaster' for example, where the satire was aimed at aspirant men about town rather than self-educating working people, and an anonymous and undated 'Frontispiece to Cumberland's British Theatre' mocked both the attractions of the popular stage and the vogue for printed play-texts. But the central focus was on self-improvement textbooks – Fig. 9.7 provided jokey illustrations of 'Arithmetical Terms' for example, and there was also a 'Parliamentary Terms', and a 'Frontispiece to the Musical Books'.

There is not space here to explore these images further and thus to evaluate the ways in which these crowded caricatures mediated the jokes and interests of Regency caricature into not just a new miniaturized format but also into the context of a wide-ranging and profound debate about the nature and significance of print culture. It is tempting to read these prints, and indeed all the images discussed here, as deeply reactionary in their social views, a sustained horrified response to, and rejection of, the possibility of a literate proletariat wealthy enough to become avid consumers, and seeking to improve their economic, cultural and social standing however misguided their chosen models of class aspiration might be. Yet I think they should rather be read as a much more open and accommodating discussion of the inevitability of a substantially and avidly literate society, and of the complexities of the politics of print culture. These prints recognize that print culture was at the same time being both contested and managed. They consider the legitimacy as well as the effrontery of a society in which dustmen read novels (even if they are short and 'not too dry') and sweeps' boys perch on chimney-tops reading *The Penny Magazine*. They also map out the ways in which the institutional and commercial exploitation of print culture in the 1830s particularly, most evidently manifested by the Society for the Diffusion of Useful Knowledge and its publications, affected the lives of working men and women. In these comic images, drawn as small-scale, often serialized publications using new-media-like lithography and the wood-engraved vignette, the domestic lives, personal ambitions and social potential of the urban workforce are fantasized out for the contemplation of a rapidly broadening consumer market for visual culture. For those who bought and enjoyed such images a traditional pleasure in old Regency jokes and visual puns was increasingly combined with a sustained set of representations of those complex social changes that were usually called the March of Intellect.

Notes

1 For the construction of the March of Intellect in relation to scientific and technological knowledge, see: J.R. Topham, 'The *Mirror of Literature, Amusement and Instruction* and Cheap Miscellanies in Early Nineteenth-Century Britain', in *Science in the Nineteenth Century Periodical: Reading the Magazine of Nature*, ed. by G. Cantor (Cambridge: Cambridge University Press, 2004), pp. 37–66; J.R. Topham 'Scientific Publishing and the Reading of Science in Nineteenth-Century Britain' in *Studies in the History and Philosophy of Science* 31 (2000): 559–612; Alan Rauch, *Useful Knowledge: The Victorians, Morality and the March of Intellect* (Durham, NC: Duke University Press, 2001). The implications of the March of Knowledge for print culture are, to name only a few obvious sources, considered by R.D. Altick, *The English Common Reader* (Chicago, IL: University of Chicago Press, 1957); R.K. Webb, *The British Working Class Reader 1790–1848* (London: George Allen & Unwin, 1955); Louis James, *Print and the People* (London: Allen Lane, 1976); Jonathan Rose, *The Intellectual Life of the British Working Classes* (New Haven, CT: Yale University Press, 2001); David Vincent, *Literacy and Popular Culture: England 1750–1914* (Cambridge: Cambridge University Press, 2001); Patricia Anderson, *The Printed Image and the Transformation of Popular Culture, 1790–1860* (Oxford: Clarendon Press, 1991); Valerie Gray, *Charles Knight: Editor, Publisher, Writer* (Aldershot: Ashgate, 2006). Much less is known about such discourses as song, even though a number of songs about the March of Intellect, such as 'The Literary Dustman', 'The Cockney University' and W.T. Moncrieff's mock-heroic verses 'The March of Intellect' were widely available in printed format as well as performance in the 1820s and 1830s.
2 Most of the key caricature images of the March of Intellect produced before 1832 are included in F.G. Stephens and Dorothy George, *British Museum Catalogue of Political and Personal Satires*, 11 vols (London: British Museum, 1870–1954). This catalogue will hereafter be abbreviated to *BMC*. For detailed descriptions

of March of Intellect caricatures in *BMC* see 15604; 15622; 15775; 15779; 15922; 15941; 16027; 16496; 16894; 17282; 17309; 17357.
3   Dorothy George's *Hogarth to Cruikshank*, first published in 1967 and several times reprinted, devotes several illustrated pages to March of Intellect prints and established their importance within the caricature canon. M.D. George, *Hogarth to Cruikshank: Social Change in Graphic Satire* (London: Viking, 1987), pp. 177–83. See also the Science and Society web site of The Science Museum, London, at www.scienceandsociety.co.uk, last accessed 28 November 2007.
4   Given the strict limitations of space in this essay, I have preferred to illustrate less well known images as part of an argument about the changing discourse of comic image making in this period. The key images can be viewed on the *BMC* microfilm, in George, *Hogarth to Cruikshank*, on www.scienceandsociety.co.uk and on the website of the Lewis Walpole Library of Yale University at www.library.yale.edu/walpole, last accessed 28 November 2007. All future references to the Lewis Walpole collection will be abbreviated to LWL followed by the call number.
5   B.E. Maidment, *Reading Popular Prints 1790–1870* (Manchester: Manchester University Press, 1996), chapter 3; B.E. Maidment, '"Penny" Wise, "Penny" Foolish – Popular Periodicals and the "March of Intellect" in the 1820s and 1830s', in L. Brake, B. Bell and D. Finkelstein (eds), *Nineteenth-Century Media and the Construction of Identities* (Basingstoke: Palgrave, 2000), pp. 104–21; and D. Hancher, 'From Street Ballad to Penny Magazine: "March of Intellect in the Butchering Line"', in Brake *et al.* (eds), *Nineteenth-Century Media*, pp. 93–103.
6   Dorothy George, in a generally withering account of the aesthetic shortcomings of these kinds of images, nonetheless acknowledges their significance for the social historian. See *BMC* vol. 11, p. xiii–xvii.
7   D. Kunzle, *The History of the Comic Strip: The Nineteenth Century* (Berkeley, CA: University of California Press, 1990), pp. 20–1.
8   *The Comic Magazine* was a weekly published by W. Marshall. It is undated, but must belong to the early 1830s.
9   R. Cruikshank, *Facetiae*, 2 vols (London: William Kidd, 1830).
10 Greg Dart, '"Flash Style"; Pierce Egan and Literary London, 1820–1828', *History Workshop Journal* 51 (2001): 180–205.
11 Henry Heath, *The Caricaturist's Scrapbook* (London: Robert Tyas, 1840). This anthology of Heath's various series of oblong-folio multi-image plates contained many images pertaining to the March of Intellect, especially the forty-eight images that made up 'Scenes in London'. *Sketches by Seymour*, initially issued in five volumes by Robert Carlile in 1836 and subsequently republished by G.S. Tregear, was later transformed by the addition of a linking, if picaresque text by A. Crowquill (Alfred Forrester), and turned into a chronicle of sporting adventures. The earlier image-only editions, however, had many March of Intellect images, including one plate (vol. 3, no. 15) which shows a weeping man fishing with his leg caught in a man-trap, together with a caption that states 'The Pursuit of Knowledge under Difficulties – Oh dear I only wanted to know if there vos any chub here'. Seymour was particularly amused by culturally ambitious dustman – in one image (vol. 5, no. 7), a disreputable-looking dustman has entered an extremely proper-looking music- and bookshop in pursuit of the popular ballad 'All Around My Hat', while another plate (Fig. 9.2) is built round an oft-repeated caricature trope of proletarian figures queuing up to read the paper or scientific reports in a low coffee shop.
12 *Everybody's Album* ran weekly from 1834 until 1835, published by Kendrick

and subsequently by Dawson. It proved an extremely popular source of scraps, and isolated images appear frequently in albums. The caricature of 'A Subscriber to the Penny Magazine' here is especially pertinent.
13. Maidment, *Reading Popular Prints*, chapter 3.
14. In one lithograph, 'Useful Knowledge', the shopkeeper is defensively located behind a panelled wooden counter. Anon., 'Useful Knowledge' (T.C. Lewis, n.d.). Lithograph, LWL 848.0.6.
15. Anonymous etching of unknown origin. (Author's collection.)
16. Anonymous engraving of unknown origin. (Author's collection.)
17. Anon., 'Useful Knowledge'.
18. C.J. Grant, *Everybody's Album* (1834). Lithograph.
19. W.T. Moncrieff, *The March of Intellect, a Comic Poem* (London: William Kidd, 1830).
20. W.N. (William Newman?), 'I say my fine uns....' (T. Dawson, 3 July 1835).
21. Anon. [C.J. Grant?], 'The March of Knowledge or Just Come from Seeing "Jack Sheppard"', *The Penny Satirist* (15 December 1839).
22. James, *Print and the People*, pp. 148–50; Hancher, 'From Street Ballad to Penny Magazine', p. 97; Maidment, *Reading Popular Prints*, pp. 81–90.
23. *Sketches by Seymour*, vol. 1, no. 10; Anon., *Tregear's Flights of Humour* 56 (G.S. Tregear, n.d.).
24. Anon., 'Fishing for the great Seal', *Sketches by Argus No. 9* (London: King, n.d.).
25. BMC 17267. See Maidment, '"Penny" Wise, "Penny" Foolish'.
26. For Grant see Richard Pound (ed.), *C.J. Grant's Political Drama: A Radical Satirist Rediscovered* (London: University College London, 1998).
27. The three images are not all dated, but the first is perhaps from October 1832, while the second can be firmly dated to 9 May 1833. Pound (ed.), *C.J. Grant's Political Drama*, pp. 120–4.
28. 21 June 1834. Pound (ed.), *C.J. Grant's Political Drama*, pp. 68–9.
29. 15 January 1835. Pound (ed.), *C.J. Grant's Political Drama*, pp. 58–9.
30. Pound (ed.), *C.J. Grant's Political Drama*, pp. 118–19.
31. See also Fig. 9.3 for another of Grant's satirical versions of *The Penny Magazine* and its readership.

10. Feeling '*Ghost*like': Carlyle and his Exposure to the 'Condition-of-England-Question'

Clare Williams

> He reminds me of that passage in Young's poems, where as Death presses closer and closer for his prey the Soul rushes hither and thither, appealing, shrieking, berating, to escape the general doom.[1]

Writing on the death of Thomas Carlyle in 1881, the American poet Walt Whitman remembered the great Victorian sage as a hysteric phantasm – an ominously haunting image of one who was celebrated by many as England's heroic man of letters, revered as a source of credible cultural authority in an increasingly industrialized, utilitarian and secular age. The Carlylean ethos of work of any kind being the means through which man could authentically realize himself as an autonomous, thinking and feeling individual had become part of an extremely influential and highly popular mythology that appeared to find its centre in the figure of Carlyle himself. 'There is no more notable working-man in England, in Manchester or Birmingham, or the mines round about', proclaimed fellow philosopher Henry David Thoreau. 'We know not how many hours a-day he toils, nor for what wages, exactly, we only know the results for us.'[2] However, while Carlyle certainly intended both his life and work to embody an ideal model of authenticity, his own endeavours to realize such a model often engendered a phantasmal sense of subjectivity from which he continually railed against. He experienced contemporary social relations in terms of an internecine impasse, and his inability to connect with society rendered him the saddest spectacle of all: a phantasm lacking the means of self-realization because bereft of any meaningful reference point in the present. So it was that, in 1837, he mournfully observed of himself in a letter to his close friend John Sterling 'There is no idler, sadder, quieter, more *ghost*like man in the world even now than I. Most weary, flat, stale seem to me all the electioneering and screeching and gibbering that the Earth is filled with, in these or indeed in any days.'[3] Paradoxically, the only way in which Carlyle could get beyond this '*ghost*like' state seemed to be to actively attempt to engage with the very contemporary society from which he observed himself alienated and rendered invisible. He had to directly confront the nemeses of himself within an immediate social context in which he felt his own subjectivity being conspicuously questioned, challenged, and tested. This essay is concerned with understanding such a phantasmal sense of subjectivity within the specific context of what Carlyle called the 'Condition-of-England-Question', which situated the social, cultural, and political state of the contemporary working classes at the centre of a radical critique of the current state of society itself. It was also a question which, while establishing for Carlyle a successful literary career with the publication of *Chartism* (1839), actually painfully exposed his real vulnerability as England's heroic man of letters to many of his readers and moreover, perhaps most detrimentally, to himself.

Carlyle's framework of secularized belief, which endeavoured to affirm the existence of some kind of divine mysticism in the external manifestations of nature, has been widely recognized as a paradox which bears within itself the seed of its own collapse. For as importantly observed by J. Hillis Miller, when one self-consciously relies upon the temporal to affirm the divine, one cannot help but suggest, 'whether one wishes to do so or not, that the whole structure may be a man-made fiction, not something based on eternal truth.'[4] When situating Carlyle's writings within the specific context of the Condition of England Question, such a philosophy appears in an extremely controversial light, where Carlyle has been criticized as a shrewd manipulator who deliberately created systems of belief through which hegemonic social, cultural and, needless to say, political relations could largely remain in tact. Yoon Sun Lee has interestingly argued that while Carlyle was all too aware that social order was ultimately dependent on the fictional constructs of fetishism, and subsequently adapted his own philosophy to found itself upon the infinite processes of human labour as opposed to the finite products of labour in themselves, he also intended such a renegotiated model of belief to primarily encourage submission as another form of fetish. Thus:

> Carlyle's success as a counter-revolutionary critic who ultimately wanted to preserve existing structures of authority depends on his conviction that knowledge and belief can be parallel ways of relating oneself to the same object. The object is the dynamic reality of human making behind the reified superficies of the present; but if *knowledge* of this history brings with it a degree of power, *belief* in this same object brings about, Carlyle suggests, a very different attitude of submission – something closer to deep and reverent passivity than to revolutionary agency. The makers of history – the workers

Carlyle and the 'Condition-of-England-Question' 173

of England – will surrender power to all that they have themselves made, illustrating precisely the dynamic of fetishism as Carlyle conceives of it.[5]

In a similar relation to the parallel Yoon Sun Lee sets up between belief and knowledge, Rob Breton has argued that Carlyle's 'Gospel of Work' established a necessarily undialectic relationship between the ideal of work (defined as relating to the spiritual act of work regardless of economic production) and the reality of labour (the mechanical act of labour within the system of economic exploitation). Breton argues that such a division enabled Carlyle to suppress the contemporary working classes by preaching to them a 'Gospel of Work' on the one hand, whilst also challenge the exploitative discourses of political economy and laissez-faire by directing a critique of labour at the bourgeoisie on the other.[6] However, if Carlyle deployed systems of belief in order to suppress working-class consciousness and largely maintain existing power relations in contemporary society, one must also recognize that such models were neither so easy to use nor so desirable to have because of Carlyle's subjective dependence upon this same social group and the painful struggles he encountered to authenticate himself in relation to them.

For Carlyle's struggle for power was always more to do with a crisis of subjectivity than any premeditated conspiracy to maintain existing power relations. In an fascinating attempt to understand Carlyle's subjective relationship with the contemporary working classes, John Plotz, in his study 'Jealousy of the Crowd in British Literature, 1800–1850',[7] has importantly argued that while Carlyle, in his essay *Chartism*, endeavoured to silence the articulate voice of Chartism, he was simultaneously aesthetically and politically jealous of what he conceived as the mysterious power of the crowd, which could crucially act as both signifier and signified, could be both subject and object in the same linguistic moment in a way that literature was unable to do. Thus Plotz observes:

> Such a truth can never exist in a narrative temporality, but only in the sort of temporal and spatial disruption that is promised by the very structure of the crowd itself. The crowd, which when it 'flares up' or 'breaks out' finds ways of melting many of the distinctions upon which conventional narrative depends: those between action and actor, between subject and object, even finally between space and time.[8]

Plotz argues that Carlyle was actually dependent upon the crowd for enabling him to create a form of language that could establish itself as a cultural authority not only over the crowd but also over the supposed socially, culturally and politically inert literature of the day. 'Interpreting Carlyle as the defender of rationalism in this text', he argues, 'requires deafness to the palpable pleas in the text for a power comparable to the power that crowds themselves have. The crowds are the muse of fire on which Carlyle's text means to rise, and that muse roars.'[9] But while Plotz shows Carlyle as successfully achieving such a dialectic between himself and the crowd, one has to question the actual validity and worth of such a success when viewed from the perspective of Carlyle himself all the while having to exist at some level outside of this specific 'temporal and spatial disruption'. Carlyle's subjective struggle with both himself and the contemporary working classes worked on many different interconnected layers of crises, and whether he managed, temporarily, to vicariously immerse himself in some kind of crowd aesthetics of the moment or was left wandering solitary yearning for some kind of external stimuli, he was always plagued, to varying extents, by the gnawing doubt that his writings were perhaps little more than phantasms after all, and that he was himself at best a phantom, at worst simply deluded.

Carlyle believed that man's engagement in the act of labour enabled him to become momentarily realized as a complete human being, a sense of entirety that was paradoxically only possible when the phantasmal presence of gnawing thoughts and feelings were finally silenced:

> Consider how, even in the meanest sorts of Labour, the whole soul of a man is composed into a kind of real harmony, the instant he sets himself to work! Doubt, Desire, Sorrow, Remorse, Indignation, Despair itself, all these like helldogs lie beleaguering the soul of the poor dayworker, as of every man: but he bends himself with free valour against his task, and all these are stilled, all these shrink murmuring far off into their caves. The man is now a man.[10]

Through his desired language of labour Carlyle endeavoured to subjectively realize such a state of completion for himself, but the problem was that his own writing of such a language not only failed to silence but even intensified the very doubts and fears that continued to dwell within him. That Carlyle endeavoured to see and believe in the working classes as being in tacit communication with nature and the mysterious silences of the universe was complicated by the fact that Carlyle himself wanted to authentically participate in such a communion from within rather than without. Nancy Armstrong has importantly shown how Carlyle, among other eminent literary figures, photographically represented themselves through 'the picturesque exterior of working-class physiognomy for the tormented masculinity of the Victorian intellectual'.[11] However, if Carlyle photographically adopted the rugged and world-weary face of working-class physiognomy in order to publicly represent his individual soul, he found it much more difficult to authentically become the very image through which he personally endeavoured to see and believe in himself.

Carlyle's writings appear to come closest to realizing this goal when he was able to vicariously see and feel himself as locating in the collective body of the working classes an innate human spirit that seemed both solid and real. Thus in *Chartism* Carlyle seemingly constructs the contemporary working classes as a massive product of intellectual labour in which he, as the consuming spectator, can apparently inhabit from the inside:

> There is in these latter, thank God, an ingenuity which is not false; a methodic spirit, of insight, if perseverant well-doing; a rationality and veracity which Nature with her truth does *not* disown: withal there is a 'Berserkir rage' in the heart of them which will prefer all things, including destruction and self destruction, to that. Let no man awaken it, this Berserkir Rage! Deep-hidden it lies, far down in the centre, like genial central-fire, with stratum after stratum of arrangement, traditional method, composed productiveness, all built above it, vivified and rendered fertile by it; justice, clearness, silence, perseverance, unhasting unresting diligence, hatred of disorder, hatred of injustice, which is the worst disorder, characterises this people; their inward fire we say, as all fire should be, is hidden at the centre Deep-hidden; but awakened, but immeasurable; – let no man awaken it![12]

Here Carlyle endows the working classes with a spiritual depth that is significantly objectified in terms of a great architectural structure, and as he pummels to the core of this structure, he is able to look up from within it to observe the many layers of being that emanate from its centre. While Carlyle cautions his readers against provoking this revolutionary core of human spirit in the working classes, he personally needs to see and write of this passion in order to vicariously participate in something that is authentic, alive, and palpable; and yet, it is also a passion that has been methodically built out of Carlyle's ordering syntax and hence becomes almost secondary because of Carlyle's very strenuous exertions to render it primary – even within the moment of such literary representations Carlyle cannot escape their literariness, their fictiveness. When one also considers what shadows plagued Carlyle's consciousness all the while outside of such vicarious, or at worst only ostensibly vicarious moments, one gains a greater sense of the meaning of Carlyle's struggle to write an authentic language which he could both see and feel himself to be authenticated.

Carlyle's *Chartism* occupies a somewhat privileged literary position as being the first book, written by an opponent of Chartism, to make the mass political movement the polemical subject of a complete work, providing a locatable forum in which the problem of social unrest could be debated within the overarching subtext of the Condition of England Question.[13] Friedrich Engels, in *The Condition of the Working Class in*

England, exhibited Carlyle as the one individual among the English bourgeoisie who, in his active criticisms of contemporary society, had surpassed the social and political efforts of both Chartist Radicals and Philanthropic Tories.[14] For other contemporary readers, Carlyle had presented a bewilderingly mystified representation of the contemporary working classes which was 'not always immediately perceptible to ordinary optics', where 'Lest the truths which he displays be too dazzling, the expositor deems it necessary to interpose a certain hazy atmosphere; or to supply the spectators with smoked glasses, to spare or aid weak vision in the season of eclipse.'[15] For Carlyle himself, well before he even wrote *Chartism*, he knew that to tackle the Condition of England Question would be to jeopardize his already tenuous subjectivity as an authentic literary worker, and it seems that it was this anticipatory knowledge that compelled him to initially resist participating in contemporary social relations when restricted within such a bewildering social context.

To have to engage with contemporary society through politics was a task which Carlyle seemed to personally wish on no man regardless of social class. While Carlyle recognized the social necessity of political activity, he simultaneously regarded it as an inferior and stifling one for the individual man, who would supposedly have no choice but to immerse himself in a phantasmal world that had lost touch with its true spiritual reality. Carlyle put forward such a perspective when, in his controversial essay 'Corn-Law Rhymes' (1832), he advised the autodidact Ebenezer Elliott to steer clear of the affairs of politics, observing 'Why should the heart of the Corn-Law Rhymer be troubled? [...] Meanwhile, is not the Corn-Law Rhymer already a king, though a belligerent one; king of his own mind and faculty; and what man in the long-run is king of more?'[16] The chief point being that amid the turmoil of contemporary social relations, Elliott (and by a parallel implication Carlyle himself) could (in theory) still see and believe in themselves as autonomous individuals working and living in the true reality of an endurable present. Paradoxically however, Carlyle was still reluctantly aware that ultimately he could not 'be at ease' with such an omniscient form of spectatorship, and his belief in himself as an autonomous agent existing in the 'Meanwhile' of contemporary social relations failed to authentically work as a form of subjective realization.

'The condition of the great body of people in a country is the condition of the country itself,' wrote Carlyle in *Chartism*, 'the alpha and omega of all!' (pp. 153–4). Carlyle's belief in the providential social commitments of a writer compelled him to endeavour to do something about the Condition of England Question, but it had to be an act of doing that would simultaneously allow for a justified realization of himself as an authentic literary worker. Thus in *Chartism*, Carlyle set about establishing a number of ultimatums that ostensibly provided him with a necessary means of differentiating between authentic and legitimate subjectivities on the one hand and unauthentic and illegitimate subjectivities on the other. He positioned his audience and also himself as either legitimate beings who spoke on behalf of the working classes or illegitimate non-entities who silenced themselves through failing to do so. '[The Governing Classes] are either speakers for that great dumb toiling class which cannot speak,' declared Carlyle, 'or they are nothing that one can well specify' (pp. 153–4). Carlyle also argued that if his readers wanted to continue to be inhabitants of England, they had to become active workers in society, while those who continued idle were to be exiled not only from the landscape of England, but also from the entire globe (pp. 162–5):

> In all ways it needs especially in these times, to be proclaimed aloud, that for the idle man there is no place in this England of ours [...]. He is doomed either to quit there habits, or miserably be extruded from this Earth, which is made on principles different from these.

However, while Carlyle publicly exhibited such beliefs, he personally shuddered under the severity of his own sentences in which he increasingly came to observe himself imprisoned.

Carlyle's beliefs were ultimately dependent upon an extensively personalized relationship with contemporary society that would allow him to find affirmation of a spiritual Ideal in the existence of the Actual through his own idealization of the working classes and their products of labour. However, this dependency entailed a disturbing process of enfeeblement that became even more conspicuous when Carlyle attempted to represent the working classes within the specific context of the Condition of England Question. His whole framework of personal and social belief became seriously destabilized when he had no choice but to recognize that his ideal of the noble manual worker had become divorced in more ways than one from the actual condition of the contemporary working classes. One could argue that the fact that Carlyle, in spite of his anticipatory knowledge and fears of such a divorcement between the Ideal and the Actual, still went on to tackle the Condition of England Question is an important testament to a painful but heroic form of authenticity that became particular to Carlyle – a form of authenticity that bewilderingly differed from but paradoxically grew out of

Carlyle's own courtroom exhibition of the 'right' and the 'wrong' way to participate in contemporary social relations.

In a letter to Mill, written six years after the publication of 'Corn-Law Rhymes', Carlyle appears uncomfortably self-conscious that he was evading the task of representing the contemporary working classes – a task that he had previously exhibited as the 'noblest and hardest work' that man could gallantly confront,[17] yet which is now seen almost as something to which he must involuntarily capitulate only when utterly defeated (*Letters*, pp. 163–4):

> Unluckily or luckily this notion of writing on the working classes has in the interim died away in me; and I have altogether lost it for the present. I have got upon Thucydides, Johannes Muller, and the Crusades, and a whole course of objects connected with my Lectures; sufficient to occupy me abundantly till that fatal time come. We will commit my Discourse on the working classes, once more, to the chapter of chances.

For Carlyle knew that he was not simply unwilling to take up this pressing social task, but was to a large extent unwilling because he already anticipated that he would be unable to effectively perform it. Thus he continues (*Letters*, pp. 163–4):

> In fact it were a right cheerful thing for me could I get to see that general *improvement* were going on there; and, I think, I should in that case, wash my hands of Radicalism forever and a day. Ah me, it is a bitter mockery to talk of 'improvement' to the men I have known! Ebenezer Elliot is with me; Machinery, and Population increasing 1200 a-day, are with me. Francis Place is against me, a man entitled to be heard. As to 'Commissioners' and their evidence, I do verily take it all to be worth almost nothing in that matter; your answer is according to your question, and your questionee, – 'as the fool thinks the bell clinks,' and all things whatsoever can be demonstrated if you choose your man.

If the corruption of contemporary social relations was regarded as an awful phantasm, it was one that seemed to be increasingly subsuming Carlyle's own sense of reality to such an extent that it had seeped into the private crevices of his innermost thoughts. Facts of working-class individuals, facts of machinery and conditions of labour, and facts of demography surrounded Carlyle as obscured shadowy symbols that were rendered largely unreadable because bereft of any visible syntax other than political cant, but the real problem for Carlyle came to do with the authenticity of his own language as much as the unauthentic nature of other people's. So it was that during the writing of *Chartism* in 1839, Carlyle confided to Mill (*Letters*, pp. 170–1):

> A great many sheets lie covered; mostly with things worthless; here and there, with a thing that might be preserved and printed. I find, in these days, that I

must bring it under some rubric, and finish it; or else tie a string about it, and shove it indefinitely into the background; perhaps, without any string, into the *fire*. Lockhart, long ago, was desirous I should put it into some reasonable shape of a pleading and protestation to the upper classes on behalf of the under. That is not perhaps impossible, tho' surely it is not very feasible. On the other hand, Benthmee Radicalism at this time seems to me like a windbladdern *rent*, lying flaccid now, probably enough forever. What am I to do? One is bested, squeezing oneself into any of the marketable shapes!

Carlyle was uncomfortably aware of the disturbing possibility that, in his very endeavours to represent contemporary social relations through applying his own ways of seeing and believing in the world, was perhaps writing of an intrinsic connection between form and content that possessed no recognized reality outside of his own imagination. Within the context of such an internecine personal and social paralysis, Carlyle's writing on the subject of the contemporary working classes becomes almost insupportable to him and continually borders on the verge of self-destruction as it appears that the only way in which Carlyle can acquire subjective release and regeneration is to physically bury or burn his own writings, in which he has perhaps involuntarily realized the phantasmal image of himself as much as anything else. Indeed, after Carlyle had written *Chartism*, he indicatively appeared to regard the work as a form of exorcism through which he had endeavoured to express his thoughts and feelings on the subject almost in order to be able to forget about them, an act of writing which had ostensibly exonerated him from any further connection with what had become to Carlyle a particularly disturbing burden of social responsibility. Thus, in 1840, in a letter to Sterling, he observes of his work (*Letters*, p. 230):

It is as bad as you like: but it utters in some way a thing that has been burning in the stomach of me these ten years, parts of it these twenty years: behold it is *out*; what more have *I* to do with it? To sweep it altogether out of my memory too [...]. The Devil and the world have now to play their part or no-part with it; mine is played.

When writing *Chartism*, Carlyle was fully aware that any subjective method of observation would be inadequate when applied to the subject of the contemporary working classes, which bewilderingly appeared as phenomena both literally and conceptually too large to remain within the representative scope of direct vision. 'Each man experiences his own hand-breath of observation to the limits of the general whole', recognized Carlyle, 'more or less, each man must take what he himself has seen and ascertained for a sample of all that is seeable and ascertainable' (*Chartism*, pp. 158–9). However, Carlyle also found himself unable to be reconciled to the forms of language that his own social class had used to represent the working classes, and consequently felt bereft of any guiding precedence. In the year that Carlyle set about writing *Chartism*, he observed to John Sterling 'I mean to read about the "working classes", if there be any book discoverable or pamphlet on that subject worth reading, – which is not the case hitherto' (*Letters*, p. 221). Carlyle felt that the abstracted language of facts and figures was being duplicitously used to encourage the reader to believe that the problem of the unemployed millions, who visibly and tangibly pervaded the English landscape, had been solved and rendered non-existent as quickly as some evaporated gaseous vapour. Where, as he ironically observes in *Chartism*, 'To read the Reports of the Poor-Law Commissioners, if one had faith enough, would be a pleasure to the friend of humanity. One sole recipe seems to have been needful for the woes of England: "refusal of out-door relief"' (p. 162). Moreover, the way in which Carlyle's own social circles abstracted the working classes in order to render their actual condition in contemporary social relations effectively invisible was personally experienced by Carlyle as a public act of violation and silencing. Hence his frustrated observation, 'With what serene conclusiveness a member of some Useful-Knowledge Society stops your mouth with a figure of arithmetic!' (p. 157).

Carlyle's social criticism was arguably written from a desire to exhibit himself as a resistant voice of authenticity as much as to authentically represent the working classes themselves. 'To believe practically that the poor and the luckless are here only as a nuisance to be abraded and abated,' observed Carlyle, 'and in some permissible manner made away with, and swept out of sight, is not an amiable faith' (*Chartism*, p. 163). He continued that this was 'A chief social principle which this present writer for one, will by no manner of means believe in, but pronounce at all fit times to be false, heretical, and damnable, if ever aught was!' (p. 164). However, while Carlyle's social criticisms endeavoured to manifest the existence of an authentic way of seeing and believing in the world, such a world remained obscured as an alternative silence whose meaning could as yet only be vicariously known and consequently continually threatened to descend into an impasse in which Carlyle was almost swallowed.

As Carlyle continued to criticize the way in which his contemporaries represented the working classes, it appeared that all visible and even conceptual presence of that social group became eclipsed by Carlyle's own voice, and while seemingly presenting an exchange of critical social dialogue, Carlyle's invisible foe appears to be as much a part of himself as of an anonymous external society (*Chartism*, pp. 194–5):

> Fifteen pence a-day; three-and-sixpence a-day; eight hundred pounds and odd a-day, dost thou call that my property? I value that little; little all I could purchase with that. For truly, as is said, what matters it? In torn boots, in soft hung carriages and four, a man gets always to his journey's end. Socrates walked barefoot, or in wooden shows, and yet arrived happily. They never asked him, What shoes or conveyance? Never, What wages hadst thou? But simply What work didst thou? –Property, O brother? Of my very body I have but a life-rent. As for this flaccid purse of mine, tis something, nothing; has been the slave of pickpockets, cutthroats, Jew-brokers, gold-dust robbers; 'twas his, 'tis mine; – 'tis thine, if thou care much to steal it. But my soul, breathed into me by God, my *Me* and what capability is there; that is mine, and I will resist the stealing of it. I call that mine and not thine; I will keep that, and do what work I can with it: God has given it me, the Devil shall not take it away!

While Carlyle sees himself as personally under attack by a society that supposedly wants to dispossess him of his God given soul, it is ironic that his own anti-capitalist discourse develops into an almost perverted form of itself as money is rejected on the grounds that it cannot be permanently possessed by any one individual and Carlyle's soul is valued because it is the one commodity that is not for sale. In a tug-of-war syntax, Carlyle's double layering of possessives with personal pronouns and exhaustive use of referential connectives reveals a desperate struggle to objectify an otherwise invisible and immaterial self in order to possess it, and show the possession of it. But this ascent of assertion is simultaneously struggling with an anticipated descent into dissolution, and what Carlyle actually produces is a formless frenzy of impassioned sound and a spectacle of his own vulnerability. It seems that it is only within the form of anticipation that Carlyle is able to achieve a somewhat deluded degree of self-realization as he ends his disguised monologue by telling society 'what I *can be* thou decidedly will not hinder me from being. Nay even for being what I *could be*, I have the strangest claims on thee, - not convenient to adjust at present!' (pp. 194–5). His state of 'being' is significantly shifted from the idea of future possibility into the actualization of that idea as a present form of 'being' in itself. For someone genuinely convinced of his own indomitable action this shift would be superfluous, but for Carlyle, who had personally placed himself on trial within his own social courtroom, it became much more than a consolation, possibly even more valuable than the actual realization of the future thing itself.

Nancy Armstrong has interestingly argued that it was ironic that the bourgeoisie chose to endow the figures of the artisan, the independent labourer and the petty trader with the qualities of individuality, durability, and autonomy when in reality these social groups were increasingly vanishing from the contemporary landscape and were therefore not representative of the modern working classes. As far as the bourgeoisie were themselves concerned, Armstrong argues, because of the context of aesthetic dematerialization, 'It was almost as if the closer to matter an individual body appeared to be, the less it actually mattered.'[18] And yet for the ever-conscientious Carlyle it seemed to matter very much that his ideal of the noble manual labourer appeared to have been rendered extinct in his own contemporary landscape as he mournfully observed: 'Are not our greatest men as good as lost? The men that walk among us, clothing us, warming us, feeding us, walk shrouded in darkness, mere mythic men' (*Chartism*, pp. 212–13). The contemporary working classes appeared to Carlyle in many respects as a dumb spectacle that he observed with a sense of dumbfounded incredulity, where, although inhabiting the same landscape, it seemed that a physical barrier had been literally imposed between them (*Chartism*, pp. 222–3):

> Were it not a cruel thing to see, in any province of an empire, the inhabitants living all mutilated in their limbs, each strong man with his right arm lamed? How much crueller to find the strong soul, with its eyes still sealed, its eyes extinct so that it *sees* not! Light has come into the world, but to this poor peasant it has come in vain. For six thousand years the Sons of Adam, in sleepless effort, have been devising, doing, discovering; in mysterious infinite indissoluble communion, warring, a little band of brothers, against the great black empire of Necessity and Night; they have accomplished such a conquest and conquests: and to this man it is all as if it had not been. The four-and-twenty letters of the Alphabet are still Runic enigmas to him. He passes by on the other side; and that great Spiritual Kingdom, the toil won conquest of his own brothers, all his brothers have conquered, is a thing non extant for him.

The metonymic working-class figure appears as an anonymous faceless phantasm dispossessed of his own materiality because of his assumed blindness to 'that great Spiritual Kingdom' that both he and his forefathers supposedly embodied through the actualized landscape of civilization. Within the literary space of this particular passage, Carlyle is able to maintain control over his act of spectatorship by showing that he still sees and believes in what the working-class figure does not. And yet there is a significant sense that Carlyle himself is stricken into an awestruck dumbness by observing this dumb figure as it almost appears that it is Carlyle who suffers from having to consciously observe such an unconscious spectacle that does not see and believe in, and therefore fails to authenticate, what Carlyle wants to see and believe in, and the more that Carlyle is exposed to such silences, the more difficult he finds it to authentically realize his own voice.

Carlyle came to increasingly recognize the fact that his language seemed without the external forms of representation necessary to authenticate it, where even the appearance of a genuine human face or the sound of an authentic human voice had become something of a conceptual memory. By the time he came to write *Past and Present* (1843), Carlyle had become so alienated from the language of his own social class that he experienced it as a spectacle that was much more distressing for him to hear than it was for him to see the hunger-stricken working classes (p. 187):

> The haggard despair of the Cotton-factory, Coal-mine operatives, Chandos Farm-Labourers, in these days, is painful to behold; but not so painful, hideous to the inner sense, as that brutish godforgetting Profit-Loss Philosophy and Life-Theory, which we hear jangled on all hands of us, in senate-houses, sporting-clubs, leading-articles, pulpits and platforms, everywhere as the Ultimate Gospel and candid Plain-English of Man's Life, from the throats and pens and thoughts of all-but all men!

Furthermore, the problem now appeared to be no longer a question of which method of observation would be the most representative or authentic, but rather that the way in which one chose to observe the contemporary working classes had almost become a matter of indifference when it seemed that all possible forms and objects of visibility produced the same bleak story. 'Descend where you will into the lower classes', mourns Carlyle, 'in Town or Country, by what avenue you will, by Factory Inquiries, Agricultural Inquiries, by Revenue Returns, by Mining-Labourer Committees, by opening your own eyes and looking, the same sorrowful result discloses itself' (pp. 3–4). Self-consciously entrapped within the context of social paralysis, attempts at subjective regeneration became paradoxically self-destructive.

In a significantly revealing passage from *Past and Present*, Carlyle observes the silence of the Workhouse Poor as an unnatural blot upon his literary vision, and yet as Carlyle also involuntarily participates in this silence he is prevented from being able to authentically realize a desirable presence of himself through his writing (p. 2):

> They sit there, these many months now; their hope of deliverance as yet small. In workhouses, pleasantly so-named, because work cannot be done in them. Twelve-hundred-thousand workers in England alone; their cunning right-hand lamed, lying idle in their sorrowful bosom; their hopes, outlooks, share of this fair world, shut-in by narrow walls. They sit there, pent up, as in a kind of horrible enchantment; glad to be imprisoned and enchanted, that they may not perish starved. The picturesque Tourist, in a sunny autumn day, through this bounteous realm of England, descries the Union Workhouse on

his path 'Passing by the Workhouse of St. Ives in Huntingdonshire on a bright day last autumn,' says the picturesque Tourist, 'I saw sitting on wooden benches, in front of their Bastille and within their ring-wall and its railings, some half-hundred or more of these men. Tall robust figures, young mostly or of middle age; of honest countenance, many of them thoughtful and even intelligent-looking men. They sat there, near by one another; but in a kind of torpor, especially in a silence which was very striking.'

Carlyle's authentic experience of the artificial theatricality of this social exhibition is revealed in his uneasy writing of it. As Carlyle moves from his generalized memories of a literary vision of the Workhouse Poor to the specific recollection of his own literal encounter with a particular group, there is disturbingly only an intensification of the phantasmal silence rather than a communicative breaking of it. The assumed consensual rules of social representation, which were seen as authorizing the supposedly necessary roles of literary spectatorship and participation, are disturbingly absent and Carlyle is uncomfortably made aware of himself as an intrusive spectator. 'The picturesque Tourist', a figure ambiguously merged with Carlyle's own narrative voice, is implicitly criticized for his consumerist treatment of the Workhouse Poor, whom he observes, passes by, and later recalls as a novel object of his country tour. Carlyle's discomfort with his language of spectatorship is revealed such exhibiting of both the working classes and himself in terms of a highly stylized and staged spectacle.

Carlyle proceeds to attempt to realize a different presence of himself as set apart from this unnatural spectacle by prolonging his place in the literary representation of his literal encounter in order to get beyond it (p. 2):

In silence: for, alas, what word was to be said? An Earth lying round, crying, 'Come and till me, come and reap me; - yet we here sit enchanted.' In the eyes and brows of these men hung the gloomiest expression, not of anger, but of grief and shame and manifold inarticulate distress and weariness; they returned my glance with a glance that seemed to say, 'Do not look at us. We sit enchanted here, we know not why. The sun shines and the Earth calls; and, by the governing Powers and Impotence of the England, we are forbidden to obey. It is impossible they tell us!' There was something that reminded me of Dante's Hell in the look of all this; and I rode swiftly away.

During this singular and dramatic moment of mutual spectatorship, the reciprocal glance is initially made to represent a tacit and intimate dialogue in which both parties reach a point of shared understanding. The glance of the Workhouse Poor, rather than represent an assertive desire for privacy, is portrayed as a subordinate plea to be overlooked because of their conscious shame of being detached from their authentic reality as active workers. As Carlyle sees himself personally recognizing the Workhouse Poor's supposed sense of personal and social alienation and eradicates any signs of hostility existing between them, he ostensibly mitigates his own consciousness of being estranged from both himself and others. Carlyle makes a literary exhibit of this point of contact so that he can fulfil both his sense of duty as a social being without jeopardizing his own beliefs and simultaneously realize a returned sense of himself as an individual human being involved in direct communication with the working classes. But this literary stage inevitably collapses when in reality Carlyle is still tied to a ubiquitous social paralysis and his cognizance of the helpless of the Workhouse Poor metamorphoses into his own impotent silence. Carlyle is exposed to himself as a phantasm whose only way of maintaining a hold over his subjectivity appears to be by paradoxically bringing about his own absence from social spaces. As his writing quite literally fails him as an effective act of doing, he abruptly flees from the scene, yet even this capitulation is rendered painfully redundant when the Workhouse Poor recede into the literary recollections of Carlyle's imagination and both he and the Workhouse Poor are consequently suspended in an intensified phantasmal silence.

What had become particularly painful to Carlyle during his exposure to the Condition of England Question was that while he observed mankind visibly making communicative signals to each other, the dumb show of social and personal paralysis nevertheless appeared to continue and Carlyle continually found himself unable to effectively do anything about it, memorably observing how (*Past and Present*, p. 274)

> Isolation is the sum-total of wretchedness to man. To be cut off, to be left solitary: to have a world alien, not your world; all hostile camp for you; not a home at all, of hearts and faces who are yours, whose you are! It is the frightfulest enchantment; too truly a work of the Evil One. To have neither superior, nor inferior, nor equal, united manlike to you. Without father, without child, without brother. Man knows no sadder destiny. 'How each of us,' exclaims Jean Paul, 'so lonely in the wide bosom of the All!' Encased each as in his transparent 'ice-palace'; our brother visible in his, making signals and gesticulations to us; – visible, but forever unattainable: on his bosom we shall never rest, nor he on ours. It was not a God that did this; no!

Carlyle saw himself involuntarily participating in the endless cycle of literary reproduction by which he was exposed as a pitiful phantasm that turned within his own confinement. Given that Carlyle observed himself rendered disturbingly amorphous during his exposure to the Condition of England Question, it is perhaps not surprising to find that his writing sometimes erupts into elaborate metaphorical constructions dogged by the implicit plea of desperate monologues as he endeavours to make and feel his desired voice seen and heard amid the impotent chatter of his own social class, the silent and always somewhat phantasmal state of the working classes, and the vicarious silences of his own social criticisms. The contemporary critic William Henry Smith had once asked in relation to Carlyle's work:

> Were it no better for those to whom philosophy has brought the sad necessity of doubt, to endure this also patiently and silently, as one of the inevitable conclusions of human existence? Were not this better than to rail incessantly against the world, for a want of that sentiment which they have no means to excite or to authorise?[19]

For Smith, exposure to Carlyle's writing was experienced as an aggressive act of violation that bordered on pitiless cruelty in its demand of society to realize a belief which it both lacked the necessary sentiment to actually bring about and was without an authentic form of authority for justifying such feelings in the first place. What Carlyle came to reluctantly realize was that his own voice was in fact part of such phantasmal silences, but the realizing and recognizing, and recognizing and accepting of such a voice were extremely difficult tasks which appeared to continue to haunt Carlyle throughout much of his life and work.

Notes

1. Walt Whitman, in the *Critic*, 12 February 1881, in *Thomas Carlyle: The Critical Heritage*, ed. by Jules Paul Seigel (London: Routledge and Kegan Paul, 1971), p. 457. All further references are taken from this edition.
2. Henry David Thoreau, 'Thomas Carlyle and his Works', in *Graham's Magazine*, March and April 1847, in *The Critical Heritage*, pp. 288–9. It is interesting to note, given Carlyle's and H.D. Thoreau's shared interest in mysticism, transcendentalism and naturalism, that at this time the American author was coming to the end of a two-year experiment in self-sufficiency, living in a wooden hut, which he had himself built, on the edge of Walden Pond, near Concord. He later published his experiences in *Walden, or Life in the Woods* (1854), in which he questions the materialism of the age and the prevailing work ethic of society. See *The Oxford Companion to English Literature*, ed. by Margaret Drabble, fifth edn (Oxford: Oxford University Press, 1985), p. 980.
3. Thomas Carlyle, *Letters of Thomas Carlyle to John Stuart Mill, John Sterling, and Robert Browning*, ed. by Alexander Carlyle (London: T. Fisher Unwin, 1923), pp. 205–6. All further references to Carlyle's letters are taken from this edition.
4. J. Hillis Miller, 'Theology and Logology in Victorian literature' (1979), in *Victorian Subjects* (Hertfordshire: Harvester Wheatsheaf, 1990), pp. 279–88 (p. 282).
5. Yoon Sun Lee, 'Making What Will Suffice: Carlyle's Fetishism', *Victorian Literature and Culture* 29: 1 (2001): 173–93 (175–6).
6. See Rob Breton, 'Gospels and Grit: Work and Labour from Thomas Carlyle to George Orwell' (unpublished doctoral dissertation, University of British

Columbia, 2001; abstract in *Dissertation Abstracts* 63:8, 2003), pp. 82–114 (pp. 89–90).
7 John Plotz, 'Jealousy of the Crowd in British Literature, 1800–1850: William Wordsworth, Thomas De Quincey, Thomas Carlyle, Maria Edgeworth, and Charlotte Brontë' (unpublished doctoral dissertation, University of Harvard, 1997).
8 Plotz, 'Jealousy of the Crowd', p. 172.
9 Plotz, 'Jealousy of the Crowd', pp. 135–82 (p. 178).
10 Carlyle, *Past and Present* (1843) (London: Chapman and Hall, 1899), p. 196. All further references are taken from this edition.
11 Nancy Armstrong, *Fiction in the Age of Photography: The Legacy of British Realism* (Cambridge, MA: Harvard University Press, 1999), p. 112.
12 Carlyle, *Chartism* (1839), in Alan Shelston's *Thomas Carlyle: Selected Writings* (Harmondsworth: Penguin, 1971), p. 172. All further references are taken from this edition.
13 See Plotz, 'Jealousy of the Crowd', on *Chartism* as being 'the first book-length work about the movement by an opponent' (p. 139).
14 See Friedrich Engels, *The Condition of the Working Classes in England*, first published in Great Britain 1892 (London: Granada Publishing, 1969), p. 318: 'Wholly isolated is the half-German Englishman, Thomas Carlyle, who, originally a Tory, goes beyond all those hitherto mentioned. He has sounded the social disorder more deeply than any other English bourgeoisie, and demands the organisation of labour.'
15 Unsigned review, in *Tait's Edinburgh Magazine*, February 1840, in *The Critical Heritage*, p. 164.
16 Carlyle, 'Corn-Law Rhymes' (1832), in *Critical and Miscellaneous Essays*, vol. 3, pp. 165–6. All further references are taken from this edition.
17 Carlyle, 'Corn-Law Rhymes', p. 163.
18 See Armstrong, *Fiction in the Age of Photography*, p. 102.
19 William Henry Smith, from an unsigned review in *Blackwood's Edinburgh Magazine*, July 1843, in *The Critical Heritage*, p. 210.

11. 'Getting Down into the Masses': Dickens, Journalism and the Personal Mode

Juliet John

On 12 June 1858, Dickens printed a now infamous statement on the front page of his journal, *Household Words*. Headed 'Personal', it announced his separation from his wife, Catherine Hogarth, and declared in his name and hers that 'all the lately whispered rumours [...] are abominably false. And that whosoever repeats one of them after this denial, will lie as wilfully and foully as it is possible for any false witness to lie, before Heaven and earth.'[1] Dickens' decision to address the public in print on so personal and controversial a topic as his marital separation and rumoured infidelity flew in the face of advice from several friends, who saw the decision as reckless and inexplicable. Subsequent commentators have been equally bemused by Dickens' conduct. Most newspapers at the time reprinted Dickens' 'personal' statement. The further publication of a letter written by Dickens to his manager Arthur Smith in the New York *Tribune* – accusing Catherine of failing in her duties as wife and mother, and hinting at mental illness – did little to improve Dickens' image in the wake of 'Personal'.[2] What was baffling then, as now, was that Dickens thought his statement appropriate, especially when the general public had no previous knowledge of his personal troubles. Dickens seemed to have lost his grip on the line between public and private, as well as on the truth.

The only explanation for his conduct has seemed to lie in Dickens' well-known belief in 'that particular relation (personally affectionate and like no other man's)' which existed between himself and 'the public';[3] 'commentators agree', according to John Drew's excellent *Dickens the Journalist*, that Dickens valued relations between himself and the public 'higher than any he had yet established in professional or private life'.[4] There is no doubt truth in this analysis, yet without in any way apologizing for his public denunciation of his wife, it is also true that Dickens' conception of his relations with the public went beyond (whilst clearly containing) the needy egocentricity that fuels today's celebrity culture. In many ways the most influential journalist of his age, Dickens saw the 'personal' flavour of his journalism as helping to militate against the increasing depersonalization that accompanied growing industrialism and commercialism. From his very early days as a journalist, Dickens aspired to control his own journal, seeing the personally conducted journal as the best means to reach a mass audience. It is easy to be cynical about Dickens' motivation for wanting what he envisaged as almost a direct line to the largest possible audience – a need to control, to be noticed, and indeed to be loved, doubtless shaped this desire for mass visibility and influence. But Dickens' belief in the importance of mass journalism was as political as it was personal. He was highly conscious throughout his career, and particularly after his ill-fated 1842 trip to the United States, of the possible demoralizing effects of unfettered commercialism and amoral press 'freedom'. The answer to what Dickens' Uncommercial Traveller describes as 'largely wholesale' economic relations was to reinstate 'a lingering personal retail interest within us that asks to be satisfied'.[5]

John Drew convincingly charts the way in which in Dickens' Uncommercial Traveller essays are not crassly anti-commercial, but advocate the supplementing of 'wholesale' with 'personal retail' values and methods.[6] This essay will argue that Dickens' journalist method, as well as his message, employs a 'personal retail' tone in a complex response to the larger 'wholesale' processes of the mass media which Dickens simultaneously resisted and accelerated. The 'personal' mode is thus not simply an antidote to 'wholesale' values but a product of them. Dickens' 'Personal' announcement was no doubt inappropriate and ruthlessly self-protective, but with the benefit of hindsight, not entirely unpredictable in the context of the complex system of belief he had developed about the place of the personal (including his personality) in mass journalism.

I

Despite editorial positions on *Master Humphrey's Clock* and *Bentley's Miscellany*,[7] Dickens' ambition to stamp his personality and vision on an influential popular journal became more focused in the wake of his first trip to the States, where the 'loathsome foul old man' on America's back (Letter to Macready, 3 January 1844; *Letters*, vol. 3, p. 11),[8] as Dickens once termed the press, had horrified him. His initial attempts to propose himself as the man to revive the newly deceased *Courier* newspaper were rejected.[9] Over time, a plan for a 'periodical' evolved, which would (ironically given his later troubles) emphasize the place of the family home as social anchor, and allow Dickens, via one of his many journalistic personae, an entrée into the homes of all:

> I would call it, sir, –
> THE CRICKET
> A cheerful creature that chirrups on the Hearth.
> *Natural History.*
>
> [...] I would at once sit down upon their [people's] very hobs; and take a personal; and confidential position with them which should separate me, instantly, from all other periodicals periodically published, and supply a distinct and sufficient reason for my coming into existence. And I would chirp, chirp, chirp away in every number until I chirped it up to – well, you shall say how many thousand! [...] I seem to feel that it is an aim and name which people would readily and pleasantly connect with *me*.[10]

The Cricket periodical in reality became two projects, *The Cricket on the Hearth* Christmas book (1845) and the newspaper Dickens established and edited, *The Daily News*. *The Daily News*, staffed in a familial fashion by Dickens' friends and relatives, had limited success and a short existence. Despite this, Dickens' plan to use his own journal to gain access to all the homes in the land, and to forge intimate relations with his readers, survived virtually unscathed to inform later journalistic projects. Feeling his way towards the concept behind the journal that eventually became *Household Words*, Dickens first revealed to Forster the fascinating idea for a shaping spirit or persona called the 'SHADOW', inhabiting and haunting the new journal and the lives of its readers:

> to get a character established as it were which any of the writers may maintain without difficulty, I want to suppose a certain SHADOW, which may go into any place [...] and be in all homes, and all nooks and corners, and be supposed to be cognisant of everything, and go everywhere, without the least difficulty [...] a kind of semi-omniscient, omnipresent, intangible creature. I don't think it would do to call the paper THE SHADOW: but I want something tacked to that title, to express the notion of being a cheerful, useful, and always welcome Shadow. I want to open the first number with this Shadow's account of himself and his family. I want to have all the correspondence addressed to him. I want to issue warnings from time to time, that he is going to fall on such and such a subject; or to expose such and such a piece of humbug; or that he may be expected shortly in such and such a place. [...] I want him to loom as a fanciful thing all over London; and to get up a general notion of "What will the Shadow say about this, I wonder? What will the shadow say about that? Is the shadow here?" and so forth. [... I]t presents an odd, unsubstantial, whimsical, new thing: a sort of previously unthought-of Power going about. [...] I want to express [...] that it is the Thing at everybody's elbow, and in everybody's footsteps. At the window, by the fire, in the street, in the house, from infancy to old age, everyone's inseparable companion....Now do you make anything out of this?[11]

The idea of an omnipresent, semi-omniscient shadow may perhaps have been less intelligible for Dickens' contemporaries than for a twenty-first-century Western public, steeped as we are in a post-Orwellian culture where the mass media shadows and surveys our lives in public and in private. The shadow is created by the human but is not itself human – a negative of humanity. Dickens' eerily prescient projection of a semi-human shadow, an absence and a presence, is as suggestive of companionship as of surveillance, however, a notion Dickens takes forward in the rationale for the journal that eventually materialized, *Household Words*.

'*Household Words*, Conducted by Charles Dickens', carried the motto adapted from Shakespeare's *Henry V*, 'Familiar in their mouths as Household Words' (*Henry V*, IV.iii.52). Its 'Preliminary Word' makes explicit Dickens' perception that personal, familial and communal affective ties are the salve to the increasing hardship and alienation of industrial society: 'We aspire to live in the Household affections', he writes:

> and to be numbered among the Household thoughts, of our readers. We hope to be the comrade and friend of many thousands of people, of both sexes, and of all faces and conditions, on whose faces we may never look. [...]
>
> No mere utilitarian spirit, no iron binding of the mind to grim realities, will give a harsh tone to our Household Words. In the bosoms of the young and old, of the well-to-do and of the poor, we would tenderly cherish that light of Fancy which is inherent in the human breast [...]. To show to all, that in familiar things, even in those which are repellent on the surface, there is Romance enough, if we will find it out: – to teach the hardest workers at this whirling wheel of toil, that theirs is not necessarily a moody, brutal fact, excluded from the sympathies and graces of imagination; to bring the greater and the lesser in degree, together, upon that wide field, and mutually dispose them to a better acquaintance and a kinder understanding – is one main object of our Household Words.[12]

'Fancy' helps to engender 'a better acquaintance and a kinder understanding' in a (reading) community. 'The mightier inventions of this age are not', Dickens argues, 'all material, but have a kind of souls in their stupendous bodies which may find expression in Household Words'.[13]

After the break-up of his marriage in 1858, it may have been a sense of his compromised position that led to what is commonly perceived as the less personal tone of the journal that replaced *Household Words*, *All the Year Round*.[14] Despite this less personal tone, as Dickens owned, edited and published *All the Year Round*, he was in many ways more 'the Chief', as his contributors called him, than ever.[15] Moreover, the less personal tone was relative rather than absolute. The title page of the last issue of *Household Words* announced 'the merger of the two publications and the prospectus of the new journal';[16] the announcement served to emphasize the connection between the two journals as much as their difference. In the extensive advertising campaign that accompanied the launch of *All the Year Round*, handbills took the form of a personal, signed address from Dickens in which he announced: 'In transferring myself, and my strongest energies, from the publication that is about to be discontinued by me, to the publication that is about to be begun, I have the happiness of taking with me the staff of writers with whom I have laboured'.[17] The first person 'I' figures largely in this advertised prospectus, just as Dickens' presence loomed large over the editorial staff. Although Dickens disavowed cronyism – writing to one correspondent, 'I know nothing about "impenetrable barrier," "outsiders," and "charmed circles"'[18] – the influence of 'Dickens' young men' (who admired and imitated Dickens) was strong on the journal.[19] *All the Year Round*, like *Household Words*, 'sought to publish essays that expressed his point of view'.[20] It is little wonder that Percy Fitzgerald deemed the journal to be 'inspired and directed, not merely edited'.[21]

II

A recurrent theme in Dickens' explanation of his journalistic vision is the importance of a personal tone as a rhetorical mode by which a cross-class audience can be reached and influenced. Key to the principles on which all Dickens' journals were conducted was the idea that they should appeal to all classes, and that they should attract, in terms of sheer weight of numbers, the largest possible number of readers, without compromising the quality of the journalism. Like 'the shadow', *Household Words* was to appeal to 'many thousands of people, of both sexes, and of all ages and conditions'. Posters announcing *All the Year Round* described the journal's purpose as 'the Instruction and Entertainment of all Classes of Readers, and to assist in the Discussion of the Social Questions of the Day'.[22] The handbills announced his plan 'for a very much wider circle of readers, and yet again for a steadily expanding circle of readers'.[23] The consistent drive to establish a mass readership was motivated by a sense of the need to elevate and 'purify' the popular press, which Dickens saw as debasing rather than improving its readers. The 'Preliminary Word' to *Household Words* makes Dickens' sense of the enemy explicit: while there are some 'tillers of the field' whose company Dickens feels it 'an honour to join', 'there are others here – Bastards of the Mountain, draggled fringe on the Red Cap, Panders to the basest passions of the lowest natures – whose existence is a national reproach. And these, we should consider our highest service to displace.'[24]

Dickens' broadside here has been taken as an attack on popular radicals such as G.W.M. Reynolds (also a plagiarist of Dickens), whose *Reynolds Miscellany* sold many times more than *Household Words*. In a reprimand to Henry Morley, one of his writers on *Household Words*, 'for not giving sufficient consideration to some of your papers', Dickens accuses Morley of not appreciating

> how severe the struggle is, to get the publication down into the masses of readers, and to displace the prodigious heaps of nonsense and worse than nonsense, which suffocate their better sense. I know of such 'perilous stuff' at present, produced at a cost about equal to the intrinsic worth of its literature, and circulating six times the amount of Household Words.[25]

Dickens' consciousness here that he is not able to compete in terms of sales figures with those he saw as pandering to the lowest common denominator, demonstrates the problems and paradoxes he confronted in attempting to combine in his journalism reformist and populist aspirations.

The pragmatics of pricing, distribution and market competition, obviously made Dickens' utopian notion of an omnipresent 'shadow' journal with a social conscience a chimerical ideal. It would be easy to read his journalistic evolution to the most commercially successful of his ventures, *All the Year Round*, as representing his capitulation to the commercialism which increasingly characterized the age. A more helpful and precisely nuanced approach, however, would be to see each of his ventures as adopting a different tactic by which to square the circle, by which 'to get the publication down into the masses of readers' in a way that would raise them up.

Thus, the *Daily News*, which Dickens edited from November 1845 to February 1846, aimed to combine 'Liberal Politics and thorough Independence' (advertisement, 1 December 1845). The reformist ideals of the paper were espoused in Dickens' opening address: its principles were those of 'Progress and Improvement', its causes education, civil and religious liberties, and 'equal legislation' for rich and poor alike.[26] In particular, it supported the repeal of the Corn Laws, backing the Manchester-based Anti-Corn Law League which had widespread support among the unenfranchised. The original fivepence price of the newspaper, however, was just one factor militating against its achieving a high circulation, especially among those sympathetic to its values.

When he established *Household Words*, he tried to bring the price closer to that of the cheap (penny) press he was attempting to supplant – in this case, to twopence. The extra penny on the price meant that Dickens was able to signal a gap in literary 'status' between his journal and 'perilous stuff'. The *Household Words* audience is commonly described as the middle-class family audience, though Michael Slater refines this category to include the 'middle-middle and lower-middle class market'.[27] Dickens seemed to have had hopes that the discerning working-class reader would have been attracted by the journal's causes and its quality. The journal 'espoused the cause of the poor and the working classes', and Anne Lohrli provides an impressive synopsis of the social issues on which it campaigned.[28] It could not compete in terms of mass readership, however, with journals like the *Family Herald* and *Reynolds' Miscellany*, which had circulations of 300,000 and 200,000 respectively (as opposed to the 40,000 of *Household Words*).[29] In practice, Dickens' hopes to supplant 'villainous' publications such as *Reynolds' Miscellany* seem to have given way to the provision of choice to the 'industrious poor' and the assumption of a 'trickle-down' effect, according to which the campaigning agenda of the journal would help to improve the lives of those it could not reach via the written word.

All the Year Round had a much wider circulation but achieved this partly by shifting the journal's focus from campaigning on British domestic issues to matters which had greater international appeal, and to the prominent serialization and marketing of original fiction. Dickens pulled out all the commercial stops to establish the enormous readership he had always dreamed of. Typical sales of the journal were 100,000.[30] Although *All the Year Round* achieved its mass circulation by becoming a more apolitical journal (vetoing at different times, for example, articles on the American Civil War and the Fenians), it was a magazine with a social conscience that resisted the sensationalist strategies of 'the Bastards of the Mountain'.

Whether or not he succeeded in appealing across classes as well as across countries, is another matter. Whereas Richard Altick argues that Dickens' journals did not appeal to the working classes, Mayhew and Binny reported that in Victorian prisons, Dickens' volumes would have been the most requested had the chaplain not banned them from the library. The *Times* credited Dickens with his great contribution to education, and with luring working-class readers away from the 'unpurified' penny journals.[31]

Dickens was notoriously vague about the particular socio-economic composition of his audience. This essay contends, however, that this vagueness was as strategic as it was naive. His sophisticated sense that the fight for social justice involves a complex interplay between issues of class, culture and commerce is most apparent in his first editorial for the *Daily News*:

> The Principles advocated by THE DAILY NEWS will be Principles of Progress and Improvement; of Education, Civil and Religious Liberty, and Equal Legislation; Principles such as its conductors believe the advancing spirit of the time requires: the condition of the country demands: and Justice, Reason and Experience legitimately sanction. Very much is to be done, and must be done towards the bodily comfort, mental elevation, and general contentment of the English People. *But, their social improvement is so inseparable from the well-doing of Arts and Commerce, the growth of public works, the free investment of capital in all those numerous helps to civilisation and improvement to which the ingenuity of the age gives birth, that we hold it to be impossible rationally to consider the true investments of the people as a class question, or to separate them from the interests of the merchant and manufacturer.*[32]

The italicized section of this quotation is as succinct a summary of Dickens' core belief in the inseparability of economics, class and cultural politics, and their combined role in shaping social justice, as can be found anywhere in Dickens' writings, or those of his critics. Dickens outlines what we have become used to calling a 'third way' between socialism and capitalism, with no sense of a naturalized opposition or hierarchy between class politics and economics, and a strong sense of the arts or culture as a crucial force in social power dynamics. The quotation furthermore makes clear the difficulty of any simple mapping modern theories of mass culture onto Dickens' work. Though cultural theory has increasingly begun to explore the ways in which commercialized 'mass' culture is not always the enemy of 'the people', the idea raised by Dickens of a mutual 'well-doing' of the arts and commerce enhancing 'the true investments of the people' has often been viewed with distrust or incredulity.

Any attempt to 'fix' Dickens' politics or cultural politics using modern assumptions and categories is as pointless, in the words of Drew, as 'trying to post Dickens into a set of political pigeonholes that seem to have been designed by Escher'.[33] Dickens' politics are not only complex and shifting in themselves; they are steeped in the kaleidoscopic political landscape of a century which saw the power of inherited privilege and agriculture superseded by the power of machines, money and the ballot box. Despite the apparently homespun or (as Mrs Gaskell might have called it) 'Dickensy' tone of Dickens' better-known journalism, Dickens was acutely aware of his political environment.³⁴ Much of Dickens' varied journalistic output (barring his *British Press* and *Examiner* contributions) was published in the 1830s, the decade that saw the first Reform Bill passed and a whole raft of legislation which helped to set Britain on its way to becoming a modern democracy. Dickens observed the major politicians of his day and rubbed shoulders with all the most influential journalists, including radicals such as W.J. Fox. Dickens was, as Drew puts it, 'a man of newspapers, and newspapery', and hence his political knowledge was topical and detailed.³⁵ His knowledge of the politics of the journalistic profession was likewise second to none, especially as Dickens, by virtue of his status and visibility, found himself called upon to commit himself to major media debates.

Perhaps the most fraught debate surrounded the so-called Taxes on Knowledge. These three taxes – excise duty on paper, a tax on advertisements, and a 'stamp' duty on newspapers, that allowed them to be sent free by post (hence aiding circulation for those who could pay) – had been in force since 1794. The taxes were obviously prohibitive for those aiming to bring print to the people, but despite Dickens' well-known support for the 'the amusements of the people', he was broadly in favour of stamp duty. As Dickens implies in his first editorial for the *Daily News*, stamp duty was to him a way of ensuring the quality of the press: 'We seek, so far as in us lies, to elevate the character of the Public Press in England [...]. The stamp on newspapers is not like the stamp on Universal Medicine-Bottles, which licenses anything, however false and monstrous.'³⁶ He elaborates his position in a letter to Thomas Milner-Gibson (12 February 1850), refusing to sign a petition against the stamp: 'the tax increases [newspapers'] respectability [...] if it were taken off we might be deluged with a flood of piratical, ignorant, and blackguard papers, something like that black deluge of Printer's ink which blights America.'³⁷

What becomes apparent in Dickens' responses to the debate about stamp duty, is that his desire to elevate the quality of popular culture was as strong as his drive to take culture to the masses. It is ironic that the *Household Narrative*, the 'spin-off' publication from *Household Words* that Dickens edited, became the centrepiece of a legal case, seen as a test case, that contributed to the eventual abolition of Stamp Duty in 1853. The *Household Narrative of Current Events* was issued, like all monthly publications, unstamped. Its mission was to present 'a vast mass of information that must be interesting to all, at a price that will render it accessible to the humblest purchasers of books'.³⁸ It was singled out for prosecution shortly after it first appeared, however, because it contained news (and newspapers were stamped) and was respectable. Dickens and his publishers ignored the ban on its unstamped publication, and eventually, the *Household Narrative* was found to be a 'chronicle or pamphlet rather than a newspaper' and remained unstamped.[39]

Dickens' position in the stamp-duty debate captures the potential for tension between two drives at the heart of Dickens' vision of mass culture: the desire to elevate the people by culture and the elevation of culture by the people (producers and consumers). The latter aim involved raising the quality as well as the status of popular culture, an objective which can be seen as both radical (in the sense that it asked for the people's culture to be valued more highly) and conservative (in the sense that it aspired to 'purify' popular culture and make it more respectable, according to standards acceptable to established guardians of culture). Dickens' agenda could be seen as a contradictory attempt to align himself with oppositional values simultaneously, or more generously, as an attempt to act as a cultural mediator, 'to bring the greater and lesser in degree, together, [...] and mutually disposed them to a better acquaintance and a kinder understanding' ('Preliminary Word', *Household Words*).

Dickens' journalistic career spans and in many ways epitomizes the more general development of the press in the nineteenth century, from the heyday of radicalism in the 1830s to the gradual rise of commercialism by the 1860s. Dickens would no doubt not have been surprised that the abolition of stamp duty in 1853 did not invigorate the radical, unstamped press. As he would have appreciated more than most, market forces had come to exert as much control as any particular act of legislation by the mid-nineteenth century. Indeed, Sally Ledger maintains that a schism between politically radical journalism and commercially popular journalism sets in as early as the 1840s, and that Dickens' ability to appeal to both kinds of 'popular' audience was unrivalled.[40]

Thus, though none of Dickens' journalist ventures achieves the perfect welding of concern for class, commerce and culture, the reason for this is not that Dickens was blind to the tensions and contradictions in his vision of mass culture as an instrument of cultural elevation and social reform. If Dickens' model of society is seen as a mobile matrix of related interests, he chooses to exert pressure on different points of that matrix in each of his journalistic ventures. Despite Elizabeth Barrett's amusing nickname for Dickens, 'Boz the universal', his sense of his of his ability to speak to all of the people all of the time on all issues of importance, was always tempered by his intricate, journalistic sense of the reality of the times.[41]

III

Dickens' 'Preliminary Word' to *Household Words* perhaps surprisingly projects a 'Dickensy', universal tone, and banishes the sophistication of the first *Daily News* editorial. *Household Words* was, however, notably more successful than its predecessor. The difference of tone between the prospectuses of the two journals arguably casts some light on their relative success. In Dickens' mind at least, a 'personal' tone became necessary in order to appeal to a mass market. Dickens' idea of the 'personal' can also paradoxically be characterized as 'universal' in the sense that his characteristically successful tone in public pronouncements (on the page or on the stage) eliminates where possible complexity and detail. When temporal details are included, Dickens' persona appears to mention them only to rise above them, presenting political views, for example, as matters of principle rather than of vested partisan interests. In *Household Words* most obviously, Dickens aimed to become as 'familiar' to his readers as 'household words' by essays that took the form of informal 'chats', 'talks' and 'gossips' that appeared to place people above politics.[42] His sense that a personal tone was paradoxically the most universal was rooted at least in part by an instinctive humanism.

Writing in a 'personal' tone was not simply a matter of writing honestly and without self-consciousness, however. On the contrary, *Household Words* and *All the Year Round* both adopted the policy of anonymous publication – despite Dickens' previous opposition to the practice – in large part so that both journals reflected Dickens' own views and writing style. Dickens would give very specific advice to contributors in order to educate them about the kind of 'personal' style that would be intelligible and interesting to a mass audience. For example, as editor of *All the Year Round*, Dickens advised a friend considering writing for the journal to:

> only fancy throughout that you are doing your utmost to tell some man something in the pleasantest and most intelligent way that is natural to you – and that he is on the whole a pleasant and intelligent fellow too, though rather afraid of being bored – and I really cannot doubt your coming out well.[43]

His conception of the desirable persona through which to address readers seems to be that of a lively and imaginative conversationalist. In his reprimand to Morley, for undervaluing the intelligence of readers, Dickens writes:

> My confidence in the ability of such people to receive and relish a good thing, is so far from being in the least shaken [...] that I only feel the more strongly that the good thing must be done at its best. [... I]t is not enough to see a thing and go home and describe it, but [...] the necessity is, for ever upon us of patiently considering *how* to describe it, so as to give it some fanciful attraction or some new air.[44]

Dickens did not see what we could call the performative personal mode of address as patronizing or insincere. He advised Wills that to patronize readers was 'as great a mistake as can be made', adding: 'dont [sic] think that it is necessary to write *down* to any part of our audience'.[45]

His conception of the desirable mode of address to a mass audience is extremely consistent with statements made in a non-journalistic context about how best to communicate with 'the people' at large. In a fascinating letter to Forster, for example, he spells out his belief, also discussed in the 'Preliminary Word' to *Household Words*, in the importance of 'Fancy' to popular literature:

> It does not seem to me to be enough to say of any description that it is the exact truth. The exact truth must be there; but the merit or art in the narrator, is the manner of stating the truth. As to which thing in literature, it always seems to me that there is a world to be done. [...] *I have an idea [...] that the very holding of popular literature through a kind of popular dark age, may depend on such fanciful treatment.*[46]

Mode of address, for Dickens, was key to inter-class communication, cultural inclusivity and social cohesion. This belief is reiterated in different contexts, and in some detail. In 'The Amusements of the People', for example, Dickens introduces Joe Whelks, the archetypal working-class cultural consumer. The melodramatic, 'fanciful' style of Dickens' novels and journalism utilizes the style that so engages Joe on the stage:

> Joe Whelks, of the New Cut, Lambeth, is not much of a reader, has not great store of books, no very commodious room to read in, no very decided inclination to read, and no power at all of presenting before the mind's eye what he reads about. But, put Joe in the gallery of the Victoria Theatre; [...] tell him a story [...] by the help of live men and women dressed up, confiding to him their innermost secrets, in voices audible half a mile off; and Joe will unravel a story all through its entanglements, and sit there as long after midnight as you have anything left to show him.[47]

In 'Two Views of a Cheap Theatre', the Uncommercial Traveller/narrator offers a fascinating critique of the rhetorical mode of a minister addressing an audience of 4,000 people at the Britannia Theatre.[48] Conceding at the outset that it is 'A very difficult thing [...] to speak appropriately to so large an audience, and to speak with tact', he concludes, 'In this congregation there is indubitably one pulse; but I doubt if any power short of genius can touch it as one, and make it answer as one.'[49] The speaker fails to communicate with a mass audience partly because the working-class section of the audience are presented by the speaker with a distorted version of themselves: 'There was a suppositious working-man introduced into the homily [...] who was not only a very disagreeable person, but remarkably unlike life – very much more unlike it than anything I had seen in the pantomime.'[50] To make things worse, 'There was a model pauper introduced in like manner, who appeared to me the most intolerably arrogant pauper ever relieved.'[51]

Perhaps the most nuanced conclusion of the essay pertaining to issues of literacy, cultural education and inclusivity comes in Dickens' discussion of the Bible. The Uncommercial Traveller recommends finally that the contents of the New Testament itself are used and transmitted thoughtfully to a mass audience:

> As to the models, imitate them, Sunday preachers – else why are they there, consider? As to the history, tell it. Some people cannot read, some people will not read, many people [...] find it hard to pursue the verse-form in which the book is presented to them, and imagine that those breaks imply gaps and want of continuity. Help them over that first stumbling-block by setting forth the history in narrative, with no fear of exhausting it. You will never preach so well.[52]

New and reluctant readers of the Bible, because they are relatively untrained, need an imaginative hook to engage their interest, and help to render complex ideas and formats accessible and unintimidating. Rendering stories and ideas accessible, to Dickens, is an ethical and social imperative.

IV

Despite the political and cultural importance Dickens attached to the personal mode of address in 'a kind of popular dark age', Morley belittled the persona he felt obliged to adopt for a series of articles on public health in *Household Words*. He told his fiancée that he had invented the persona of 'a gossipy old lady with conceits and prejudices, giving *my* view of things, characteristic and laughable, but so put as to inculcate sanitary truths. [...] Writing as an old woman, there will be no polished composition wanted – only a quizzical slip-slop.'[53] Morley's attitude is partly informed by condescension towards his audience, and partly by a sense of the inauthenticity of the performative personal tone that writing for Dickens seemed to demand of him. Morley is not alone in his discomfort with Dickens' vision of mass journalism, Mrs Gaskell's adjective

'Dickensy' capturing most succinctly and acidly the artificiality some have associated with Dickens' projection of himself to a popular audience. Anne Lohrli, the scholar from whom today's Dickensians have perhaps learned most about *Household Words*, displays a marked critical distance from her subject when she identifies a 'superficiality' and 'a kind of dishonesty' in the journal.[54] This dishonesty she associates with 'the attempt to make *Household Words* lively reading', or from Dickens' perspective, to communicate with a mass audience.[55]

In the current postmodern, mature age of mass culture, it is a commonplace to associate mass culture with inauthenticity and dishonesty. Tabloid newspapers and reality television shows, to name just a couple of the more extreme manifestations of mass culture, are routinely accused of distorting and sensationalizing reality and of 'dumbing down'. Today's mass culture is of course a long way from a Victorian family journal like *Household Words*. But what Dickens' vision of mass culture has in common with postmodern manifestations is that all trade on the performance of the personal. Tabloid newspapers today are more about celebrities than about politics (however inflected by the interests of political parties and newspaper owners) and reality television, like soap opera, owes its success to the idea that we are watching 'real people' – albeit larger-than-life representations of people who are like and unlike ourselves.

In retrospect then, the elevation of the personal is a product of 'wholesale' or mass culture, and not simply an antidote to it. The valorization of the individual, the subjective, and the inward, has been interpreted by many commentators (most notably Foucault) as an effect of the shift towards a secular, bureaucratic, capitalist democracy. For Dickens, the personal is valuable as a means of connecting people; for the personal to be moral, it must be social. Anti-social, self-reflexive individualism is, to Dickens, tantamount to a social evil.[56] Dickens' view of the personal mode is thus always bi-focal, aware of a speaker and a social audience. It is therefore, by definition, performative and self-conscious. He memorably describes the double vision which attends the Dickensian personal in his late essay, 'A Fly-Leaf in a Life' (1869): 'Being accustomed to observe myself curiously as if I were another man', he throws out as if in passing.[57]

This uncharacteristically autobiographical essay was published in Dickens' name, but as part of a new series of essays entitled 'New Uncommercial Samples', whose title associated its author with the persona of the 'Uncommercial Traveller'. Thus, despite putting his name to the essay, Dickens' authorial identity hovers in a space between person and persona. This invocation of person and persona was of course not uncommon in Dickens' career, and in many ways, the public perception of Dickens as an author is a conjuring trick involving various projections of himself 'in person' and disguised as 'another man'. Dickens' adoption of various writerly personae is obviously connected to his better-known love of the theatre and performance – not simply because Dickens' performances on stage added to a certain composite picture of Charles Dickens the author and showman familiar, but also because it shows the extent to the display of a fractured and metamorphic identity was natural (and even compulsive) to Dickens rather than 'inauthentic'.

What is interesting, though, is the way in which the various pieces of Charles Dickens presented to the public seemed to add up to a reassuring whole. To confine ourselves for the moment to print personae, Dickens presented himself to the public as 'Boz', 'Master Humphrey', a lazy apprentice and an 'uncommercial traveller', to mention just a few of his more obvious incarnations. Most of his journalism, whether for his own journals or publications such as the *Examiner*, was published anonymously. In the case of the journals he 'conducted', the anonymous, multi-authored format had the effect of subsuming other voices beneath his own identity, especially when uniformity of style and opinion was so encouraged. The edited journal is thus in some ways a symbol for the way in which Dickens managed to present a definite, solid identity or 'brand' to the public which was in reality the product of multiple voices. Even when writing in the first person in his own person, there is a sense in which Dickens' sense of himself is always metamorphic and infused with a sense of his own cultural mediation.

The 'dishonesty' that Lohrli attributes to Dickens' personalized journalistic projections does not then represent the whole truth. Dickens' strategic public speech emanates from an unusual sense of himself as both a reformer and a celebrity. As a reformer, Dickens believed it his political and ethical duty to direct and help the public by the most effective means. If we accept Dickens' idea that 'fancy' and imagination are key to social and personal change, then it is only by projecting ideals that we can reshape reality. According to Dickens' logic, it is by figuring the cultural public as cross-class and unified, and the personal mode as a salve to the problems of mass culture, that progress towards social cohesion can be made.

In her excellent essay on Dickens' public readings, Helen Small explores Dickens' 'active management' of the idea of a unified reading public transcending class.[58] She argues that the readings, like the liberal reform movement, 'aimed to assist [...] an incorporation of meritorious members of the working classes into middle-class culture', and that, despite evidence to the contrary, Dickens and his promotional team 'believed they were facilitating a true melding of working, middle and upper classes into one reading culture'.[59] Dickens' rhetoric about his journalism pre-dates the rhetoric surrounding the reading tours, and presents us with the same questions: were Dickens' attempts to 'get down into the masses' motivated as much by an impulse to control 'the masses' as by an egalitarian social vision? Did Dickens' audience really include and unify all classes, and did he believe this to be the case?

Small's emphasis on Dickens' impulse to control and manage the lower classes was an important corrective to naive celebrations of Dickens' populism. However, any suggestion that Dickens' cultural project was naively paternalistic risks underestimating Dickens' sophistication in matters of class, culture and rhetoric, and rendering the Victorian liberal project one-dimensional – a project driven more by considerations of power than by ideals and beliefs. A one-way emphasis on the idea of cultural control likewise renders metamorphic cultural formations static. In reality, if Dickens controlled the idea of the public, for example, the idea of the public also controlled him. Dickens' control of his own sense of self depended on his consciousness of, even need for, the idea of a mass audience. His celebrity depended on being all things to all people, and this malleability gave rise to a sense of self-fragmentation without the presence of a unifying audience. The public Dickens – appearing one-dimensional and reassuringly whole in any particular context – is the product of the mass audience as much as the mass audience is the product of Dickens.

The idea of Dickens and the Dickensian that is still so prominent in mass culture owes its potency not simply to Dickens' personality or myth-making, however. Dickens happened to exist at a historical cusp where paternalistic and humanist cultural models were beginning to give way to a commercialized, mass culture that has received its fullest expression in the postmodern era. Ever the journalist, he was porous to all these currents, offering sustenance to modern and nostalgic sensibilities, to realists and idealists. Thus, what appears on the surface to be the uncomplicated promotion of a bourgeois individualism in Dickens' world-view, in fact has complex roots in his reformist agenda and his commercial sensitivity to the new mass culture, as well as in his willed humanism. His promotion of the 'personal' is, as we have seen, inextricable from his consciousness of the 'wholesale'. The Dickens persona emerges from a shadowy sense of fracture in himself, his audience and his social and cultural theory – or, indeed, the persona, is the shadow. Dickens became accustomed (and addicted), to paraphrase his own words, 'to observing himself curiously as if he were another man'.

Dickens then, like the Uncommercial Traveller, did 'travel for the great house of the Human Interest Brothers', and had 'rather a large connexion in the fancy goods way'.[60] Or to put it in the harsh words of Harriet Martineau, he was a 'humanity-monger' who sold himself.[61] But the idea that his commercial humanism is either sincere or insincere, personal or wholesale, is misguided. Dickens' continued mass appeal owes much to the fact that he embraced humanism and commercialism simultaneously. Likewise, the Charles Dickens projected to the public was both himself and not himself, as was the Charles Dickens projected privately. It is perhaps most appropriate to end with Dickens' own idea of the 'shadow' – real yet intangible, pervasive yet absent, it symbolizes much about Dickens' public persona, and about the mass culture it both inhabited and haunted.

Notes

1 *Household Words* 17 (12 June 1858): 601.
2 Sir Frank Thomas Marzials, *Life of Charles Dickens* (London: Walter Scott, 1887), p. 137.
3 John Forster, *The Life of Charles Dickens*, ed. by J.W.T. Ley (London: Palmer, 1928), p. 646.
4 John Drew, *Dickens the Journalist* (Houndmills: Palgrave Macmillan, 2003), p. 134.
5 'Refreshments for Travellers', *AYR* 2 (24 March 1860): 512–16, in *'The Uncommercial Traveller' and Other Papers, 1859–70*, ed. by Michael Slater and John Drew, The Dent Uniform Edition of Dickens' Journalism, 4 vols (London: Dent, 2000), vol. 4, pp. 74–83 (p. 83). See Drew, 'The Nineteenth-Century Commercial Traveller and Dickens' "Uncommercial" Philosophy' (Part Two), *Dickens Quarterly* 15 (1998): 83–110 (88).
6 Drew, 'The Nineteenth-Century Commercial Traveller'.
7 Dickens edited *Master Humphrey's Clock* from April 1840 to December 1841; it was a journal conceived and written by him. He edited *Bentley's Miscellany* from January 1837 until January 1839.
8 All quotations from Dickens's letters are taken from *The Letters of Charles Dickens*, Pilgrim edition, ed. by Madeline House and Graham Storey, 12 vols (Oxford: Clarendon Press, 1965–2002).
9 Drew, *Dickens the Journalist*, pp. 67–8.
10 Letter to John Forster [early July 1845?], Pilgrim *Letters*, vol. 4, pp. 327–8 (p. 328).
11 Letter to John Forster [7 October 1848]; (Pilgrim) *Letters*, vol. 5, pp. 621–3 (pp. 622–3).

12 *Household Words* 1 (30 March 1850): 1–2 (1).
13 *Household Words* 1 (30 March 1850): 1.
14 Ella Ann Oppenlander (ed.), *Dickens' All the Year Round: Descriptive Index and Contributor List* (Troy, NY: Whitston, 1984), pp. 25–6.
15 Oppenlander (ed.), *Dickens' All the Year Round*, p. 37.
16 Oppenlander (ed.), *Dickens' All the Year Round*, p. 14.
17 Repr. in Harry Stone (ed.), *The Uncollected Writings from 'Household Words', 1850–1859*, 2 vols (Bloomington, IN: Indiana University Press, 1968), vol. 1, p. 26.
18 [To Unknown Correspondent], (27 December 1866), Pilgrim *Letters*, vol. 1, p. 289.
19 J.W.T. Ley, *The Dickens Circle* (London: Chapman and Hall, 1918), p. 292.
20 Oppenlander (ed.), *Dickens' All the Year Round*, p. 35.
21 *Memories of Charles Dickens* (Bristol: J.W. Arrowsmith, 1913), pp. 108–9.
22 Repr. in Stone (ed.), *Charles Dickens' Uncollected Writings*, vol. 1, p. 26.
23 Repr. in Stone (ed.), *Charles Dickens' Uncollected Writings*, vol. 1, p. 26.
24 *Household Words* 1 (30 March 1850): 1. Dickens' description of Reynolds as one of the 'Bastards of the Mountain, draggled fringe on the Red Cap' invokes the context of French Revolutionary politics, 'the Mountain' being the radical wing of the Jacobins, and the 'Red Cap' the symbol of the sans-culottes.
25 Letter to Morley (31 October 1852); (Pilgrim) *Letters*, vol. 6, pp. 790–1 (p. 790).
26 *Daily News* (21 January 1846): 4, col. 1.
27 Introduction, '*Gone Astray' and Other Papers from Household Words, 1851–59*, ed. by Michael Slater, The Dent Uniform Edition of Dickens' Journalism, 4 vols (London: Dent, 1998), vol. 3, p. xi.
28 Anne Lohrli, 'Introduction' to Lohrli (ed.), *Household Words: A Weekly Journal, 1850–1859, Conducted by Charles Dickens: Table of Contents, Lists of Contributors and Their Contributions, based on The Household Words Office Book in The Morris L. Parrish Collection of Victorian Novelists, Princeton University* (Toronto: University of Toronto Press, 1973), pp. 4–5.
29 Slater, Introduction, '*Gone Astray' and Other Papers from Household Words*, p. xi.
30 *AYR* letter book; cited by Oppenlander, Introduction, *Dickens' All the Year Round*, p. 49.
31 Richard Altick, *The English Common Reader* (Chicago, IL: University of Chicago Press, 1957), p. 347; Henry Mayhew and John Binny, *The Criminal Prisons of London and Scenes of Prison Life* (1862; London: Frank Cass, 1968), p. 219; George H. Ford, *Dickens and his Readers* (Princeton, NJ: Princeton University Press, 1955), p. 79. All references cited by Oppenlander in Introduction, *Dickens' All the Year Round*, p. 29.
32 *Daily News* (21 January 1846): 4, col. 1. Italics mine.
33 Drew, *Dickens the Journalist*, p. 192.
34 Elizabeth Gaskell, Letter to Charles Eliot Norton (9 March [1859]), in *The Letters of Mrs Gaskell*, ed. by J.A.V. Chapple and A. Pollard (Cambridge: Cambridge University Press, 1967), pp. 534–9 (p. 538).
35 Drew, *Dickens the Journalist*, p. 188.
36 *Daily News* (21 January 1846): 4, col. 1.
37 (Pilgrim) *Letters*, vol. 6, pp. 35–6 (p. 36).
38 Quoted by Slater, Introduction, '*Gone Astray' and Other Papers from Household Words*, p. xii.
39 Drew, *Dickens the Journalist*, p. 185.
40 Sally Ledger, 'From Queen Caroline to Lady Dedlock: Dickens and the Popular

Radical Imagination', *Victorian Literature and Culture* (2004): 575–600 (576)
41 Letter from Elizabeth Barrett to Miss Mitford (21 November 1854), quoted in (Pilgrim) *Letters*, vol. 4, p. 438n, from Betty Miller (ed.), *Elizabeth Barrett to Miss Mitford* (London: John Murray, 1954), p. 261.
42 Lohrli (ed.), *Household Words*, p. 8.
43 Letter to Thomas Beard (25 March 1861); Pilgrim *Letters*, vol. 9, p. 395.
44 Letter to Morley (31 October 1852); (Pilgrim) *Letters*, vol. 6, pp. 790–1.
45 Letter to Wills (12 October 1852); Pilgrim *Letters*, vol. 6, pp. 776–7 (p. 776).
46 Forster, *Life of Charles Dickens*, pp. 727–8. See Juliet John, *Dickens' Villains: Melodrama, Character, Popular Culture* (Oxford: Oxford University Press, 2001), p. 6.
47 'The Amusements of the People', *Household Words* (30 March 1850): 13–15 (13). See John, *Dickens' Villains*, p. 5.
48 *All Year the Round* 2 (25 February 1860): 416–21; repr. in Slater and Drew (eds), *'The Uncommercial Traveller' and Other Papers*, pp. 52–62.
49 Slater and Drew (eds), *'The Uncommercial Traveller' and Other Papers*, p. 59.
50 Slater and Drew (eds), *'The Uncommercial Traveller' and Other Papers*, p. 59.
51 Slater and Drew (eds), *'The Uncommercial Traveller' and Other Papers*, p. 59.
52 Slater and Drew (eds), *'The Uncommercial Traveller' and Other Papers*, pp. 61–2.
53 H.S. Solly, *Life of Henry Morley* (Arnold, 1898), p. 151; quoted by Drew, *Dickens the Journalist*, p. 176.
54 Lohrli, Introduction, *Household Words*, pp. x–xi.
55 Lohrli, Introduction, *Household Words*, p. x.
56 See John, *Dickens' Villains*.
57 In 'New Uncommercial Samples, by Charles Dickens', *All the Year Round*, new series 1 (22 May 1869): 589-91; repr. in Slater and Drew (eds), *'The Uncommercial Traveller' and Other Papers*, pp. 386–91 (p. 388).
58 'A pulse of 124: Charles Dickens and a pathology of the mid-Victorian reading public', in James Raven, Helen Small and Naomi Tadmor (eds), *The Practice and Representation of Reading in England* (Cambridge: Cambridge University Press, 1996), pp. 263–90 (p. 269).
59 Small, 'A Pulse of 124', pp. 271, 275.
60 'His General Line of Business' and 'The Shipwreck', *All the Year Round* 2 (28 January 1860): 321–6; excerpted in Slater and Drew (eds), *'The Uncommercial Traveller' and Other Papers*, pp. 28–40 (p. 28).
61 Harriet Martineau, *The Factory Controversy: A Warning against Meddling Legislation* (Manchester: National Association of Factory Occupiers, 1855), p. 44.

12. 'Scrupulously Empty Phrases' and the Silent Work of Matthew Arnold: Belief in the Action of Writing

Kate Campbell

> direct political action is not the true function of literature[1]

As the author of 'Dover Beach' (1867) and other poems that speak of the loss of religious belief, who became a critic with faith in literature, Matthew Arnold has an obvious place when considering the role of belief in Victorian writing. In his first public utterance as a critic in 1853, in the 'Preface' to his third volume of poetry, he repudiated the doubt in his writing and elaborated how poetry should in fact 'rejoice and inspire the reader' (vol. 1, p. 2). In a period in which Christianity was increasingly discredited, Arnold's subsequent criticism continued to stress the ethical action of literature and then culture in shaping individuals and society. Yet his criticism uses religious language to advance secular forms, not least when it looks to the 'promised land' of literature (vol. 3, p. 285). His essay on 'The Study of Poetry' (1880) explicitly proposes that 'most of what now passes with us for religion and philosophy will be replaced by poetry' (vol. 9, pp. 161–2). As a critic, then, Arnold readily exemplifies the transference of religious belief to literature.

The current hold of such readings owes much to the American critic J. Hillis Miller, and, before that, to T.S. Eliot. Eliot discerned a modern hollow writer who lacks belief in religion and philosophy, whose ambitions for poetry to be a substitute for religious faith exemplify his unsoundness.[2] For Miller, not so much lack of proper religious belief, but relentless, theological belief in lost harmony is Arnold's weakness and the source of his vagueness. Here Arnold's sense of modern fragmentation is seen as the source of negative criticism that denies the content of philosophy; as it accordingly employs 'scrupulously empty phrases', it 'beckons' to the future 'promised land' of creative writing.[3] This account of Arnold's belief in lost harmony discounts the secular redirection of his gaze from his 1853 'Preface', and so he (p. 268):

must hover in the void, in one direction waiting for lightning to strike, the dawn to come, and in the other direction sternly and implacably criticising all present cultural forms as false. Through his strategy of withdrawal from practical involvement, he attains at last what he has sought from the beginning. Arnold's final platform is the absence of God.

In the long run this passive, literary-theological Arnold of Miller has contributed to the continuing association of Arnold with a metaphysical belief in Literature, and his identity as a detached critic or hoverer.[4]

Recent cultural critics are more likely to foreground the strategic role of Arnold's well-known ideas and phrases in the institutionalization of English studies. One essay for instance proposes his identity as a 'master-strategist' who is 'largely responsible for establishing the discipline of '"English"'.[5] Yet here, as in other accounts since the 1980s, Arnold moves in a mysterious way in his institutional performance. While they both perceive his catchwords and his vagueness, cultural critics no less than literary critics have tended to neglect his action in writing and its context.

In contrast to Miller's theologically minded hoverer and the cultural critics' conjurer of institutional English, this account examines Arnold's secular belief in writing as a form of action that advances democracy and the modern state. This secular project, which arose from his dedication to action and his work as a Schools Inspector, can be glimpsed in his short book, *A French Eton* (1863–1864), which seeks state interference in middle-class education as a step towards greater equality. This book's concluding projection of a promised land in terms of a better *society* foregrounds Arnold's strong social and political belief, and his desire to move readers. In this rhetorical prose the 'lower class' is thus hailed as an 'obscure embryo, only just beginning to move', that needs 'a practicable passage to all the joy and beauty of life' (vol. 2, pp. 324–5). Far from being one who 'beckons' to future literary activity, Arnold's self-conception appears here as a type of midwife who seeks to facilitate a 'practicable passage' to a more equal society. In this context, *Culture and Anarchy*'s call for a stronger state a few years later (1867–1868; 1869) is hardly abstract, since this is a means of further educational provision that will advance the cause of democracy.

The entries on belief in the *Oxford English Dictionary* include 'mental assent to or acceptance of a proposition, statement, or fact, as true'.[6] On many grounds, belief can seem an obsolescent category in postmodern times. Twentieth-century accounts of pragmatism, and of neo-Marxist hegemony, post-structuralist power relations, Wittgensteinian rule-following, and the liberal self have together largely relocated belief in and around social practices – in behaviour, discourses, habits and atmosphere.⁷ We will see how Arnold was party to such shifts: for him, like many of his contemporaries, belief resides in atmosphere and embedded states as well as ideas that become 'catchwords' or slogans, and state intervention and democracy can be advanced by producing appropriate atmosphere and phrases in writing.

As a critic who was a poet, he was sensitive to the many ways in which writing indirectly acts on readers. In the following account, his belief in atmosphere and praxis at a turning-point in his life are examined first, then the way that his belief in writing as a form of action evolved from this moment at the mid-century until the late 1860s, in the context of a new cultural politics. His own writing in his essay, 'Democracy' (1861), and in *Culture and Anarchy*, his vaguest text, is also briefly considered. It is an account of how a critic negotiates his belief in mind and matter, and avoids having his hands tied by either of these.

Acquiring Belief in *Praxis*

Apart from his experience of poetry's effects and contemporary politics, the background of Arnold's belief in writing as a form of action lies in the discourses of influence that circulated after the French Revolution, where the power of words, ideas and beliefs, and poetry and journalism, were scrutinized. He encountered such discussion through his reading and conversations at Oxford, where John Henry Newman's sermons demonstrated the power of religious words in practice. From 1847 he was able to pursue his interests in the power of writing through his acquaintance with associationist psychology and theological and philological studies at London University.⁸

During his stay in Paris in the 1848 Revolution ,Arnold witnessed how writing acted on others politically. Socialist philosophers are here seen by him as marginal to political activity compared with the influence of French popular culture – 'novels as opposed to Comte & them of that kidney – Figaro as opposed to the Contrat Social'; 'amongst a *people* of readers the litterature [sic] is a greater engine than the philosophy'. Journalism's special strength as an 'engine' of praxis appears as it supplies 'applied ideas' for more educated readers in the fortnightly *Revue des deux mondes*.⁹ The identity of 'litterature' as an engine suggests how its popular forms break with the orthodox intellectual transmission of ideas and effect material change; and the misspelling, 'litterature', underlines this writing's difference from the texts of polite society.

Arnold's excitement indicates his fascination with the social action of writing and questions of influence. His letter evokes John Stuart Mill's recent reading of French history in particular:

> some notions of a progressive unfolding of the capabilities of humanity – of a tendency of man and society towards some distant result – of a *destination*, as it were, of humanity – pervade, in its whole extent, the popular literature of France. Every newspaper, every literary review or magazine, bears witness of such notions. They are always turning up accidentally, when the writer is ostensibly engaged with something else; or showing themselves as a background behind the opinion which he is immediately maintaining.[10]

Mill's prose quite calmly proposes that influence operates involuntarily and through 'background' expression – where atmosphere prevails. Arnold's private response during a climax of such action revels in the inversion of established hierarchies, which his idiomatic and bathetic use of 'kidney' underlines. His mention of this vital organ, and an engine, registers the palpable effects of writing in bringing mind and matter, and intellect and feeling, together.

Eighteen months later he proposed how a 'moral atmosphere' could be the basis of his own purposeful action or praxis, and hence overcome these oppositions in himself. The letter in which this appears was written in September 1849 when Arnold finally abandoned his interest in the woman who prompted his love poetry. Its importance here lies in his simultaneous affirmation of practice and sensory cognition. Until Cecil Lang's edition of his *Letters*, the word praxis was taken for 'prayer' – a word which hardly makes sense in view of Arnold's declared aversion to 'mighty spiritual workings' (*Letters*, vol. 1, p. 156):

> What I must tell you is that I have never yet succeeded in any one great occasion in consciously mastering myself: I can go thro: the imaginary process of mastering myself & see the whole affair as it would then stand, but at the critical point I am too apt to hoist up my mainsail to the wind and let her drive. However as I get more awake to this it will I hope mend for I find that with me a clear almost palpable intuition (damn the logical senses of the word) is necessary before I get into praxis: unlike many people who set to work at their duty, self-denial &c. &c. like furies in the dark hoping to be gradually illuminated as they persist in this course. Who also perhaps may be sheep but not of my fold, whose one natural craving is not for profound thoughts, mighty spiritual workings &c.&c. but a distinct seeing of my way as far as my own nature is concerned.

Apparent weakness here becomes a source of strength, as the external routes of right conduct, intellect and 'mighty spiritual workings &c.&c' are all relegated in ascertaining his own practice, or praxis. As Arnold detaches himself from standard routes his future practice purportedly derives from an intuitive, independent process based on his senses – 'almost palpable', 'seeing of my own way'. He thus outlines an existential task of finding the right course, unaided by outside authorities and abstract beliefs. The context in which he writes suggests this praxis refers to his 'way' or direction in writing, and his poetry becomes bolder from this point. The term's Aristotelian derivation however implies thought and action in ethical and political life, and Arnold's tendency to praxis was more evident in his turn from poetry to school inspecting, and then criticism, a few years later.

Aptly, then, earlier in this letter of 1849 he appears 'snuffing for a moral atmosphere to respire in' (*Letters*, vol. 1, p. 155). Such sensory activity recalls Newman's understanding that belief can be lodged within behaviour in his sermon on 'The Theory of Developments in Religious Doctrine', which Arnold certainly knew. As a complex meditation on how persons come to hold ideas, this sermon proposes that some belief is unconscious, and some belief entails 'implicit reception' rather than 'explicit statement'.[11] Like Arnold's allusions to 'moral atmosphere' and the effects of 'literature', Newman's sermon belongs among the discourses of influence that Robert Douglas-Fairhurst has traced. While many writers thought of writing in terms of the silent – since unarticulated – effects that 'influence' denoted, the singularity of Arnold's thinking as a Victorian intellectual centres on his election of atmosphere and practical wisdom in the determination of his own way. His writing has moreover a neglected investment in making words 'real', so that reality corresponds to them. In his later essay on 'Heinrich Heine' (1863; 1865), this 'real' imperative – that also owes much to Newman – is conveyed in Arnold's approval of a writer for whom 'ideas were not counters or marbles, to be played with for their own sake' (vol. 3, p.120). Such investment in transformative praxis also echoes German philosophers, whose work Arnold knew by the late 1840s.

His practical emphasis broadly aligns him with the resistance to intellectualist understanding in the much later work of Pierre Bourdieu and Ludwig Wittgenstein. In an essay that brings together the late-twentieth-century French social theorist and the earlier philosopher, the present-day philosopher Charles Taylor elaborates the understanding of those for whom representations are not 'the primary locus of understanding, they are only islands in the sea of our unformulated practical grasp of the world'. For Taylor such departures from 'intellectualist' approaches turn on grasping how understanding and oneself are embedded and embodied, so that 'the representations we do make are only comprehensible against the background provided by this inarticulate understanding'.[12] Although Taylor does not use the word 'belief', his use of the word understanding suggests how this word has taken its place. While representations are far from precluded in Taylor's anti-intellectualist scheme, they are sourced very differently than has been usual in intellectual history – as 'islands in the sea' of what is not expressly articulated. For Arnold in 1849, atmosphere, or background 'sea', and action are inextricably linked, and belief becomes implicit in the 'way' or direction that he determines through his 'snuffing', or 'almost palpable intuition'.

The salience of Taylor's account of 'practical grasp' here is reinforced by the direct quotation from Aristotle's *Ethics* in Arnold's letter. Where this appears, Arnold enjoins: 'Let us be neither fanatics or yet chalf blown by the wind' but let us be as the man of practical wisdom would define it, and not as any one else would define it' (vol. 1, p. 156). As one mode of practical reason, 'snuffing' requires sign-reading or semiotic skill, since it silently picks up clues. Leaning on *mores* or how things are done, it locates ideas, and 'my way', in 'moral atmosphere' or background, so that they are not found through 'profound thoughts' but instead scented out. This affirms a kind of embedded thought in atmosphere: from this one can sift a direction, an idea, or a belief, with *praxis* working backwards from practice. Freedom, epistemology and materialism are all at stake in the odd expression, an index of Arnold's empirical, anti-metaphysical course that led to caricatures in the 1860s in which he was seen holding his nose. A positive use of the small, vernacular word 'clue', which runs across his writing, from his early poem 'To the Duke of Wellington' (1849) to his biblical criticism in the 1870s, likewise tells of these values and how deeply Arnold held them.

Writing as a Means of Action

As Taylor reminds us, 'A way is essentially something you go through in time', and Arnold's belief in writing as a form of action was built up from his understanding of atmosphere and writing's effects (p. 176). Much as he saw his own 'way' or direction that implies a goal, or belief, from inductive 'snuffing' for a 'moral atmosphere' – as if seeking clues – so he would propose that others could similarly be led towards the right way in 'The Function of Criticism' (1864; 1865). But his earliest criticism was more taken up with specifying *what* was needed than attending in practice to the manner of utterance and writing as a form of action. Indeed his 1853 'Preface' persists in denigrating any local 'striking' effects of writing. In that this text formally valorizes a plain style, architectonic form, and grand human actions, it seems he would like to dispense with language altogether. His lectures and essays from his appointment as Oxford Professor of Poetry in 1857 further advocate a plain, transparent style, to secure an intellectual rescue of modern confusion and the sources of transformation from this state are primarily located in the formulation of standards.

Nonetheless, his observation of the role of public opinion in French politics in 1859 brought new appreciation of the political action of writing. In particular his pamphlet, 'England and the Italian Question' (1859), discerns the importance of the way in which political ideas are embedded, and conversely how they function as 'catchwords' or slogans. The pamphlet grasps how 'the ideas of 1789' – 'Liberty' and 'Equality' especially – have become the framework of modern political activity, where authority derives from 'the people': since 1789, 'no politician has played a great part without taking them [the ideas] into account' (vol. 1, p. 81). The different linguistic registers of the rulers and ruled make it necessary for rulers to encode their expression for those in a different sociolinguistic group: 'The masses of the people are strongly susceptible to certain powerful ideas. When a ruler is himself susceptible to these ideas, he not only knows how to speak to the people a language which they will comprehend, but how to speak it with the force and effectiveness of conviction' (vol. 1, p. 121). The abstract words or ideas that rally the French people, like liberty and equality, are thus read as emotive signs that must be embedded in suitable sociolinguistic registers which tacitly press the people into accepting their ruler's authority.

The pamphlet's account of the force of the Enlightenment ideas broadly corresponds with a late-twentieth-century account of their peremptory effects. Here such ideas as liberty constitute a form of 'thin' but compelling moral argument that no modern politician can neglect: as headlines in the media, they rally support. Their power depends on vagueness, whereby difficult questions of the detailed application of the principles that they represent are avoided.[13] Their vagueness is hence a strength in daily political life, since potentially conflicting sources of support are combined under them. Arnold's pamphlet considers this conglomerating effect in France. And his next political text, 'Democracy' (1861, the Introduction to his work on *The Popular Education of France*), conceptualizes the state in similar unifying terms, as an ideal that is 'a rallying-point for the intelligence and for the worthiest instincts of the community' (vol. 3, p. 19). In ideas or slogans that provide a focus for different interests – like 'the State' – atmosphere comes to a head, in words that 'catch' consensus.

In 'Democracy' Arnold's analysis of signs and writing as a form of action yields to his own confused use of them to gain middle-class support for state interference in education. This essay encapsulates his 1860s educational agenda: the installation of public spirit or disinterestedness through such state control will advance democracy's staggered realization. First the working classes will acquire grounds for respecting the middle-classes as they become disinterested, then the middle-class disinterest will ensure equal educational provision that will end class differences. Arnold's private references to his 'tact' in writing this essay attest to his immediate middle-class objective – he even writes of 'licking' it into shape. His tactful devices include a long conciliatory introduction. A subsequent long passage begins in appeal to middle-class readers on behalf of the working-classes: 'Can it be denied, that to be heavily overshadowed, to be profoundly insignificant, has, on the whole, a depressing and benumbing effect on the character?' (vol. 2, p. 9). However a page of such eloquent psychological appeals potentially dispels class altogether by hailing middle-class readers in a more or less buried life of oppression that they also know. In its fierce antipathy to subordination, and the essay's later Enlightenment conception of the English democracy tending to 'throwing off the tutelage of "aristocracy", we see a pull to a different, more equal order, rather than simply a more contained one – a place *without* class distinctions' (vol. 2, p. 17). The presentation of persons 'without extraordinary gifts or exceptional energy, and who will ever require, in order to make the best of themselves, encouragement and directly favouring circumstances', thus touches on experiences that cross class boundaries (vol. 2, p. 9). As such language points beyond class, it creates a 'moral atmosphere' of great force that is at odds with the deferment of equality for all. In the vagueness, idealism and inconsistency of this passage, Arnold's weaknesses as a political thinker are apparent.

Yet the belief in a common humanity and the sense of moral obligation which make up the atmosphere of 'Democracy' were then becoming major forces in English politics. For the commercialization of the press which followed the abolition of the stamp duty on journals in 1855 brought more extensive political reporting, in which liberal politics began to be conducted on a high moral ground where 'the people' were important. William Ewart Gladstone's public profile as a Liberal leader in the early 1860s rested on this conjunction of a moralized politics and modern forms of publicity, which produced a newly 'mediated political field' and cultural politics.[14]

The same year 'Democracy' was published, Gladstone became known as 'The People's William' for his abolition of the tax on paper. The liberal *Daily Telegraph* exploited the appeal of a moral, egalitarian stance by attaching this label to him for his action in thus ending the 'taxes on knowledge'. Such labels and slogans played a growing role in political struggle. Arnold's first journal article, 'The Twice-Revised Code' (1862), resisted Robert Lowe's controversial scheme for allocating funds to elementary schools that was widely known as 'payment by results'.

Earlier radical and working-class interests were accommodated in the popular Liberalism that exuded a moral atmosphere, where religious belief and language were transferred to politics. The revisionist historian Patrick Joyce contentiously takes this ethos further in arguing that a sense of equality underlay a new 'democratic imaginary' that emanated from the ex-Chartist popular Liberal, John Bright, especially. The key point about this 'imaginary' is that it brings a 'feeling of living in a democratic culture and society', whereby social and material differences appear insignificant.[15]

The extent of Arnold's belief in action through writing and his sensitivity to this moralized politics emerge in his literary essays of 1863 and 1864, most of which were collected as his *Essays in Criticism* (1865). These essays identify different sources of power, and as Arnold reads the current force of morality back in the Reformation it begins to sound like some Gladstonian campaign. Accordingly, in 'The Bishop and the Philosopher' (1863), it was not by 'intellectual truth' that 'the Reformation touched and advanced the multitude: it was by the moral truth of its protests' (vol. 3, p. 44). In 'Marcus Aurelius' (1863) this affective capacity is linked to 'the ordinary man', who responds positively to dogmatism because of the warmth it conveys (vol. 3, pp. 134–5). As Arnold continues his exploration and distinguishes between the popular literary work that acts as a 'critical hit', and the better type of hit that has critical power since it is 'capable of emitting a life-giving stimulus', it can seem that the value of a work depends on how much its ideas are taken up in practice (vol. 3, pp. 278, 183). In his essay on the French writer, Joubert (1864), he sees from his subject's notebooks how 'familiar words' especially catch contemporary readers and gain credence: 'style takes hold of the reader and gets possession of him. It is by means of these that great thoughts get currency and pass for true metal' (vol. 3, p. 195). Overarching all of these methods is tone, which aims at 'a spiritual and intellectual effect' in which atmosphere has been brought to a definite pitch (vol. 3, p. 249). In its action of influence, tone approximates to Bourdieu's concept of the *habitus* – the cluster of assumptions that constrain and generate conduct and belief.[16] When Douglas-Fairhurst observes how tone appears as 'both diagnosis and therapy', he indicates how Arnold views and practises writing as a form of action through this feature specifically (p. 118).

But 'Heinrich Heine' explicitly relates tone to the indirect *political* action of writing: this 'brilliant soldier in the Liberation War of Humanity' turned away from 'direct political action' against 'the German Governments' and his 'propagandism took another, a more truly literary character' (vol. 3, p. 119). Literature is here not remote from politics but its modern 'theatre of operations'; as he operates indirectly, through influence, Heine shows 'there is so much power' (vol. 3, p. 122, p. 132). In his partisan article against Lowe's 'Revised Code' Arnold had broken with the neutrality of civil servants at some risk, and his exuberance in his writing now turns on the possibilities of criticism that looks neutral but is surreptitiously partisan and effective. The tacit, indirect methods formally become central to critical writing in the last-written of these essays, 'The Function of Criticism', where the critic's role is to proceed 'insensibly, and in the second place, not the first, as a sort of companion and clue, not an abstract lawgiver' (vol. 3, p. 283). 'Insensibly' allows for effects that operate beneath explicit statement and observation, as the sounds and features of a critic-companion 'touch' others like clues – and here we can seem back in 1849 with Arnold's 'almost palpable intuition'. In private, in the 1860s when he was still quite new to journal publication, he exulted in his new ability to act indirectly on others (*Letters*, vol. 2, p. 238):

> It is very animating to think that one at last has a chance of *getting at* the English public – such a public as it is, and such a work as one wants to do with it; partly nature, partly time & study have also by this time taught me that everything turns upon one's exercising the power of *persuasion, of charm*; that without all this fury, energy, reasoning power, acquirement, – are thrown away and only render their owner more miserable. Even in one's ridicule one must preserve a sweetness and good-humour.

Not long after Arnold wrote of this 'sweetness', he suggested his own role in facilitating a 'practicable passage' for the lower classes to a more fulfilled life in *A French Eton*. This text of 1864 for the general public urged state intervention in education; his subsequent criticism for the general public, however, neglected the topic of education, though it maintained the need for a stronger state.

Culture and Anarchy, Indirect Action and Politics

Before he started on *Culture and Anarchy* Arnold was busy finishing his report on secondary *Schools and Universities on the Continent* (1868), where again he advocated such intervention. A copy of this report was 'on hand' for Members of Parliament when the first instalment of *Culture and Anarchy* was in circulation. As in much of his educational work, in producing this report Arnold had worked closely with politicians. Further state provision in education was highly contentious, even within the Liberal Party. More awareness of Arnold's educational texts should dispel the image of his Olympian detachment as they indicate his practical political engagement on this issue, and his belief in writing's action on others.

For his school reports reiterate the importance of good literature in 'animating and moving' pupils, instigating desire for learning: reason alone is insufficient to motivate most of them.[17] A comparable understanding of arousal as a stimulus to knowledge informs the passage in *Culture and Anarchy* that objects to the 'ordinary popular literature' which can be seen 'working on the masses' (vol. 5, p. 112). Such literature tries 'to indoctrinate the masses with the set of ideas and judgments constituting the creed of their own profession or party'; 'culture works differently', as it does not provide 'an intellectual food' at all, but 'an atmosphere of sweetness and light', that may whet appetites for ideas and judgments – though this atmosphere may also serve in default of such ideas among general readers, it seems (vol. 5, pp. 112, 113). In his precise distinction between forcing beliefs and providing atmosphere lies Arnold's legitimation of the silent action of his own writing.

Culture and Anarchy is unambiguous about the need for 'doing good' as well as right belief; *Schools and Universities* maintains that 'the aim and office of instruction' is to supply men with the knowledge that is 'the only sure basis for action' (vol. 5, p. 91; vol. 4, p. 290). Arnold's insistence on critical disinterest has however eclipsed his understanding of disinterest as a prelude to action, and his own political ambition to move public opinion – not least dismissive Liberal MPs – towards state interference. To have argued for the state *and* educational reform would have been obviously partisan on the part of a Schools Inspector, and Arnold scrupulously avoided sustained attention to education in his published social and political writing. Through indirection, however, it seems that he can operate disinterestedly *and* practically in these texts. He only calls for a stronger state, and gestures towards his practical action in a way that makes it sound vague and empty: 'we have told silently upon the mind of the country, we have prepared currents of feeling which sap our adversaries' position when it seems gained' (vol. 5, p. 106).

In conclusion, then, this account suggests that *Culture and Anarchy* has a political investment in Liberal interventionism, which Arnold tries to take forward through his criticism. This resembles the new cultural politics in its attempt to produce catchwords or slogans, and to create an effective 'moral atmosphere' where class is immaterial and the public interest prevails. Here, as one of 'the true apostles of equality', he can be seen playing back a version of Gladstone and Bright's 'democratic imaginary' (vol. 5, p. 113). In his egalitarian rhetoric, the 'best self', for whom class is immaterial, embodies this mental state (vol. 5, p. 134). As he pronounces how 'the great men of culture' have spread the 'best that has been thought and said in the world', his vagueness circumvents disabling differences of opinion (vol. 5, p. 113). More generally, he presents a levelling moral discourse where weaknesses and strengths are considered equally in each of the social classes. Familiar words and phrases elaborate culture further, until it comes to seem empty: 'Not a having and a resting, but a being and becoming', 'sweetness and light', 'the study and pursuit of perfection' (vol. 5, pp. 94, 113, 115). If his words now seem preachy, this underlines the correspondence between Arnold's methods and contemporary politicians', and his belief in writing's indirect political action through working on his readers.

Notes

1 Matthew Arnold, in *The Complete Prose Works of Matthew Arnold*, 11 vols, ed. by R.H. Super (Ann Arbor, MI: Michigan University Press, 1960–1977), vol. 3, p. 118. Further references to this collected edition are given after quotations in the text. Most of the chapters in Arnold's books were first published as essays in journals: where the date of first publication of an essay differs from the date of its book publication, both dates are indicated in the text.
2 T.S. Eliot, *The Use of Poetry and the Use of Criticism* (London: Faber, 1933), pp. 113–16.
3 J. Hillis Miller, *The Disappearance of God* (Oxford: Oxford University Press, 1963), pp. 210–69 (p. 265). Further references to this edition are given after quotations in the text.
4 Francis Mulhern, *Culture/MetaCulture* (London: Routledge, 2000), for instance, sees advocates of culture such as Arnold as journeying 'through the waste land in search of lost virtue', p. 174.
5 Graham Holderness, in G. Day, (ed.), *The British Critical Tradition* (Basingstoke: Macmillan, 1993), p. 29.
6 *Shorter Oxford English Dictionary*, 2 vols, ed. by C. T. Onions, third edn (Oxford: Clarendon Press, 1970 [1944]), vol. 1, p. 165.
7 On pragmatism see, for instance, *The Cambridge Dictionary of Philosophy*, ed.

    by Robert Audi (Cambridge: Cambridge University Press, 1999), pp. 730–1.
8   See Franklin Court, *Institutionalising English Literature* (Stanford, CA: Stanford University Press, 1994), p. 106.
9   Matthew Arnold, *The Letters of Matthew Arnold*, 6 vols, ed. by Cecil Lang (Charlottesville, VA: University Press of Virginia, 1996–2001), vol. 1, p. 92. Subsequent references to this edition are given after quotations in the text.
10 Quoted in Robert Douglas-Fairhurst, *Victorian Afterlives* (Oxford: Oxford University Press, 2004), p. 117. Further reference to this book is given after quotation in the text.
11 John Henry Newman, 'The Theory of Religious Developments', in *Newman's University Sermons: Fifteen Sermons Preached before the University of Oxford, 1826–1843* (London: SPCK, 1970), p. 327.
12 Charles Taylor, *Philosophical Arguments* (London: Harvard University Press, 1995), p. 170. Subsequent references to this edition are given after quotations in the text.
13 See M. Walzer, *Thick and Thin: Moral Argument at Home and Abroad* (Notre Dame, IN: Notre Dame University Press, 1994).
14 On the 'mediated political field', see John Thompson, *Political Scandal* (Cambridge: Polity, 2000), p. 198. More generally on these developments see Kate Campbell, 'W.E. Gladstone, W.T. Stead, Matthew Arnold and a New Journalism', *Victorian Periodicals Review* 36:1 (2003): 20–40; also, especially on recent historiography, Catherine Hall, Keith McLell and Jane Randall, *Defining the Victorian Nation* (Cambridge: Cambridge University Press, 2000); also Eugenio Biagini, *Gladstone* (Basingstoke: Macmillan, 2000).
15 Patrick Joyce, *Democratic Subjects: The Self and the Social in Nineteenth-Century England* (Cambridge: Cambridge University Press, 1991), pp. 4–5, 136–7.
16 On the *habitus* see for instance Pierre Bourdieu, *Distinction: A Social Critique of the Judgement of Taste*, trans. by Richard Nice (London: Routledge and Kegan Paul, 1984), pp. 101–2, 114.
17 Matthew Arnold, *Reports on Elementary Schools: 1852–1882*, ed. by Francis Sandford (London: Macmillan, 1889), p. 89.

Index

Alford, Revd Henry 12
Altick, Richard 195
Aristotle 62, 214
Armstrong, Nancy 174, 181, 182
Arnold, Matthew xxi, xxii, xxix, 22, 141, 209–21
   'Bishop and the Philosopher, The' 217
   Culture and Anarchy xxi, xxii, 210, 211, 219–20
   'Democracy' 211, 216
   'Dover Beach' xxi, 209
   'England and the Italian Question' 215
   Essays in Criticism 217
   French Eton, A 210, 218
   'Function of Criticism, The' 214
   'Heinrich Heine' 213, 218
   Letters 212–14, 218
   'Marcus Aurelius' 217
   Popular Education of France, The 215
   'Preface' 209, 210
   Schools and Universities on the Continent 219, 220
   'Study of Poetry, The' 209
   'To the Duke of Wellington' 214
   'Twice-Revised Code, The' 217
Atlantic Monthly 75

Baldick, Chris 119
Baird, Robert 73
Barnett, Henrietta 31
Barrett Browning, Elizabeth xix, 7n, 198
Baudelaire, Charles 120
Bebbington, D. W. 6, 14
Beckford, James 8n
Beecher, Henry Ward 84
Bentley's Miscellany 190
Binny, John 195
Blake, William 57, 58, 67
   Marriage of Heaven and Hell, The 57
Bourdieu, Pierre 213, 217
Bosco, Ronald A. 103
Bradwell, Albert 3
Breton, Rob 173
British Critic 136
Bright, John 217, 220
Brown, Callum 3, 7, 8
Browning, Robert 7n, 137n

Bryant, M. Darrol 8n
Butler, Joseph 67
Butler, Josephine xxv n, 22, 24, 30, 37
   Autobiographical Memoir 37
Byron, George Gordon, Lord 120

Carlyle, Thomas xxviii, 60, 171–87
   'Characteristics' 60
   Chartism 172, 175–82
   'Corn-Law Rhymes' 176, 178
   Letters 171, 178–80
   Past and Present 174, 183–85
Carroll, Lewis 59, 77
   Alice's Adventures in Wonderland 77
Certeau, Michel de 16, 88, 90, 91
   Heterologies 91, 93
   'Mystic Speech' 88
Christian Remembrancer 48, 52
Cixous, Hélène xix n
Clough, Arthur Hugh xxiii, xxiv, 60–63, 65
   Amour de Voyage 60
   'Dipsychus' 61
   'Hymnos ahymnos' 63
   'It fortifies my soul to know' xxiii, xxiv
   Roma Notebook 62
Coakley, Sarah 22
Cobbett, William 163
Coleridge, J. T. 135
Coleridge, Samuel Taylor 23, 25, 26, 27, 29, 30, 36
   Friend, The 26, 29
   'Frost at Midnight' 29
Comic Magazine, The 152, 159
Cruikshank, Robert 152

Dante Alighieri xi
Darwin, Charles 4n
Davis, Philip xviii, xix
Derrida, Jacques 4
Dewey, John 69
Dial 99
Dickens, Charles xxix, 83, 84, 189–205
   All the Year Round 192–95, 199–202, 205
   Bleak House 83, 84
   Cricket, The 191

Cricket on the Hearth, The 191
Daily News 191, 194, 196, 197, 199
'Fly-Leaf in a Life, A' 202
Household Narrative 197, 198
Household Words 189, 191–95, 197–202
Letters 190, 191, 194, 197, 199, 200
Master Humphrey's Clock 190
'New Uncommercial Samples' 202
Uncommercial Traveller 190, 200, 201, 202, 205
Dickinson, Emily xxiii, xxvi–xxvii, 73–91
'Bumble-Bee's Religion, The' 78–79, 84
'Come slowly – Eden!' 86–87
'Drunkard cannot meet a Cork, A' 87
'Fame is a Bee' 90
'From Cocoon forth a Butterfly' 80–83
'His feet are shod with Gauze –' 79–80
Letters 74–76, 80, 83
'Those – dying then' xxiii
'To make a prairie it takes a clover and one bee' 89–90
Douglas-Fairhurst, Robert 213, 218
Drew, John 189, 190, 197
Durandus, William 132, 138

Eagleton, Terry xix
Ecclesiologist, The 131, 135
Edwards, Jonathan 85
Edgecombe, Rodney Stenning 136, 137
Egan, Pierce 153
Eliot, George (Marian Evans) 58, 63
Daniel Deronda 63
Elliott, Ebenezer xxii, 176, 178
Emerson, Ralph Waldo xxvii, 73–74, 87, 95–109
'Circles' 103
'Emancipation in the British West Indies' 98, 99
Essays: Second Series 99
'Experience' 99–101
'Humble-Bee, The' 74, 87
Journals and Miscellaneous Notebooks 98
Later Lectures 102, 105
Nature 97–98, 101
Poems 99
'Poet, The' 99–101
'Poetry and Imagination' 103–09
'Times, The' 98
Engels, Frederich 175
The Condition of the Working Class in England 175, 176
Evangelical Magazine 11

Faber, Frederick 132–35
Cherwell Water-Lily, The 134

'St Mary's at Night' 134, 135
Family Herald 195
Faraday, Michael 102, 103
Farr, Judith 85, 86
Feuerbach, Ludwig 58, 67
Essence of Christianity 58
Finney, Charles, G. 3
Fitzgerald, Percy 193
Frankenstein 115
Freud, Sigmund 113, 117, 127
'On the Uncanny' 113
Totem and Taboo 117

Gaskell, Mrs 196, 201, 202
Girard, René 113, 117, 118, 125
Scapegoat, The 117
Violence and the Sacred 113
Gladstone, William Ewart xi–xiii, xxiv, 22, 216, 220
Grainger, R. D. xxvi n, 40–49, 53
'Evidence' 41, 42, 44
Second Report 41–47
Grant, C. J. 155, 166, 167

Haldane, Revd James 12
Hampson, Daphne 22
Hardy, Thomas 68
Hartshorne, Charles 101, 104
Haslam, Richard 119
Haywood, Ian 44
Heath, Henry 155
Heine, Heinrich 213n, 218n
Henderson, Heather 4
Herbert, George 136, 137
Higginson, Thomas Wentworth 73, 74, 76
Hill, Octavia xxv n, 22, 24n, 27, 30–37
'Letters to Fellow Workers' 34
Life of Octavia Hill: As told in her Letters 32–36
Hillis Miller J., xvi–xvii, 172, 209, 210
Disappearance of God, The 209, 210
Victorian Subjects xvi–xvii
Hilton, Boyd 45
Hilton, Tim 141
Hindmarsh, D. Bruce 6
Hogg, James 119
Hollingsworth, Revd A. G. H. 11
Homer xi
Hood, Thomas 152
Hope, A. J. B. 132
Hopkins, Gerard Manley 141
Hume, David 29
Huysmans, Joris-Karl 125

Irigaray, Luce xix n, 88, 90
'Divine Women' 88

Jack Shepherd 164
James, William xv, xxvi, 64–69
   Selected Writings 65, 66
   Varieties of Religious Experience, The xv, 65, 68
   Will to Believe and Other Essays, The 66
Johnson, James 44
Johnson, Samuel 62
Joyce, Patrick 217

Kallenberg, Brad 6
Keats, John 64
Keble, John 129, 132–35, 137
   Christian Year, The 129, 133, 135
   Lectures on Poetry 1832–1841 129
   Lyra Innocentium 135
   'Trinity Sunday' 133, 134, 137
Kingsley, Charles 11, 34

Lamb, Christopher 8n
Lang, Cecil 212
Law, William 61–62
Laycock, Thomas 43
Lease, Benjamin 76
Lechevalier, Jules 22
Lee, Yoon Sun 172, 173
Lessing, Doris 69
Lofland, John 9, 10, 11, 14
Lohrli, Anne 195, 205, 203
Lubbock, John 76
Luther, Martin 119

MacDonald, George xxvi n, 62–63, 65, 68, 69
   Dish of Orts, A 68
   Wilfrid Cumbermede xxvi, 62–63
Macmillan's Magazine 11, 35
Magee, William 116
Maistre, Joseph de 114–16
   'Enlightenment on Sacrifices' 114
Mallock, W. H. 64
Malthus, T. R. 48
Mansel, H. L. 67
Martineau, Harriet 153, 154, 205
Maturin, Charles xxvii n, 113–26
Maurice, F. D. xxv, 22–37
   Friendship of Books, The 24, 25
   Kingdom of Christ, The 22, 23, 24, 25
   Life of Frederick Denison Maurice 26, 28
   Sketches of Contemporary Authors 24, 25
   Theological Essays 28, 29
Mayhew, Henry 195
McFague, Sallie 8

McFarland, Thomas 30
Michel, O. 6
Mill, John Stuart xx–xxii, 57, 178, 212
   Autobiography 57
   'Utility of Religion' xx
Millar, John 48
Milton, John 29
Moncrieff, W. T. 152, 163, 164
   'Literary Dustman, The' 164
   March of the Intellect, The 152, 163
Morgan, R. C. 13
Morris, Jeremy 23

Neale, John Mason 131–34, 138, 142
   Few Words to Church Builders, A 131
   Few Words to Church Wardens, A 131
   Letters 132
   Symbolism of Churches 132, 138, 142
Newman, John Henry 4n, 5, 7, 11n, 16n, 132, 133, 135, 136, 211, 213
   Apologia Pro Vita Sua 4
   'Gospel Palaces, The' 136
   'Sudden Conversions' 5
   'Theory of Developments in Religious Doctrine, The' 213
   'Visible Church an Encouragement to Faith, The' 136
   'Visible Temple, The' 136
New Testament 6, 9, 79, 201
Nietzsche, Friedrich xvii n
Nock, A. D. 5
Norton, Charles Eliot 7n

Old Testament 7, 79, 118
Orr, J. Edwin 13
Owen, David 31

Paget, Francis xxvi, 40, 41, 45, 47, 48–54
Pageant, The 40, 47, 48, 50–51, 53
Paine, Thomas 163
Patmore, Coventry 141–43
   'Architectural Styles' 142
   'Essay on English Metrical Law' 143
Patrick, James 132, 136
Penny Magazine, The 150, 155, 156, 164–68
Penny Satirist 164
Percy, Martin 8n
Pickard, John B. 86
Plotz, John 173, 174
Prickett, Stephen 23, 28
Pugin, A. W. N. 130, 131, 136, 138, 141
   Contrasts 130, 136, 138
   True Principles of Pointed or Christian Architecture, The 131
Pusey, Edward Bouverie 132

Rambo, Lewis 8n, 14, 15, 16
Ramsbottom, Joseph xxiv
Rank, Otto 126
Religious Tendencies of the Age, The 10
Retz, Gilles de 125
Reynolds, G. W. M. 194
Richardson, Robert D. 99, 157
Robertson, Roland 5
Rossetti, Christina xix n, 141
Ruskin, John xxviii, 4, 7–10, 13, 14, 16, 27, 28, 31, 130, 138, 141–43
  Diaries of John Ruskin, The 9
  Fors Clavigera 7
  Modern Painters II 9
  Notes on the Construction of Sheepfolds 9
  'Notes on the Turin Gallery' 7
  Praeterita 7, 14
  Seven Lamps of Architecture, The 9, 130, 141, 142
  Stones of Venice, The 141, 142
Ruskin, John James 7

Saint Augustine xxvi, 48, 49, 114, 126
  Confessions 126
  De Trinitate 126
Saint Paul xxvi, 5, 10, 49, 51, 116
Sewall, Richard B. 76
Schad, John xix, 4
Schleiermacher, Friedrich Daniel Ernst 29
Scott Holland, Henry 59
Scott, Sir Walter 119
Scudamore, Revd W. E. 12
Seymour, Robert 155, 165
Shakespeare, William 192
Shaw, W. David. xvi, xvii
Shuttleworth, Sally 40
Skonovd, Norman 9, 10, 11, 14
Slater, Michael 195
Small, Helen 203, 204
Smith, Adam 48
Smith, William Henry 186
Southey, Robert 39, 50, 54
Spurgeon, Charles Haddon 3, 13, 16
Stevenson, Robert Louis 126
Stowe, Harriet Beecher 82

Taussig, Gurion 29
Taylor, Brian 8n, 15
Taylor, Charles 213, 214
Taylor, Jeremy 23, 29

Tempest, The 121
Tennyson, Alfred, Lord 59, 137
Tennyson, G. B. 133
Thoreau, Henry David 99, 171
Tonna, Charlotte Elizabeth xxvi, 40, 41, 45–54
  Milliners and Dress-Makers 40, 45–52
Tracts for the Times 132
Turner, Victor 8

Viswanathan, Gauri 8n

Walter, James 6
Watts, Isaac 77, 78, 82
  'Against Idleness and Mischief' 77, 78, 82
  Divine and Moral Songs for Children 78
Webb, Beatrice 31
Webb, Benjamin 131, 132, 138, 142
  Symbolism of Churches, The 132, 138, 142
Wheeler, Michael 7
White, James F. 132
White, William 142
Whitehead, Alfred North 101
Whitman, Walt 171
Wilde, Oscar xxvii n, 113, 120–25
Williams, Isaac xxvii, 129, 130, 132, 133–41, 143
  'Athanasian Creed, The' 140
  Baptistery, The 129, 140, 141
  Cathedral, The xxvii, 130, 133, 136–41
  'Doxology, The' 137
  'Forms' 140
  'North Aisle, The: The Lord's Prayer' 139
  'North Porch, The' 137
  'North Transept' 130
  'On Reserve in Communicating Religious Knowledge' 132
  'South Aisle, The: The Creed' 139
Wilson, Eric 102
Wittgenstein, Ludwig 213
Wolffe, John 6
Wordsworth, William 25, 68, 136
  Recluse, The 136
  Excursion, The 136

Yeats, William Butler 126